APPLYING ANDRAGOGICAL PRINCIPLES TO INTERNET LEARNING

APPLYING ANDRAGOGICAL PRINCIPLES TO INTERNET LEARNING

Susan Isenberg

CAMBRIA
PRESS

YOUNGSTOWN, NEW YORK

Copyright 2007 Susan Isenberg

All rights reserved
Printed in the United States of America

No part of this publication may be reproduced, stored in or introduced into a retrieval system, or transmitted, in any form, or by any means (1, mechanical, photocopying, recording, or otherwise), without the prior permission of the publisher. Requests for permission should be directed to permissions@cambriapress.com, or mailed to Permissions, Cambria Press, PO Box 350, Youngstown, New York 14174-0350.

This book has been registered with the Library of Congress.
Isenberg, Susan
   Applying Andragogical Principles to Internet Learning
        p. cm.
   Includes bibliographical references
   ISBN-13: 978-1-934043-19-6

For my family

Table of Contents

Foreword xv

Preface xxvii

Acknowledgements xxxvii

Chapter One: Overview of the Study 1

    Lifelong Learning 2

    New Demands on the Adult Learner 2

    More Adults Using Computers and the Internet 3

    Andragogical Principles and Adult Learning 3

    Andragogy and the Internet 4

    Statement of the Problem 5

    Purpose of the Study 8

    Importance of the Study 8

    Definition of Terms 9

    Limitations 10

Delimitations 11

Assumptions 11

Chapter Two: Background 13

Principles of Adult Learning 13

Technology of Adult Learning 20

Issues with Face-to-Face Teaching / Learning 27

Issues without Face-to-Face Teaching / Learning 28

Whole-Mind Learning 32

The Four Pillars of Learning 34

    Learning to Know 35

    Learning to Do 36

    Learning to Live Together 36

    Learning to be 37

The Role of Creativity in Innovation 37

Internet Learning 39

Table of Contents ix

    Internet Learning and Andragogy:
        Making the Connection 44

    Conclusion 46

Chapter Three: Research Methodology 49

    Interpretive Inquiry 50

    Phenomenology 51

    Grounded Theory 51

    Case Study 52

    Action Research 53

    Subjects 54

    Instrumentation 57

    Procedure 59

    Data Analysis 61

Chapter Four: Presentation of Data 63

    Making the Connection Between
        Research and Interview Questions 63

    Aligning the Interview Questions
        with the Appropriate Research Sub-Question 65

Merging the Research Questions
    with the Interview Questions 65

Issues with face-to-face teaching / learning 65

Issues without face-to-face teaching / learning 75

Can an Internet program stimulate
    whole-mind thinking? 81

How does the design meet the goal of the
    International Commission on Education
    for the Twenty-first Century? 87

Emerging Themes 101

Emerging theme: Interest 101

Emerging theme: Legalities 105

Emerging theme: Money 109

Emerging theme: Skill 113

Emerging theme: Relationships 115

Emerging theme: Doubt 119

Emerging theme: Trust 121

Emerging theme: Fun 123

Table of Contents xi

    Emerging theme: Leadership 125

    Emerging theme: Getting it right 126

    Emerging theme: Educational constraints........................ 131

    Emerging theme: Situational constraints 137

    Emerging theme: Evaluation... 142

Chapter Five: Conclusions and Recommendations 153

    Discussion 153

        Issues with face-to-face teaching / learning..................... 154

        Issues without face-to-face teaching / learning................ 158

        Can an Internet program stimulate
           whole-mind thinking? 163

        How does the design meet the goal of the
        International Commission on Education
        for the Twenty-first Century?.. 166

        Emerging theme: Interest.. 173

        Emerging theme: Legalities 176

        Emerging theme: Money... 177

        Emerging theme: Skill 179

Emerging theme: Relationships 181

Emerging theme: Doubt 182

Emerging theme: Trust 182

Emerging theme: Fun 183

Emerging theme: Leadership 184

Emerging theme: Getting it right 185

Emerging theme: Educational constraints 188

Emerging theme: Situational constraints 190

Emerging theme: Evaluation 193

Protocol 194

Protocol elements resulting from the
    lived experience 198

Integrated protocol 200

Answering the Research Questions 200

Current Status of Virtual Health Coach 209

Recommendations for Future Research 210

Appendix A: Interview Questions for the Author / Researcher, the Programmer, and the Graphic Artist 213

Appendix B: Interview Questions for the Air Force Lieutenant Colonel and Pharmaceutical Company Regional Account Manager 215

Appendix C: Consent 216

Appendix D: Verbatim Transcripts (in sequential order) 221

Appendix E: Author / Researcher's Virtual Health Coach Implementation Kit Letter 283

Appendix F: Military Surveys on Animation and Voice of Virtual Health Coach Character 284

Appendix G: Example Provider and Patient Letters in Virtual Health Coach Implementation Kits 294

References 297

Index 307

FOREWORD

Two distinct ideas are present in this title: andragogy and Internet learning. The history and origination of each started about the same time—1833. In this book, they are ultimately brought together as a "cutting-edge movement" and show great promise of benefit for the adult learners and society that will be served in this and coming generations.

Internet learning has its historical roots, background, and foundation in educational technology, dating back to more than a century. Correspondence Study in various content areas was the first among distance education offerings in numerous countries, states, cities, and institutions: Sweden in 1833, England in 1840, Germany in 1843, the United States in 1873, Illinois Wesleyan University in 1877, Edinburgh in 1878, New York in 1883, University of Wisconsin in 1885, London in 1887, University of Chicago in 1892, Moody Bible Institute—Chicago in 1901, Benton Harbor, Michigan in 1923 (the city where I was born), University of Nebraska in 1929, and prior to World War II in France.

Electronic Communications was next to come on the scene and has been changing ever since. Some systems stayed and some faded out with others taking their place. Europe had audio recordings for the blind and language teaching for all. Laboratory kits were used in teaching electronics and radio engineering. U.S. radio stations, in the 1920s, were first to be involved in education. Experimental television teaching programs were introduced in the 1930s, with broadcast television courses coming in 1951. Satellite technology came in 1960, having varying success, and became cost-effective in the 1980s.

In the late 1980s and early 1990s, with the coming of fiber-optic communications systems, there was expansion of live, two-way, high-quality audio and video interaction in distance education. Full-motion, two-way interactive video, data (Internet), and voice services were beamed to an untold number of locations at the same time. All this became the backbone for computer telecommunications and asynchronous, Internet-based programs offered to distance learners. In addition, computer-mediated communications, computer conferencing, and computer networks have all become convenient ways to distribute materials to learners all over the world.

Numerous other things that appeared included short-wave radio, telewriter, audio teleconferencing, videoconferencing, multimedia technical centers, one-way television transmission with "talking heads," two-way audio (radio), two-way video / audio (TV), audio telephone and lecture notes, video satellite and telephone call back, telephone networks with printed materials and discussion at multiple sites, and others too numerous to mention.

All of these distance education systems have had writers like Holmberg (1986) identify numerous political, economic, and educational reasons for offering distance learning, including: (a) to increase educational offerings, (b) to serve educational needs of adults with jobs and family responsibilities in addition to social commitments, (c) to offer individual adults including disadvantaged groups and society-study opportunities, (d) to provide professionals with advanced-level learning, (e) to support educational innovation, and believing that this would be an economical use of educational resources.

'Andragogy' as a term was coined and first appeared in published form in 1833 by a German School Teacher, Alexander Kapp (a replica may be found at the following website: www.andragogy.net) Andragogy became popularized in the 1970s and 1980s in the United States, primarily through the work of Malcolm Knowles and others. However, Lindeman (1926) was credited with its original introduction into the United States.

Knowles (1970, 1980) defined andragogy as the "art and science of helping adults learn." The main structure of Knowles (1995) andragogical expression took the form of a process design instead of a content design, with assumptions and processes. The six assumptions about adult learners are: (a) they are self-directing, (b) their experience is a learning resource, (c) their learning needs are focused on their social roles, (d) their time perspective is one of immediate application, (e) they are intrinsically motivated and want to problem-solve, and (f) they want to know a reason that makes sense to them as to why they need to learn something. The eight learning processes that adults want to be actively and interactively involved in are: (a) preparing for the adult learning experience, (b) a climate conducive to learning, (c) cooperative planning, (d) diagnosing their needs, (e) setting objectives, (f) designing the pattern and sequence of techniques, (g) conducting the activities, and (h) evaluating their progress to rediagnose their learning needs.

Later, Mezirow (1981) added to Knowles' conception of andragogy and developed a critical theory of adult learning and education that laid the groundwork for what he called a charter for andragogy that included 12 core concepts. Suanmali (1981) focused on the agreement of 174 adult educators, including professors and practitioners, and on 10 of Mezirow's core concepts that all related to self-direction in learning. The major theme of his study was that in assisting adults to enhance their capability of functioning as self-directed learners, the adult educator must: decrease learner dependency, help learners use learning resources, help learners define their learning needs, help learners take responsibility for learning, organize learning that is relevant, foster learner decision-making and choices, encourage learner judgment and integration, facilitate problem-posing and problem-solving, provide a supportive learning climate, and emphasize experiential learning methods.

In support of Knowles' ideas, Zmeyov (1994) clearly stated that Knowles' concept of andragogy scientifically finds the activity of the learners and teachers in the process of the determination of goals and tasks; of content, forms, and methods; of organization, technology, and realization of learning, and is considered now by many scholars and teachers as a fundamental theoretical base for adult education. Dover (2006) suggests that although Malcolm S. Knowles was not the first to use the term, his popularization of andragogy explains why Knowles is one of the most frequently cited theorists in adult education and is often referred to as "the father of adult learning."

With the emergence of Internet learning, many adult educators have sought to apply sound andragogical learning theory to its use. Numerous adult educators have emphasized their perception of how andragogy and Internet learning may be brought together.

Burge (1988) was one of the first to make a connection between andragogy and Internet learning. She said that one reason for distance educators to look at andragogy is the concept of quality. She asks the question: would an andragogical learner-centered approach contribute to or undermine academic rigor? She believed that a closer examination of the key implications of andragogy and a learner-centered view within the new classrooms of distance education contributes to academic rigor. It will also expand the definitions of helping adults learn to include more of the subtle qualitative aspects of learning. The quality of counseling and tutoring, as distinct from quality of course content, is another professional issue that benefits from a closer look at andragogy.

Bullen (1995) offered some words of caution on the use of andragogical principles in distance education. She suggested that distance educators need to examine the mandate of their operation, the purpose and nature of the courses, and the preferences and characteristics of their learners. Their application of andragogy needs to be moderate rather than radical. If andragogy were adopted on the strength of its underlying assumptions about adults, distance educators would do well to validate those assumptions in their own contexts.

Conner (1997–2003) strongly declared that andragogy refers to learner-focused education for people. Thus, in the information age, the implications of a move from teacher-centered to learner-centered education are staggering. Postponing or suppressing this move will slow our ability to learn new technology and gain competitive advantage. To succeed, we must unlearn our teacher-reliance.

Green (1998) comments on some important factors for consideration in online learning, and suggests that in andragogy, learners must balance life responsibilities with the demands of learning. Teachers guide learners to their own knowledge rather than supplying them with facts. Learners need to connect their tremendous amount of life experiences to their knowledge base and recognize the value of the learning.

Foreword xix

In seeking to bring numerous factors together in online learning, *Andragogy* addressed the question of how to put the pieces together: learner, institution, and technology. He also focuses on who the learner is and that andragogy must be learned, designed to fit the learner, to incorporate technology positively (Thorpe, 1999).

Dewar (1999) articulated what she deems to be the important principles of andragogy / adult learning for consideration when facilitating adult learning online. Increasing and maintaining ones' sense of self-esteem and pleasure are strong secondary motivators for engaging in learning experiences. New knowledge has to be integrated with previous knowledge, which means active learner participation. Adult learning must be problem and experience centered. Effective adult learning entails an active search for meaning in which new tasks are somehow related to earlier activities. A certain degree of arousal is necessary for learning to occur. Stress acts as a major block to learning. Collaborative modes of teaching and learning enhance the self-concepts of those involved and result in more meaningful and effective learning. Adults generally learn best in an atmosphere that is nonthreatening and supportive of experimentation and in which different learning styles are recognized. Adults experience anxiety and ambivalence in their orientation to learning. Adult learning is facilitated when: (a) the learner's representation and interpretation of their own experiences are accepted as valid, acknowledged as an essential aspect influencing change, and respected as a potential resource for learning; (b) the teacher can give up some control over teaching processes and planning activities and can share these with learners; (c) teaching activities do not demand finalized, correct answers, and closure; (d) teaching activities express a tolerance for uncertainty, inconsistency, and diversity; and, (e) teaching activities promote both question-asking and question-answering and problem-finding and problem-solving. Adult skill learning is facilitated when individual learners can assess their own skills and strategies to discover inadequacies or limitations for themselves.

Osborn (1999) declared that andragogy has the potential to play an important role in distance learning. However, she found that students need to be coached in the principles of the approach so they understand the teacher's expectations. Most students have been trained to rely on their teachers for leadership. Some need to be shown how to take responsibility for their own learning and become self-directing.

Moore (n.d.), in listing adult learner characteristics, provided the following implications for technology use: (a) Adults should be provided with adequate resources and technology tools to direct their own learning; (b) Adult learners should regularly be required to relate classroom content to actual life experiences; (c) Appropriate beliefs about learning are developed over time by providing students with many opportunities to ask their own questions and engage in personal inquiry; and, (d) Motivation and interest can be supported by designing authentic projects or tasks that the learner can see are relevant to their future needs.

Fidishun (n.d.) asserted that to facilitate the use of andragogy while teaching with technology, technology must be used to its fullest. In addition to the arguments of online being flexible for learning, self-paced, anytime, and anywhere, learners may also adapt the lessons or material to cover what they need to learn and eliminate the material that is not appropriate or that they have already learned. The design must be interactive, learner-centered and facilitate self-direction in learners. Educators must become facilitators of learning, and structure student input into their design and create technology-based lessons that can easily be adapted to make the presentation of topics relevant to those they teach.

Commenting additionally on the value of andragogy in technological learning, Rossman (2003) posits that andragogy provides (a) a context for developing distance education programs, (b) a framework to build a climate conducive to adult learning, and (c) a process for involving the adult learner more actively in the distance learning process.

Gibbons and Wentworth (2001) expressed a concern about colleges and universities that are rushing at an alarming rate to answer the call of the growing number of online learners. They raised a crucial question: Can faculty make effective use of the online learning platform to design, construct, and deliver a meaningful online course that addresses the motivations, needs, learning styles, and constraints on nontraditional learners, while achieving the same learning outcomes as "on ground"? They seek to address this question by revealing the need for substantive differences between online and "on ground" teaching methodologies. They declare that dialogue is the methodological heart of the online learning paradigm. They also support the idea that learning a subject well requires intensive discourse in any field or discipline and that the learners' need for individual dialogue contributes as much to the teaching and learning structure as the teacher offers in the way of course content or design. They further assert that those who teach online need to be trained (helped to learn) to respect the maturity of the adult learners and their motivations for learning. In this process of their being helped to become online faculty, they evolve from being an instructor and content expert to a facilitator and resource person. The new facilitator learns to create a course that emphasizes the primacy of the learner, grants a substantial measure of control to learners, and places learning directly in the context of learners' own experiences.

Barclay (2001) made it clear that Knowles' concept of andragogy became infused with humanistic psychology. Although subjected to much debate as to whether it should be considered a theory, method, technique, or simply a set of assumptions, andragogy now occupies an important place in the adult education field. It has engendered awareness of the learning needs of adults and is now emerging as a base of concepts applicable for learning at a distance.

Akande and Jegede (2004) made the case that adults in Nigeria are far behind children in achieving technological literacy. Their perspective to improve adult computer literacy skills in Nigeria holds the view that describes andragogy as one of the new sciences of education that is now gaining ground in many areas. It is democratic in the sense that the learner is seen as an active participant in the whole learning process. Thus, they conclude that andragogical methods are highly appropriate for adult education in computer literacy.

Oduaran et al. (2003) asserted that among other transformations in African university adult and continuing education, andragogy is taught as a mainstream course. Andragogy is also applied as the major principle guiding interactions among Information and Communication Technologies (ICT) and diversity.

Simonson et al. (2006) declares that most now consider Malcolm Knowles' work to be the theory of distance education because many times adults are involved in distance education and andragogy addresses frameworks for

Foreword

programs designed for the adult learner. Brookfield (1986) asserts that the core of attaining adulthood is quite similar to adults perceiving themselves as self-directing persons.

Building on the previously stated assumptions and processes of andragogy as set forth by Knowles, Simonson et al. (2006) suggest a number of characteristics needed in distance / Internet education systems designed for adults. They are:

- The physical environment of the learning setting used by adults should enable them to be comfortable, the materials need to be in the letter size for them to see, and they need to be able to hear any sound connected with the program;
- The physiological environment should be one that promotes respect and dignity for the adult learner;
- Adult learners must feel supported and encouraged by the contents and ideas of the materials;
- A starting point for a program, or module of a program, should be the needs and interest of the adult learner;
- Program plans in the material should include clear course descriptions, learning objectives, resources, and sequences of the activities;
- General to specific patterns of content presentation work best for adult learners; and
- Active participation should be structured and fostered through the design of the materials.

Isenberg (2005) developed and tested the "Virtual Health Coach" Internet program that combines andragogical principles with Internet technology. It has numerous health issues being dealt with such as smoking, cessation, and weight loss. It is being used with the military, health care institutions, and is available online through website technology. The research indicates excellent success with the participants in dealing with health issues.

This original edition of *Applying Andragogy to Internet Learning* by Susan Isenberg represents a milestone in bringing together these two concepts—andragogy and Internet learning. Others have made suggestions about what is needed for bringing them together, but she has conducted the

Foreword   xxiii

research and knows what is needed. The book presents the "cutting-edge" requirements of lifelong learning for adults to retain mastery of their own destinies in a world of an accelerating rate of change and rapid globalization. It is a landmark in the presentation of a scientific foundation for research in andragogy and its roots in relationship to the very practical aspects of Internet learning. This is the only book I know that delivers such in-depth information and research actually applying andragogy to Internet learning—and it does that in the very crucial area of a Virtual Health Coach and health related concerns.

This book provides a break-through framework for bringing together the interaction of andragogy and Internet learning, while blending the practical and theoretical, the practice and research, and the technology and learning process. It presents a dynamic design to meet the goal of the International Commission on Adult Education for the Twenty-first Century, focusing on four pillars of learning: To know, to do, to live together, and to be. A fifth pillar of learning, learning to change, was added after the writing of this book to emphasize the lifelong nature of learning (Nurturing the treasure: Vision and strategy 2002–2007, UIE UNESCO Institute for Education, Hamburg, Germany). It addresses the multisided issue of "learning with a face-to-face teacher," and "learning without a face-to-face teacher." It presents a state-of-the-art picture of the themes that emerged during the human process: Interest, legalities, money, skill, relationships, doubt, trust, fun, leadership, getting it right, educational constraint, situational constraint, and evaluation. This book sets forth the integrated protocol elements of building this kind of Internet learning program that resulted from merging the protocol elements of thse literature review and the protocol elements of the lived experience. Finally, this book is a very important contribution to the literature of adult education as well as a valuable resource for those individuals and teams who wish to build other adult / lifelong learning programs and systems, dealing with a variety of subject areas that will help in applying andragogy to Internet learning.

John A. Henschke
University of Missouri, St Louis, MO
and
University of Missouri Extension

REFERENCES

Akande, J. O., & Jegede, P. O. (2004). Andragogy and computer literacy: The Nigerian perspective. *The African Symposium: A Journal of Educational Research on Africa, 4*(2). Retrieved April 4, 2006, from http://www.ncsu.edu/ncsu/aern/andralog.html

Barclay, K. (2001). *Humanizing learning at a distance.* Unpublished doctoral dissertation, University of Hawaii, Honolulu, Hawaii.

Brookfield, S. (1986). *Understanding and facilitating adult learning.* San Francisco: Jossey-Bass.

Bullen, M. (1995, June). *Andragogy and university distance education.* Paper presented to the 17th conference of the International Council for Distance Education, Birmingham, UK. Retrieved from http://www.cstudies.ubc.ca/~bullen/bullen1.html

Burge, L. (1988). Beyond andragogy: Some explorations for distance learning design. *Journal of Distance Education/Revue de l'enseignement a distance, 1–14.* Retrieved November 18, 2005, from http://cade.icaap.org/vol3.1/burge.html

Conner, M. L. (1997–2003). Andragogy + Pedagogy. *Ageless Learner, 1997–2003.* Retrieved January 13, 2004, from http://agelesslearner.com/intros/andragogy.html

Dewar, T. (1999). *Adult learning principles (a selection).* Retrieved November 13, 2005, from http://www.calliopelearning.com/adult.html

Dover, K. H. (2006). Adult learning theorist: Malcolm S. Knowles—Biography. *Adult/Continuing Education: A Free Newsletter Guide.* Retrieved April 4, 2006, from http://adulted.about.com/cs/adultlearningthe/a/knowles.html

Fidishun, D. (n.d.). *Andragogy and technology: Integrating adult learning theory as we teach with technology.* Unpublished manuscript, Penn State Great Valley School of Graduate Professional Studies, Malvern, PA.

Gibbons, H. S., & Wentworth, G. P. (2001). Andragogical and pedagogical training differences for online instructors *Journal of Distance Learning Administration, 4*(3).

Green, J. (1998). Andragogy: Teaching adults. In B. Hoffman (Ed.). *Encyclopedia of educational technology.* Retrieved February 11, 2006, from file:///C:/Documents

Holmberg, B. (1986) *Growth and structure of distance education.* London: Croom Helm.

Isenberg, S. (2005, April). *The experience of applying principles of andragogy to Internet technology.* Unpublished doctoral dissertation at the University of Missouri—St Louis. Division of Educational Leadership and Policy Studies.

Kapp, A. (1833). Die Andragogik oder Bildung im männlichen Alter. *Platons Erziehungslehre, als Pädagogik für die Einzelnen und als Staatspädagogik.* Germany: Minden und Leipzig: Ferdinand Essmann.

Knowles, M. S. (1970). *The modern practice of adult education* New York: Association Press and Cambridge Book Publishers.

———. (1980). *The modern practice of adult education* (2nd ed.). New York: Association Press and Cambridge Book Publishers.

———. (1995). *Designs for adult learning: Practical resources, exercises, and course outlines from the father of adult learning.* Alexandria, VA: American Society for Training and Development.

Lindeman, E. C. (1926). Andragogik: The method of teaching adults. *Workers' Education, 4,* 38.

Mezirow, J. (1981). A critical theory of adult learning and education. *Adult Education, 32*(1), 3–24.

Moore, J. (n.d.). *Site philosophy: Learner-focused education, andragogy.* Retrieved October 13, 2004, from http://www.edtech.vt.edu/edtech/is/ocs.introp2.html

Oduaran, A., Lekoko, R., & Oduaran, C. (2003). *Learning transformations in university continuing education and the African response.* Retrieved October 24, 2005, from http://www.face.stir.ac.uk/Paper12AkpovireOduaranR2.html

Osborn, S. (1999). *Andragogy.* Belgrade, Yugoslavia: Faculty of Philosophy Forum. Retrieved October 24, 2005, from http://ifets.gmd.de/

Rossman, M. (2003, Winter). Andragogy and distance education: Together in the new millennium. In N. Gadbow (Ed.). *New horizons in adult education*—ISSN 1062-3183, Vol. 14, No. 1.

Simonson, M., Smaldino, S., Albright, M., & Zvacek, S. (2003). *Teaching and learning at a distance: Foundations of distance education* (3rd ed.). Columbus, OH: Merrill Prentice Hall.

Suanmali, C. (1981). *The core concepts of andragogy.* Unpublished doctoral dissertation. Columbia University Teachers College. Dissertation Abstracts International, University, No. 8207343.

Thorpe, Dr., E. (1999). *Andragogy and technology.* This PowerPoint is accessible through one of two places: e-mail directly to thorpet@mail.mohawke.on.ca, or go to the following website http://www.umsl.edu/~henschke, then click on 'andragogical concepts' and go through the alphabetical listing to the name 'Thorpe'.

Zmeyov, S. I. (1994). Perspectives of adult education in Russia. In P. Jarvis & F. Poggler (Eds.), *Developments in the education of adults in Europe: Vol. 21* (pp. 35–42) Bern, Switzerland: Peter Lang.

PREFACE

Since this study applying andragogical principles to Internet learning, there has been much written about technology and Internet learning but less about applying andragogical principles to Internet learning. Current literature on the topic of technology and Internet learning appears to have three themes: e-learning barriers, distance education, and interactivity. A brief discussion of each will be followed by a discussion on how new thinking adds value to this book's original study.

The first barrier to applying andragogical principles to Internet learning may be an inadequate exposure of would-be teachers of adults to computer learning as children. "Public school students' use of technology for instructional purposes remains at a lower than optimal level even though computers are more readily available in schools" (Mayo, Kajs, & Tanguma, 2005, p. 11). A current lack of public school teacher preparation may be resulting in upcoming adult educators who are not comfortable with computers and Internet technology (much less applying andragogical principles to Internet learning), and therefore less likely to use technology in preparing adult learning activities.

A three-year study (2001–2003) looked at the success of integrating technology training within a teacher preparation program to prepare preservice public school teachers to use technology in classroom instruction.

"The ability to incorporate technology within the curriculum is one of the most difficult tasks for classroom teachers" (Benton Foundation, 1997; Driskell, 1999 cited in Mayo et al., 2005, p. 3). The authors further say that

> While college students may be familiar with the every day practical use of technology, they need specific preparation to develop technology-integrated curricular lessons. A major focus of the educational reform movement has been to develop teacher education programs that emphasize pedagogical practices to prepare classroom teachers to incorporate technology into classroom learning (Mayo et al., 2005, p. 3).

In addition, the authors say that "technology education for teacher candidates has been to teach them computer skills leaving the application in the classroom to their own initiative" (p. 11).

Results of the study found that technology training for future teachers provided not only the skills but also the attitudes to promote students' use of technology. "The training taught future teachers to effectively integrate technology into lesson plans" (p. 11). The future teachers with the training were more comfortable using technology and moreover had a higher frequency of technology use. Though training is likely to help future teachers to use more of technology, teachers of children seem to be focusing on integrating technology into the lesson plans instead of integrating lesson plans into technology.

The second barrier is access issues, sometimes known as the digital divide. Although much has been written about the digital divide, the Pew Internet & American Life Project reports that the number of American people using the Internet continues to increase (Fox, 2005a). According to Fox, as of May and June 2005, 68% of the adult U.S. population (137 million) used the Internet. "A new type of digital divide has been created by different access speeds ... those truly offline (22% of adults), those with relatively modest connections such as dial-up (40%), and those who are the highly wired broadband elite (33%)" (Evers, 2006, p. 2).

Internet learning is the fastest growing market segment of adult education (Carr-Chellman, 2005). "Although this area only amounted to somewhere around $550 million of the adult education market in 1998, the growth expectations are phenomenal" (p. 2). In 2000, there were more than 3 million college and university students participating in distance education (National Center for Education Statistics, 2003, ¶ 7).

Access issues are minor in the United States compared with other parts of the world. Carr-Chellman (2005) discusses access issues related to e-learning in countries outside the United States such as Taiwan, where the cost of Internet access, the lack of basic computer skills, and the lack of Internet literacy widen the access gap. Jia Qi (Carr-Chellman, 2005) says that "the [Taiwan] government should commit itself to achieving equity in technical support, equalized use and public access to the resources on the Internet, and promote literacy of information and computer skills through collaboration with academia, industry, and local government" (p. 48).

The third barrier in e-learning is identified as a problem in the United Kingdom—retention and drop out (Simpson, 2005). Regarding lower retention rates in e-learning, the author says

> Once again there does not appear to be much research into the reasons for low retention on e-learning courses as distinct from conventional distance education. Clearly, many of the reasons will be similar, but if dropouts from e-learning are higher, then characteristics of the technology must be involved (p. 97).

Simpson describes yet another barrier in an e-mail he received from a student who wrote, "If you sit at a pc all day at work then doing it in the evening as well can not only be very fatiguing but positively harmful" (p. 98). To add to the story, Simpson describes a student at the institution where he works who spent five hours on an e-learning Spanish course, "roughly half an hour of which she had spent speaking Spanish, the other four and a half hours had been spent trying to get the software to work" (p. 98).

Simpson (Carr-Chellman, 2005) seems to think that the solution to retention and drop out is more of student support such as help lines, tutors, and online support. "Or it may be that answers will lie in the creative use of other forms of technology … for example … m-learning using mobile devices such as palmtop computers and WAP-enabled mobile phones that can access the Web" (p. 99).

To restate the e-learning barriers, they are (a) an inadequate exposure of would-be teachers of adults to computer learning as children, (b) access issues, and (c) retention and drop out. Possible solutions to the above barriers are (a) technology training for future teachers; (b) collaborations between academia, industry, and local government; and (c) more student support or other creative uses of technology. The possible solutions seem reasonable, but are difficult to implement.

The second theme arising from the current literature on applying andragogical principles to Internet learning is distance learning. "Distance education represents a major revolution" (Latchem, 2005, p. 194). Although Latchem believes distance education "provides a great opportunity for institutions that ... can see beyond the mere digital transmission of content ... to the fuller possibilities of global e-learning" (p. 194), the challenge is "not simply to provide teaching that is as good as in the traditional classroom but to use the instructional tools and methods in ways that achieve *better* or *different* learning outcomes" (p. 190).

The efficiencies of distance education are alluring—time is saved, money is saved, and presumably educational goals are met. The Internet is a very good tool for information and communication but "not so useful for other forms of learning" (Carr-Chellman, 2005, p. 150). Carr-Chellman further says

> [The Internet] tends to disconnect people rather than connect them. So, we try to retrofit the basic nature of the thing so that it *can* connect people. The basic nature of the tool, however, the existential nature of the experience of online learning is isolating. It is more isolating than if you were to go to a classroom and attend face-to-face learning experiences (p. 150).

Carr-Chellman (2005) ends with a warning:

> Technology will indeed enhance individual choice. The issue is that we have to carefully design it to do that; otherwise, it will serve the purposes of the most powerful factions in American society. The innate nature of technology will serve our American instincts for efficiency, individualism,

and vocation rather than liberation, democracy, diversity and community. A careful study of unregulated markets and deregulation in America may serve to help us predict failures and design online learning technologies that truly advance democracy (p. 157).

Effective distance education must do more than inform and communicate. "Today's online students need appropriate guidance for their assignments and relevant class discussions and activities" (Muirhead, 2004, ¶ 3). Further, "instructors can diminish student motivation by assigning an excessive number of assignments and having numerous discussion questions in their weekly dialogs" (2004, ¶ 3).

Distance education is popular and successful in the area of adult health promotion and disease management. Roughly 8 out of 10 Internet users have used the Internet to search for health information (Fox, 2006). "Many national groups, including the Robert Wood Johnson Foundation and the Science Panel on Interactive Communication and Health, have repeatedly emphasized the need for more evaluation research in this area" (Evers, 2006, p. 3). Evers (2006) examined the research on the impact and efficacy of Internet programs on health behavior and the results were promising.

> A meta-analysis was conducted in 2004 to examine the effectiveness of web-based interventions on behavior-change outcomes.... Effects-size comparisons in the use of web-based interventions when compared with no-web-based interventions showed an improvement in outcomes for knowledge and behavior change for several different behaviors (p. 4).

Further research is needed in the area of distance learning and health promotion. Recruitment and retention continue to be a problem. "Developers and researchers need to move beyond a narrow focus on early adopters and produce a population perspective on recruitment and retention of participants in programs" (Evers, 2006, p. 6). Until the field of eHealth engages a larger percentage of the at-risk population, "they will not be able to realize their potential to be the lowest cost modality for delivering tailored communications that can have the highest potential impacts on health promotion, disease prevention, and disease management" (p. 6).

The following is a summary of the adult distance learning issues found in the literature: (a) more work is needed to find methodologies that achieve better or different learning outcomes than from traditional classrooms; (b) technology will enhance individual choice only if we design it to do that; (c) students in distance education need guidance and relevant discussions and activities, not assignment overload to compensate for lack of face-to-face teaching; (d) eHealth is a popular form of distance education but used mostly by early adopters who represent a small percentage of the at-risk population. The studies indicate that distance learning is being done extensively but there is concern that this methodology is not always meeting the learning needs of the distance learner.

The last theme emerging from the current literature on applying andragogical principles to Internet learning is interactivity. "Effective online courses use interactive instructional strategies and learning events that flow from and support course learning objectives" (Merrill, 2006, p. 13). Technologies that make interactivity possible are called information communication technologies, or ICT. It allows both synchronous (same-time) and asynchronous (different-time) delivery and communication.

> Examples of synchronous delivery include two-way audio (via computer, telephone or radio) or two-way video, IM, text messages and online chat. Examples of asynchronous delivery include e-mail, listservs, online bulletin boards, blogs, videotapes, CD-ROMS or archived audio and video streams (p. 13).

High-speed bandwidth Internet capacity is converging with ICT to carry content. The result is course management systems called CMS, such as Blackboard, WebCT, Angel, and eCollege (Merrill, 2006). The role of the facilitator is important as content and process expert, manager of the structure and process, and developer of effective groups. The author notes the importance of the facilitator developing an engaging voice and personalized tone. "Using student names and inclusive language (we, you, our) in emails, forum postings, chat exchanges, and rubric or other assessment feedback helps build relationships" (p. 15).

Preface

A member Website called The Virtual Learning Space (VLS) (2006) is an example of self-directed interactive learning. It is "an environment dedicated to facilitating learning in information and communication technologies via online collaboration" (¶ 1). It allows professionals to come together to share best practices and new ideas. A Discovery section includes general references, space to support eWorkshops, and eNewsletters.

"Ontologies can support group interaction and discussion, role-playing, team learning, and other forms of collaborative, cooperative, and conversational learning" (Beck, 2006, p. 32). Ontologies are concept maps that represent a single concept and links between pairs of nodes that express relationships between them (Beck, 2006). They could be called tools for the construction of e-learning systems. One example of how ontologies can create a tailored adult learning experience is when "the topic ontology drives the overall search whose results are organized to give precedence to elements that match students' learning styles" (pp. 35–36). The idea of ontologies as databases are new but the connection between computer-based knowledge representations and cognitive processes involved in learning looks promising (p. 37).

"Informal and less structured, e-learning has done wonders for learners' ability to be self-directed" (Chapnick & Meloy, 2005, p. 33). Yet "when an asynchronous, off-the-shelf type of e-learning is used that has a teacher-knows-best tone, it not only is *not* self-directing, it is actually disempowering" (p. 33). Interactivity alone is not enough to engage adults in online learning. Chapnick and Meloy (2005) introduce a new learning theory created by Stewart Hase, an Australian professor of organizational learning, called heutagogy. As a relatively new theory, it adds to andragogy by giving special emphasis to one of its cardinal principles—self-directed learning. Heutagogy supports the following:

- Learning how to learn—the process of acquiring knowledge, not just with more knowledge;
- Double loop learning—learning how to examine one's own internal assumptions, values, and beliefs, a key part of learning how to learn;
- Universal learning opportunities—a heightened emphasis on the importance of organic and informal learning experiences, anything from internships to everyday activities or events;

- Nonlinear process—most learning does not follow a logical process but many of its steps are done either subconsciously or not at all;
- True learner self-direction—self-determined learning is not teacher-centered like most other e-learning. People learn when they are ready and this happens randomly, chaotically and in the face of ambiguity and need (pp. 37–38).

Heutogogy puts the learner truly in charge of what they learn and when. The vast majority of e-learning still does not even approach being self-directed (Chapnick & Meloy, 2005, p. 39). Heutogogy provides a framework for e-learning that puts the adult in charge of "much more than whether they press the forward or back button" (p. 39).

Here is a restatement of the interactivity issues arising from the current literature: (a) effective online courses use interactive instructional strategies, (b) online learning facilitators must develop an engaging voice and tone, (c) the website VLS is an example of self-directed interactive learning for professionals, (d) ontologies can support group interaction and cooperative learning, and (e) e-learning supports a new learning theory called heutogogy that adds to and supports andragogy by emphasizing true self-directed learning.

Recent literature therefore demonstrates more progress in the area of interactivity than e-learning barriers and distance education. It is not surprising that interactivity is progressing at a rapid rate. Society demands it for businesses and personal lives. But, as the literature demonstrates, e-learning requires more than just being in touch. It seems that current distance learning is not meeting the expectations of the learners. The new learning theory heutogogy emphasizes andragogy's self-directed learning principle and is advancing the thinking for e-learning. The learner must be in charge of what they will learn and how they will learn it. Ontologies seem to have promise in the area of tailoring the e-learning experience. Merrill (2006) recognized the importance of the e-learning facilitator's tone and voice.

Of high importance in applying andragogical principles to Internet learning, is climate setting—or creating an online physical and psychological environment that is respectful. There is evidence that the opposite is true. It seems that facilitators and students of distance learning spend too much time online with too little return for their effort. It should not be that way. In this recent research, there was no literautre that pointed to evidence of Internet learning resulting in *better* or *different* learning outcomes.

The following study on applying andragogical principles to Internet learning describes a promising new approach to Internet learning at a time when a *better* or *different* idea seems to be sorely needed. Interactivity is here—it is just waiting for a process to connect adult learners (with or without a teacher) to what they need to learn, how they need to learn it, in the way they like to learn.

Acknowledgements

My husband unselfishly and without fail gave his full support and encouragement while I worked. My children, as my biggest fans, set the expectation that I would succeed.

John Henschke, Ed.D. guided and supported my development over many years and taught me how to be an adult educator. Mary Cooper, Ph.D., Carl Hoagland, Ph.D., and George McCall, Ph.D. together with Dr. Henschke, advanced and at times redirected my work through their intelligence, encouragement, and dedication.

Dan Shoemaker, President of ExpressiveTek, took my idea and made it work with his technological wizardry. Tony Marshall, ExpressiveTek Graphic Artist, gave the idea life with his creativity and graphic design. The Air Force and their collaboration with a major drug company took a risk in partnering on this project and gave unselfishly of their time, talent, and resources. After the lived experience, all of the above stakeholders willingly and generously allowed me to interview them, telling the story as they knew it with richness and detail that far exceeded my expectations.

Applying Andragogical Principles to Internet Learning

CHAPTER ONE

OVERVIEW OF THE STUDY

It is important for adults to be lifelong learners. In the 1998 report to the United Nations Educational, Scientific and Cultural Organization (UNESCO) of the International Commission on Education for the Twenty-First Century, Jacque Delors, the chairman of the commission called education the necessary utopia and sees education as an "indispensable asset in its attempt to attain the ideals of peace, freedom and social justice" (p. 13). Maintaining a knowledge status quo is not an option for those who want to pursue their unalienable rights as defined by Thomas Jefferson in the Declaration of Independence—life, liberty, and the pursuit of happiness. To sustain and nurture life requires valuing good health and personal safety and understanding what it takes to sustain them. Liberty, or freedom to think and do as we please, requires an understanding of personal rights and limitations, which positions members of a society to be in control of their destinies. And, pursuit of happiness, which could be described as the ability to realize a personal vision, always requires gaining new competencies that are a dynamic interplay of knowledge, understanding, skill, attitude, value, or interest (Becker, 1977). "So, the pursuit of happiness is a journey we take from within; liberty is the freedom we allow ourselves;

and life is the vessel which carries both our happiness and our freedom" (Casper, 1996, ¶ 2). There are things adults *ought* to learn in order to survive, to work, to be happy, and to be good citizens (Knowles, 1980).

Lifelong Learning

Lifelong learning has become a necessity, not only to realize the full benefits of our rights as citizens but also because, "In an era of breathtaking change, it is truly impossible to acquire early in life the knowledge that adulthood will require" (Smith, 1982, p. 15). Delors (1998) reports that the concept of learning throughout life emerges as one of the keys to the twenty-first century because it meets the challenges posed by a rapidly changing world. Further, "the only way of satisfying it is for each individual to learn how to learn" (p. 22). According to Delors, the term learning how to learn is the sum total of four separate and powerful components he refers to as the four pillars of learning: *learning to know, learning to do, learning to live together, and learning to be.*

And learning can also be a lifelong process. Smith (1982) said, "Because learning itself involves processes, understandings, and skills that can be learned and taught, one *can* learn how to learn more effectively and efficiently at any age" (p. 15). In summary, lifelong learning is a means for controlling personal destiny and keeping pace with society, regardless of age. More specific to this study, Smith (1982) further said, "Because if lifelong learning is absolutely essential and learning how to learn is feasible, then learning about learning takes on real importance. Time and energy given over to it stand to yield rich returns" (p. 15).

New Demands on the Adult Learner

This new knowledge-based society calls for mass-knowing of standard information just to participate and thrive. "In a world in which the accelerated rate of change and rapid globalization are transforming each individual's relationship with both time and space, learning throughout life is essential for people to retain mastery of their own destinies ..." (Delors, 1998, pp. 100–101). An information explosion has accelerated the pace of adult learning. In 1999, Merriam and Caffarella reported that the amount of information in the world doubles every seven years (p. 15). Longer life spans translate into more jobs and career changes over a lifetime with experts predicting that "today's graduates will work for as many as five different employers in as many as 10 different jobs ..." (McBride, 2003, ¶ 2), thus escalating the need for continuing education. Additionally, a longer life span produces a greater need to pay attention to healthy living.

MORE ADULTS USING COMPUTERS AND THE INTERNET

Adult learners are using computer technology and the Internet at an increasing rate to communicate, as well as to get and send information. A report on the Internet that used census data to track its use in the United States found that more than half the nation is now online. "In September 2001, 143 million Americans, or about 54 percent of the population, were using the Internet, and new users were adopting the technology at a rate of more than two million per month" (NTIA and the Economics and Statistics Administration, 2002, ¶ 1). Currently, according to Don Evans, Secretary of Commerce, "new census data shows that more than half of American households and more than half of all Americans are now connected to the Internet" (¶ 2). The report further states that the increased use of the Internet is rising among all people regardless of income, education, age, race, ethnicity, gender, or location (rural or urban). Lastly, Americans are conducting an expanding range of activities on the Internet with a notable 46% using e-mail, 36% searching for product and service information, 39% making online purchases, and 35% searching for health information (¶ 4). "The Internet is simply modern technology of communication" (Ryan, 1997, p. 1178).

ANDRAGOGICAL PRINCIPLES AND ADULT LEARNING

There is research that supports the notion that following the principles of adult learning improves adults' ability to learn. "Many research findings have tended to lend credibility to the conventional wisdom commonly associated with andragogical principles" (Ross, n. d., p. 32). There are many educators, scientists, and theorists who have attempted to explain why andragogical principles facilitate effective learning among adults. For example, Brookfield (1986) proposed six principles that underlie effective facilitation of learning—participation, mutual respect, collaboration, praxis, critical reflection, and self-direction. MacKeracher (1996) believes that it is the interaction of cognitive, affective, physical, social, and spiritual aspects that make andragogy effective in facilitating learning. A neuroscientist, Joseph LeDoux (2002) supports the principles of andragogy by declaring that learning occurs only when the whole mind is engaged—cognition, emotion, and motivation. Knowles (1996) described elements of the adult learning process design—climate setting, mutual planning, diagnosing needs, translating needs into objectives, designing learning experiences, and evaluating the extent to which the objectives have been achieved and called them "a set of procedures for facilitating the acquisition of content by the learners" (pp. 259–261). Further, Knowles said, "teaching is a process of guided interaction between the teacher, the student, and the materials of instruction …" (Knowles cited in Carlson, 1998, p. 4). Experts seem to agree that in order to facilitate adult learning, more than just the content must be considered.

ANDRAGOGY AND THE INTERNET

Clearly, the Internet expands the possibilities of meeting the growing learning needs of adults. However, though information rich, the Internet alone does not attend to the process of learning. Merriam and Caffarella (1999) believe that "having access to unlimited information is not the same as being able to search efficiently for the most significant information, or to even know what is most significant" (p. 17). Ratinoff (1995) believes that the information overload created by the Internet has resulted in "a social craving for simplifications, a popular demand for translating simplicity into action…" (p. 165). Further, Ratinoff sees "too many alternatives and information overload" (p. 173). Isenberg and Titus (1999) describe today's adults as information surfers that surf the net like they switch channels on the television. The authors' concern is "that many adults are engaging in passive learning with a tool that requires active participation and interaction to accomplish objectives" (p. 3).

Overview of the Study 5

STATEMENT OF THE PROBLEM

Described in 1999 as a practitioner concern by Isenberg and Titus:

> Adult learners are provided with a plethora of information at their fingertips through the Internet. However, the accessibility, volume, and speed of information and the practice of "surfing the net" raise a practitioner concern over the user's ability to meet learning needs. Because online adults can get the information they need at the time they need it and in the way they need it, the Internet would seem to be one of the ultimate learning tools. However, until adults learn how to learn, the "link to the world" may merely be an information box, not a tool for learning (p. 1).

According to Isenberg and Titus (1999):

> The importance of the concern is threefold: 1) many adults' educational background has left them ill-equipped to be lifelong learners; 2) failure to learn on the Internet may lead to frustration, anger, and a fear of trying again; and 3) communication technology is expanding so rapidly that adult education research is not able to keep pace with Internet learning practice (p. 1).

This previous threefold concern still prevails today for adult education practitioners. The traditional linear model, research to practice, is a deductive approach where premises lead to conclusions. This implies that practice arises from research. In reality, practice to research, which is an inductive approach where conclusions lead to premises, also occurs. Isenberg and Titus (1999) further describe the concern and suggest a new practice model:

> The phenomenon of research falling behind practice is not a new discussion topic in the profession. As recently as the 1998 Midwest Research-to-Practice Conference, a panel discussion addressed the importance of thinking in terms of a model that reflects the reciprocal or back-and-forth

relationship between research and practice. ... Henschke (1987) identified a number of literature sources that looked to practice as an important resource for research. ... Shön's idea of reflection in action is better understood by his 1983 statement, "When someone reflects-in-action, he becomes a researcher in the practice context" (p. 68). Building theory, according to Kenny and Harnisch in 1982 (cited in Deshler & Hagan, 1989, p. 152), is not an either / or approach, but instead, a blending of deductive and inductive approaches called action research described as researching what you are doing while you are doing it ... for the purpose of solving a problem. Perhaps the new action research model (Figure 1) that reflects the blending of research and practice, better reflects today's practitioners research concerns (p. 4).

Regarding the practice of adult learning, Isenberg and Titus (1999) believe that there must be a change in "the dominant static linear model, from research comes practice, to reflect the current reality that the opposite is also true (from practice comes research), resulting in a new dynamic,

FIGURE 1. Isenberg and Titus' new research / practice model

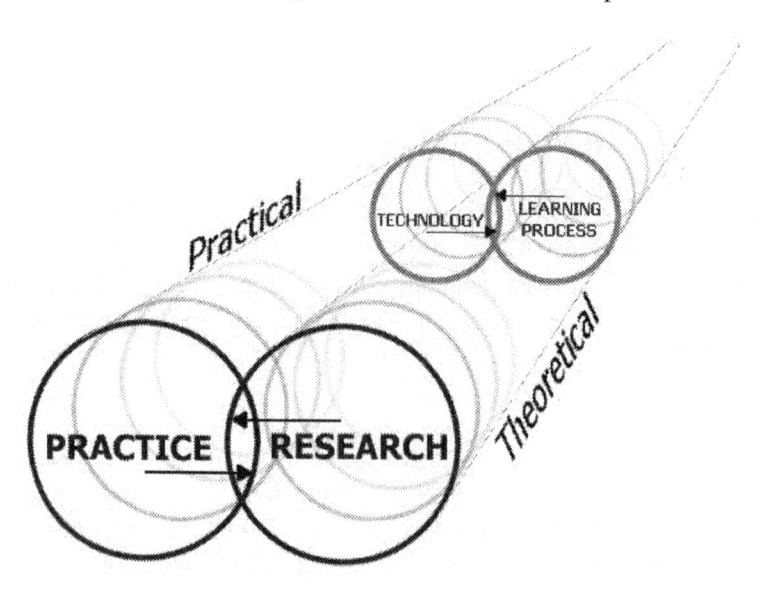

Overview of the Study 7

three-dimensional model illustrating a blending of the two" (p. 1). The back-and-forth relationship between practice and research is clearly demonstrated by the model.

The authors describe the model as follows:

> [Regarding the practice of adult learning] ... The two largest circles show an order reversal by putting *practice* in the left circle. This demonstrates that practice is ahead of research. The second set of blended circles (technology to learning process) is placed directly behind to show a blending of sets as well. Just as practice is ahead of research, technology is ahead of the adult learning process. The *theoretical*, research and the learning process, overlap with the *practical*, practice and technology. From an adult learning perspective, the overlap of the *practical* and *theoretical* aligns with the interactive dimension of the contextual perspective. The pairs of circles disappearing into infinity depict a research / practice model that is future oriented and protected from obsolescence. Future practitioners will fill in related concepts for their own time (pp. 4–5).

Because educators of adults are not physically present to facilitate effective Internet learning, it seems logical that creators of adult Internet learning experiences should follow andragogical principles when creating the programs to increase the likelihood that the adult's learning needs will be met. Lewin (1951) said, "There is nothing so practical as a good theory" (p. 169). But, the practice of Internet learning is ahead of the theory of adult learning. Educators of adults lack a how-to guide for applying adult learning principles to Internet learning. Presently, practitioners use adult learning techniques in classroom settings and may supplement learning with a traditional Internet-based learning program. However, the experiences remain separate, existing side-by-side and not integrated.

Ratinoff (1995) recognizes a need for order among the information chaos and suggests considering "the interaction between the quantity and quality of knowledge" (p. 165). It can be assumed that andragogical principles are applied to adult learning experiences by those trained in the field where and whenever possible. But, presently, there seems to be no protocol for how to integrate theory and practice in this area, or, in other words, how to apply the principles of adult learning to the practice of Internet learning.

Purpose of the Study

To create a protocol to facilitate adult Internet learning requires an education expert and a technology expert. Both have different training, background, and experience yet both are very process-oriented but perhaps with two different goals. Education's goal is learning and technology's goal is functionality. Dissecting the path taken to create a prototype for an adult Internet learning experience may add to the development of knowledge, understanding, skill, attitude, value, or interest (Knowles, 1980) needed to create a protocol on how to build a technologically functioning program (no matter what the subject or curriculum) that has the necessary process elements to facilitate learning.

This study will explore whether it is possible to support the principles and technology of adult learning, while creating an Internet learning experience?

Other issues that will be examined include:

1. What are the issues with face-to-face teaching / learning during the development of the program?
2. What are the issues without face-to-face teaching / learning during the development of the program?
3. Can an Internet program stimulate whole-mind thinking (cognition, emotion, and motivation) to learn?
4. How does the design meet the goal of the International Commission on Education for the Twenty-First Century (UNESCO) for learning throughout life as described by the four pillars of learning: learning to know, learning to do, learning to live together, and learning to be?

Importance of the Study

The results of this study may be important to adult education practitioners who are attempting to change traditional classroom learning experiences

Overview of the Study 9

into Internet-based learning experiences. The study addresses the practitioner concern that adult learners may not be getting their learning needs met with today's Internet technology.

The findings of this study will also be important to adult learners who specifically use the Internet to intentionally learn. As end-users, they may benefit directly from Internet learning experiences that incorporate the principles of andragogy.

Other stakeholders interested in the results of this study will be persons or organizations (commercial or non-profit) that are interested in helping adults learn and change on the computer such as colleges and universities, corporations, librarians, social workers, counselors, community health organizations, politicians, parent educators, and medical patient educators.

DEFINITION OF TERMS

Andragogy—Andragogy is the art and science of helping adults learn (Knowles, 1980, p. 40). Alexander Kapp, a German educator, coined the term andragogy in 1833. Smith (1982) defines the term adult as follows: "The person who regards himself or herself as an adult and has assumed the responsibilities associated with adulthood (worker, spouse, parent) is considered to be an adult and, therefore, is fair game for adult educators and likely to learn best under conditions that take into account the characteristics of adults as learners" (p. 38). Smith further says, "... then, adult education refers to a purposeful effort to foster learning by persons who have become largely responsible for their own comings and goings ..." (p. 38).

Change—Learning and changing are used synonymously in this study. Making a change requires learning something new. Tough (1982) said, "Learning is a fundamental concept and is always involved in some kind of change" (p. 10). Change consultant and author, Richard Beckhard (1997) said, "all learning is transactional and all learning is change" (pp. 159–161).

Learning—Smith (1982), defines learning as "a transformation that occurs in the brain; problem solving; an internal process that leads to behavioral change; the construction and exchange of personally relevant and viable meanings; a retained change in disposition or capability that is not simply ascribable to growth; and a process of changing insights, outlooks, expectations, or thought patterns" (p. 34). Further, Smith says that learning has three different meanings—learning can be thought of as a product, as a process, and as a function. As a product, learning emphasizes outcomes. As a process, learning explains what happens when learning takes place. And, as a function, learning describes important aspects that produce learning (like motivation) (p. 34). In this study, the focus will be on learning as a process and function, not as a product.

Proof-of-concept—A proof-of-concept is the product that is a result of a first attempt to turn an idea into a product. When an inventor looks to implement a new technology, he or she naturally seeks assurance that it works and that it will really deliver the claimed benefits.

Learning contract—A learning contract is a way to help learners structure their own learning. Knowles (1980) illustrates a construct that is a table with five columns—learning objectives, learning resources and strategies, target date for completion, evidence of accomplishment of objectives, and criteria and means for validating the evidence. "Contract learning solves, or at least reduces, the problem of dealing with wide differences within any group of adult learners" (Knowles, 1980, p. 381).

LIMITATIONS

Change is either intentional or unintentional. Human changes occur as a result of both. Sometimes the steps to achieve the change require a great deal of effort. Breaking a habit, learning a complex skill, or understanding economic affairs are examples of difficult intentional change. This study will focus on highly deliberate efforts to learn or what Tough calls learning projects. Allen Tough (1979) defined a learning project as:

> simply a major, highly deliberate effort to gain certain knowledge and skill (or to change in some other way). Some learning projects are efforts to gain new knowledge, insight, or understanding. Others are attempts to improve one's skill or performance, or to change one's attitudes or emotional reactions. Others involve efforts to change one's overt behavior or to break a habit (p. 1).

In this study, the teaching / learning that occurred during the development of the Internet program is understood to be the process of guided interaction, not classroom instruction.

DELIMITATIONS

In this study, unintentional change that happens as a result of shock or evolution will not be addressed. Instead, the focus will be on intentional change, which can be thought of as anticipated change.

ASSUMPTIONS

There will be an underlying assumption in this study that learning leads to change, and change leads to learning, and that one does not happen without the other.

CHAPTER TWO

BACKGROUND

Many adult educators and theorists have written about andragogy, the art and science of adult learning. Internet learning is a much newer concept than andragogy and many topics related to it have been explored in the literature. However, few researchers have examined the integration of the two. To study the application of andragogy principles to Internet learning, several topics will be explored in the literature. There is a sequential order to the topics, each building on the previous one to build a scaffold of logic, upon which suggestions for a protocol are based. The topics reviewed move from general to specific as follows: principles of adult learning, technology of adult learning, issues with face-to-face teaching / learning, issues without face-to-face teaching / learning, whole-mind learning, the four pillars of learning, the role of creativity in innovation, Internet learning, and making the connection between Internet learning and andragogy.

PRINCIPLES OF ADULT LEARNING

Educators of adults have described the uniqueness of adult learners since Kapp first used the term "andragogy." Prior to this, there is evidence that well-respected historical figures knew there was a difference between adult and youth learners in the way they described how they transmitted knowledge, understanding, skill, attitude, value, and interest to adults. To begin a quest for how to integrate andragogy and Internet learning, it is important to first understand what is known about the adult learner.

Examples of andragogy can be found early in the recorded history of the world. Before it was named, the art and science of adult learning was practiced as evidenced by early writings about Socrates. Known only through the writing of his students Plato and Xenophon, an Ancient Greek historian, Socrates (480 B.C.) used conversation for the "dialectic improvement of the learner" (LoveToKnow Corp., 2002a, ¶ 16). Understanding that the answer comes from the learner, and not the teacher, he invented the Socratic method or the asking of probing questions to promote learning. He promoted self-assessment or know thyself, a cornerstone of adult learning and understood that adults' past learning and experience contributes to new learning through reflective and critical thought. Socrates perceived learning as a process of active mental inquiry. Socrates' inquiry method is described as a dialectical method with two distinguishable processes: the destructive process, by which the worse opinion is eradicated; and the constructive process, by which the better opinion is induced (LoveToKnow Corp., 2002b, ¶ 6). Further, Socrates found that many learners "stopped short at the stage of perplexity" when, in fact, "the constructive process was the proper and necessary sequel" (¶ 10). Socrates carried his learners to positive conclusions—conclusions that are concerned with practical action. Therefore, in general, there is a process from the known to the unknown. Taylor (1986) would agree that not facilitating the movement of the learners past the stage of perplexity results in less than positive conclusions.

In light of what is known about the Socratic method, a Socratic Internet learning experience could be described as a process that takes the learner from the known to the unknown by asking probing questions in a conversational way, honoring past experiences, and promoting reflective thought. Ending with a practical action plan will increase the possibility that a constructive process follows the destructive one.

In the 17th century, Comenius demonstrated his understanding of the principles of adult learning by being an advocate of systematizing all knowledge (Columbia Electronic Encyclopedia, 2000). Savićević (1991) suggests that Comenius also supported the comprehensiveness of education and learning for the purpose of developing, to the full degree of humaneness, all people regardless of age, gender, culture, class, or nationality. Comenius promoted teacher innovation to make learning interesting and practical, and he also believed that learning comes through the senses. Additionally, he saw the need for personal motivation in learning (Columbia Electronic Encyclopedia, 2000). Important to this study is Comenius' recognition that learning involves portions of the mind other than cognition—preferred learning style and motivation.

Benjamin Franklin stressed the importance of self-education and informed citizenry that led him to encourage the founding of public libraries. The idea started from his love of books and the creation of Junto in 1728. The Junto was a weekly and guided discussion group of citizenry who were interested in pursuing truth and advancing mankind by sharing ideas and knowledge. He took climate setting into account when he declined to have the Junto's meetings in a tavern but "consented to the members downing a glass of wine before moving from one discussion topic to another" (Smith, 1982, pp. 48–49).

Franklin decided that members of the Junto would bring together books from their personal collections as they could best spare because their books were so often referred to in their discussions. Franklin was chosen to be librarian and this was the beginning of public libraries. Important to this story is the fact that the Internet is like a library that never closes, and is a library without a librarian. Just as important to this story is how successful the climate was for learning by truly treating the members as adults. The Junto was active and vital under Franklin's leadership for 30 years. A protocol for integrating andragogy and Internet learning must serve not only as a learning process guide but also like a librarian directing users to appropriate resources in a climate of respect.

As an adult education philosopher, Lindeman (1961) was concerned about the meaning of adult education. He called for "a new kind of education with its initial assumption affirming that education is life—not a mere preparation for an unknown kind of future living" (p. 4). Lindeman can be summarized as a visionary who saw beyond technique to describe the "quintessential format" (Brookfield, 1984, p. 195) of program planning. So, it might be that a protocol for integrating andragogy and Internet learning must go beyond technique to address the higher needs of the adult. Brookfield (1984) said, "… we can ill afford to ignore the contemporary relevance, intellectual elegance, and inspirational vision of the major American philosopher of adult education [Lindeman]" (p. 195).

A long time before the Internet was invented, Verner (1962) differentiated between general dissemination of knowledge and systematic diffusion of knowledge. He said, "The field of mass communication is developing the specialized knowledge about general dissemination while systematic diffusion is the special area of adult education" (p. 2). Further, learning may be the result of both "but it is assumed here that learning, which can take place only within the individual, is more apt to occur when processes that facilitate learning are applied systematically" (p. 2). The objectives of the institution will determine which method is used. Some will use both. "Basically, the choice is determined by the degree to which the institution is willing to accept conformity to its objectives or the alteration of values, attitudes, and behavior that results from an individual's exercise of his own rational discretion as a consequence of learning" (p. 2).

Automobile companies seeking changes in the behavior of their new customers that result from rational thought follow procedures for the systematic diffusion of knowledge. A glove-box automobile owner's manual is an example of systematic diffusion of knowledge, a clear and simple way for the user to learn how to operate the car. It begins with how to open the door and moves to how to start the engine, etc. The section on normal maintenance of the car comes before the section on specific problems that could occur with the car. Imagine if new owners were given the automobile's detailed specifications book, which is a big thick catalog of the new car's parts and repair details that are listed in alphabetical order. These manuals are designed for use by trained automobile mechanics only. The average new car owner would most likely be overwhelmed with so many details. Institutions seeking changes in behavior that result from rational thought follow procedures for the systematic diffusion of knowledge. The Internet could be thought of as what Verner labeled as general dissemination of knowledge. Creating an Internet learning protocol could be thought of as a way of changing general dissemination of knowledge into a systematic diffusion of knowledge. Thus, facilitation of learning on the Internet would be enhanced and not just left to chance.

Freire (1973) wrote about critical consciousness as essential for transforming a person's reality and contends that a change in consciousness is the defining characteristic of learning in adulthood. He said, "... to every understanding, sooner or later an action corresponds" (p. 44). He further says, "Once man perceives a challenge, understands it, and recognizes the possibilities of response, he acts" (p. 44). According to Freire, helping people move from naive to critical transitivity requires a process that uses an active, dialogical, criticism-stimulating method. To summarize what can be gleaned from the work of Freire, an Internet learning process that intends to transform the learner may benefit from using a challenging dialog methodology.

Knowles, assumptions about adult learners lend an understanding of what elements may be helpful to include when creating an Internet learning experience. He uses comparisons to distinguish youth from adult learners as well as traditional from andragogical models of teaching to demonstrate how adults learn best. First, the following Table 1 (Knowles, 1973, p. 119) illustrates the differences between youth learners and adult learners regarding assumptions and design of education programs. The comparison clearly demonstrates that pedagogy is teacher centered and andragogy is learner centered.

Additionally, Knowles (1973) describes the andragogical model as a process model, in contrast to the content models employed by most traditional educators. "A process can be seen as a value chain, with each step adding value to the preceding steps" (Knowles, Holton, & Swanson, 1998, p. 257). In Knowles' original depiction of a process model, the andragogical teacher prepares in advance a set of procedures for involving the learner in a process that involves the following elements: (a) establish a climate conducive to learning; (b) creating a mechanism for mutual planning; (c) diagnosing the needs for learning; (d) formulating program objectives (which is content) that will satisfy these needs; (e) designing a pattern of learning experiences; (f) conducting these learning experiences with suitable

TABLE 1. A Comparison of the Assumptions and Designs of Pedagogy and Andragogy

	Assumptions		Design Elements	
	Pedagogy	Andragogy		Pedagogy	Andragogy
Self-concept	Dependency	Increasing self-directiveness	Climate	Authority-oriented Formal Competitive	Mutuality Respectful Collaborative Informal
Experience	Of little worth	Learners are a rich resource for learning	Planning	By teacher	Mechanism for mutual planning
Readiness	Biological development social pressure	Developmental tasks of social roles	Diagnosis of needs	By teacher	Mutual self-diagnosis
Time perspective	Postponed application	Immediacy of application	Formulation of objectives	By teacher	Mutual negotiation
Orientation to learning	Subject centered	Problem centered	Design	Logic of the subject matter Content units	Sequenced in terms of readiness Problem units
			Activities	Transmittal techniques	Experiential techniques (inquiry)
			Evaluation	By teacher	Mutual re-diagnosis of needs Mutual measurement of program

techniques and materials; and (g) evaluating the learning outcomes and rediagnosing learning needs (p. 102). Later, Knowles (1995) added an eighth element that precedes the others, preparing the learners for the program / course. In light of this, a protocol for transforming curriculum into an Internet adult learning experience could be called an andragogical model (process model) if it involved these eight elements. In contrast, the Internet alone could be thought of as merely content in a content model.

Smith (1982) also describes how adults learn best. Smith's six conditions that must be met for optimal learning include two that Knowles described, climate setting and mutual planning. Additionally, Smith discusses the importance of tailoring the learning experience to (a) the learner's life stage; (b) the amount of autonomy the learner demonstrates; (c) the learner's past experiences; and (d) the learner's preferred learning style (pp. 48–49). A protocol that allows a facilitator to tailor an Internet learning experience to unique characteristics of the learner may improve learning.

Brookfield (1986) warns practitioners to be wary of any standardized approach to learning because "every learning group contains a configuration of idiosyncratic personalities, all with differing past experiences and current orientations, all at different levels of readiness for learning, and all possessing individually developed learning styles" (p. 122). This statement supports Smith's (1982) belief in the need for tailoring of the educational experience, whether traditional or on the Internet.

Tough makes the link between learning and changing. Tough (1982) believed that "learning is a fundamental concept and is always involved in some kind of change" (p. 10). With this statement, Tough sanctions the interchangeability of learning and change. Tough (1982) also says that intentional change is a normal, natural process and that learners are surprised to discover their own planning processes, competencies, power, and success. "Most people have a very low opinion of their capacity for bringing about changes in themselves and their lives" (p. 99). Tough (1982) believes that facilitators of change / learning should "help people see the effectiveness of their own natural change process" (p. 99). It would seem that a protocol for creating an Internet learning experience should follow the learner's own natural process for intentional learning and changing and, at the same time, make the learner aware of the benefit of doing so.

Mezirow (1981) promotes self-directedness by identifying a potential risk for adult educators who do not promote it. He says:

> we must attempt to provide the specialized educational resource adult learners seek when they choose to use an adult educator, but our professional perspective needs to be unequivocal: we must respond to the learner's educational need in a way which will improve the quality of his or her self-directedness as a learner. To do less is to perpetuate a dysfunctional dependency relationship between learner and educator (p. 21).

Mezirow (1981) is quick to add that the adult educator is not value-free. "His [the adult educator's] selection of alternative meaning perspectives will reflect his own cultural values ..." (p. 20). Regarding a protocol for creating an Internet educational experience, Mezirow supports the notion that the educator will have an impact on the learner through his or her selection of alternative meaning perspectives. To think about an application of this piece, self-directedness in an Internet learning experience may not mean unlimited choices but instead controlled decision-making.

To restate the review of the literature on adult learning principles, it seems that intentional learning among adults happens as a result of a systematic process: one that involves the learner through challenging dialog, is respectful of past experiences, is modeled after a normal natural process, allows controlled decision-making, is tailored to learner's unique needs, and creates a climate that makes the learner feel welcome and safe to experiment. Hence, these principles might provide criteria for successfully integrating andragogy and Internet technology. The byproduct of this research could be a proof-of-concept software program and perhaps it could be measured against the principles identified in this section.

TECHNOLOGY OF ADULT LEARNING

The assumptions about adult learners have implications for the practice or technology of andragogy. Knowles (1980) said, "Methods and techniques, which involve the individual most deeply in self-directed inquiry will produce the greatest learning" (p. 56). Adults are themselves the richest learning resource for one another for many kinds of learning (Cooper,

Henschke, & Isaac, 2003). Verner (1962) said, "Institutions seeking changes in behavior that result from rational thought employ procedures for the systematic diffusion of knowledge" (p. 2). To do this, Verner said it is necessary to design and construct specific situations for learning that are characterized by a "continuous and direct exchange between the institution through its agent and the learning public" (p. 2). If one applies the work of these authors to this study, a protocol for creating an Internet adult learning experience that results in behavior change must promote rational thought. And to promote rational thought, one must lead the learner through a systematic diffusion of knowledge by way of a continuous exchange between the *virtual* teacher and the learner.

The Whole-Part-Whole (WPW) Learning Model (Knowles et al., 1998) purports that there is a "natural whole-part-whole rhythm to learning" (p. 186). This systematic approach starts with the first whole by introducing new content to give the learner a framework to absorb the concept(s) or part(s) that come next. Then, the facilitator links these parts together to form the second whole. The first whole could be thought of as an advance organizer (Ausubel, 1968), used by the facilitator as a technique to prepare and motivate the learner for the lesson by doing such things as giving background information and defining new terms. The parts are the details of knowledge, techniques, and skills. The second whole is considered the most important of the three components. According to Gestalt theory, the whole is greater than the sum of its parts (Elias & Merriam, 1980). Understanding how everything links together is what the authors refer to as forming the "instructional whole" (p. 191). Furthermore, "using active learning in the 'second whole' will allow students to practice all of their skills in one continuous procedure" (p. 191). To apply the WPW Learning Model to this study, it might be most important to ensure that the Internet learner is allowed to practice all skills in one continuous procedure in the second whole. Perhaps this could be accomplished through the online creation of an action-oriented learning contract.

Knowles (1984, 1995) offers practical and concrete suggestions for creating an andragogical model. Knowles describes eight elements of an andragogical process design by which one could measure progress toward having one. The first two elements are: (a) preparing the learner and (b) establishing a climate conducive to learning, both the physical and the psychological atmosphere. A room that is bright, cheery, well lighted, and well ventilated where there is mutual respect, collaboration, mutual trust, openness, fun, support, and humanness would satisfy both the physical and psychological climate needs.

Regarding establishing a climate conducive to learning, colors are more than the combination of red and blue or yellow and black. Colors have symbolism and color meanings as non-verbal communications. "... It is helpful to keep in mind how the eye and the mind perceive certain colors and the color meanings we associate with each color" (Bear, 2004, ¶ 1).

Knowles (1984) remaining six elements are process-oriented and learner-centered: (a) having a mechanism for mutual planning; (b) involving the learners in diagnosing their own learning needs; (c) formulating their own program objectives; (d) designing their own learning plans; (e) helping the learners carry out their own learning plans; and (f) involving the learners in evaluating their learning (pp. 15–18).

An andragogical climate can be created in an Internet learning experience by using bright, cheery colors, and by using a psychological tone of acceptance and caring in the text that demonstrates mutual respect, collaboration, mutual trust, openness, fun, support, and humanness. Additionally, it seems that a protocol for andragogical Internet learning should address Knowles remaining six elements, as listed in the preceding paragraph, in a systematic and sequential way that seems natural to the learner.

To provide structure to the learning and give even more control to the learner, Knowles (1975) recommends using learning contracts:

> The learning contract is a means of reconciling [these] imposed requirements from institutions and society with the learners' need to be self-directing. It enables them to blend these requirements in with their own personal goals and objectives, to choose their own ways of achieving them, and to measure their own progress toward achieving them. The learning contract thus makes visible the mutual responsibilities of the learner, the teacher, and the institution (p. 130).

According to Knowles (1975), a learning contract is created as follows: the learner (a) translates a diagnosed learning need into a learning objective; (b) identifies resources and strategies for accomplishing the objective; (c) specifies what evidence will be collected to show accomplishment; and lastly (d) states how the evidence will be validated. Present Internet technology makes the creation of an online learning contract not only possible but also rather easy to do. A series of carefully crafted pre-programmed questions and answers could result in the creation of a learning contract that could be printed for portable use, revisited and changed at any time.

Galbraith (1991) describes adult learning as transactional. He states that when "facilitators and adult learners are engaged in an active, challenging, collaborative, critically reflective, and transforming educational encounter, a transactional process is occurring" (p. 1). Further, "the desired result, because of the interaction, is that all involved participants will think and act differently, whether it be about the personal, professional, political, social, or recreational aspects of their lives" (p. 1). It is reasonable to say, then, that an interactive Internet adult learning experience should also transform users and cause them to be changed forever. Galbraith (1991) provides adult educators with six guiding principles for creating a transactional process: (a) follow a philosophy; (b) recognize and understand diversity among the learners; (c) create a climate conducive to learning; (d) provide challenging teacher—learner interactions; (e) foster critical reflection and praxis; and (f) encourage independence (p. 16). There is support for individual elements of Galbraith's six principles (Knowles, 1984; Mezirow, 1981; Verner, 1962).

Galbraith brings to the study a direction to maintain a philosophy. Elias and Merriam (1980) said, "philosophy raises questions about what we do and why we do it" (p. 5). Further, they said that:

> A philosophy of education does not equip a person with knowledge about what to teach, how to teach, or how to organize a program. It is more concerned with the why of education and with the logical analysis of the various elements of the educational process (pp. 16–17).

Key to this study is the importance of including an adult education philosophy statement and description in a protocol for creating an Internet learning program. For, "… philosophy will help focus on the ethical issues associated with the relationship of adult learning facilitation and adult learning ..." (Elias & Merriam, 1980, p. 17).

Prochaska, Norcross, and Diclemente (1995) studied change readiness. In this study, recall that change and learning are synonymous. Therefore, change readiness is the same as learning readiness. They identified six stages of change that most people move through to successfully make a change: (a) the precontemplation stage, when individuals are not even thinking about making a change; (b) the contemplation stage, when people are thinking about making a change in the next six months; (c) the preparation stage, when those who are ready to change develop a plan; (d) the action stage finds people in the middle of making a change; (e) the maintenance stage or the period of time at least six months after change; and (f) the termination stage, which is the period of time when it is not likely that people will go back to the old behavior and usually requires a five-year period of time to pass after the change is made. The importance of these authors' research may be the potential benefit of tailoring answers to the learner's stage of change as well as the potential risk of not tailoring the answers.

Consistent with the idea that adult learning is composed of process elements described as tasks (Knowles, 1984, 1995; Smith, 1982; Verner, 1962), Taylor (1986) studied learning toward self-direction, as the *learners* experience it. Taylor found that what previously was only observed to be true was indeed true as reported by the learner him or herself. Her work resulted in three distinct findings. First, she found that self-directed learning, as the learners experience it, is a connected flow of events over time with a specific chronological pattern. Taylor's study supports the notion that there is "an inherent order in what the learner is experiencing" (p. 68).

A second finding of Taylor (1986) is that learning is a major psychosocial reorientation and that the learner is "literally changing an interpretative framework within which reality is understood and which affords a wider range of behaviour [*sic*]" (p. 69). Similarly, Parkes (1971) talks about the restructuring of "the assumptive world" as a major element of psychosocial transitions toward greater personal responsibility-taking and self-direction. Papert (1993) thinks that contact with the computer can open access to knowledge, not instrumentally by providing people with processed information but by challenging the constraining assumptions that they have about themselves. Parallels could also be drawn to Mezirow's (1978) study of women returning to school who were found to have greater self-determination. Evident is the fact that learning is far more complex than acquiring skills and knowledge through tasks. Learners engaged in self-directed learning go beyond surface level content to deeper level interpretive processing (Taylor, 1986). LeDoux (2002) agrees that there is an emotional component of learning. The significance of this finding has implications for the design of an Internet learning experience. It suggests that efforts to promote self-direction include special social and psychological understanding and expertise.

And third, Taylor (1986) finds that, according to the learner, "the learning process was related to, but not simply a direct consequence of, the initiatives of others" (p. 70). She finds that self-direction is not brought about solely by the individual learner and not solely by the educational environment but instead, a delicate balance of both. Taylor (1986) said, "Since courses and educational programmes [sic] are temporary environments, one of the practical implications is the importance of promoting learner's awareness of relational contingencies so that transitions to other settings are understood and effectively managed" (p. 70). Taylor may agree that an implication for Internet programs is that there could be value in creating critical points in the movement toward self-direction regarding the learner's relationship with the program's events and the learner's perceptions and emotions.

Billington (2000) investigated which factors in adult learning environments best facilitate adult growth and development. A summary of her research described the only learning environment that resulted in significant personal growth. Unique to the author's findings was the importance of learning environments "... where individual needs and uniqueness are honored, [and] where life achievements are acknowledged and respected" (¶ 6). Therefore, a protocol for creating an Internet adult learning experience that addresses the above aspects of the learning process could be desirable. Allowing online learners to tailor their learning experience to meet unique needs can be accomplished through the use of a text box answer option to most multiple-choice questions. Including a section that asks learners about life achievements in categories that make sense to the intended learning would be easy to do.

Regarding the difference between the technology of pedagogical learning and the technology of adragogical learning, Marotta (1999) distinguishes power-over from power-with in a discussion about effective living for women. She said, "Too often, power has been viewed in a hierarchical way of power-over others. ... Power-with promotes the well-being of self and others, and is inspirational and considerate of others" (Marotta, 1999, ¶ 5). This implies that traditional pedagogical teaching techniques give teachers power-over the learner, and in contrast, andragogical teaching techniques give teachers power-with the learners.

The concept of distance learning should be mentioned as adult learning technology. Cooper and Henschke (2003) identify similarities between Knowles' description of a traditional adult learning environment (that comes from the concept of andragogy) and Simonson et al.'s (2003) description of characteristics needed in distance learning for adults. The characteristics are as follows:

> the physical environment of a television classroom used by adults should enable them to see what is occurring, not just hear it; the physiological environment should be one that promotes respect and dignity for the adult learner; adult learners must feel supported; a starting point for a course, or module of a course, should be the needs and interest of the adult learner; course plans should include clear course descriptions, learning objectives, resources, and timelines for events; general to specific patterns of content presentation work best for adult learners; and active participation should be encouraged, such as by the use of work groups, or study teams (p. 5).

These characteristics provide support for the notion that andragogical principles can be addressed in a non-traditional adult learning environment that is similar to Internet learning—both distance learning and Internet learning require learners to sit in front of a screen without a teacher in the room.

Bullen (n.d.) warns practitioners to be moderate rather than radical in their application of andragogical principles in distance education. According to

Bullen, moderate application means that practitioners should validate adult learner assumptions in their own contexts. Bullen implies that practitioners are not able to literally apply the principles of andragogy to distance learning. Similarly, this warning should be heeded when applying the principles of andragogy to Internet learning—be moderate and validate adult learner assumptions in the context of the Internet classroom.

Issues with Face-to-Face Teaching / Learning

Traditional education describes the situation when a teacher teaches a classroom of students. McLagan (1978) knows that the job of a teacher is to help others learn. She believes that teachers do this by making programs learnable. According to McLagan (1978), program learnability involves: (a) helping learners become motivated to change; (b) helping learners effectively handle course information and experiences; (c) helping learners develop knowledge, skills, values and attitudes, and / or creative ideas; and (d) helping learners transfer their learning to the application environment.

Knowles (1980) views learning as guided interaction. The role of the adult educator is to manage the educational process. Teaching, like medical practice, is mostly a matter of cooperation with nature. Initially defined as, "the art and science of helping adults learn," (Knowles, 1996, p. 254) andragogy has come to be understood as an alternative to pedagogy; a learner-focused approach for people of all ages. Implications for practice are twofold: (a) pedagogs are concerned with transmitting the content and (b) andragogs are concerned with facilitating learning. Sims and Sims (1995) believe that another aspect of taking a learner-focused approach is taking into account the learning differences among learners. "Learning styles, especially when used in conjunction with the nature of adult learning, do not begin and end in the training classroom. They become a natural part of education and life" (Sims & Sims, 1995, p. 170). Teachers who can help their students learn how to learn may give them advantages that extend way beyond the classroom (Smith, 1982). Just as classroom teachers follow a process to deliver content and, at the same time, assist students in following their preferred learning style, so might virtual teachers.

Henschke (1998) makes an andragogy theory / practice connection in his promotion of modeling what is taught. When the suggestion is made that theory and practice needs to be congruent when working in any regard with the development and / or education of adults, it is a process of modeling that would appear to be the most consistent way to be. Some of the earmarks indicated of being a model are in speech, manner of life, love, and trust. "Do what you say you will do, (DWYSYWD) is the critical difference of what leadership credibility is all about, which is the bottom line of a theory and practice connection" (Kouzes & Posner, 1993, p. 47).

Savićević (1999), like Knowles (1980), sees the adult educator as manager of the educational process. Savićević (1999) profiles the adult educator as a universal type that can organize and prepare the educational process, draw up plans and programs, counsel, direct, and evaluate the educational process. Further, "this broader type of adult educator would also more easily promote the desired creative integration of the educational and cultural elements of adult education" (p. 133). Implications for creating a protocol for integrating adult learning principles and Internet technology are that such a protocol might be able to take the place of the adult educator as manager of the educational process. And, perhaps, of equal significance, is the potential ability to creatively integrate educational and cultural elements with a manager protocol.

Issues without Face-to-Face Teaching / Learning

The subject of self-directed, self-paced learning, has been well studied and written about in education literature. There is support for the concept of adult learning as a self-structured process. Self-learning occurs alone or in a group without a face-to-face teacher.

Group learning is learning without face-to-face teaching / learning. Lewin (1951) believes that both personal traits as well as the group traits influence learning. Though people come to a group with very different dispositions, if they share a common objective, they are likely to act together to achieve it. He describes behavior as a result of both personal traits and surrounding environment. Lewin's work seems important to this study because people who come to the Internet are individuals with unique personal traits, but, if they have a common learning goal, they are members of a virtual group as well. This virtual group membership advantage might be realized through a chat room function where individuals working toward a common goal could support one another.

"Allen Tough and Cyril Houle were the first to produce a clear image of the self-directed learner" (Kidd cited in Tough, 1982, p. 9). "Study after study has now demonstrated that virtually all adults engage in self-planned learning, which is about 7 times more common than classroom learning" (Tough, 1981, Intro, p. 2). Tough found that 95% of college graduates conducted at least one self-directed teaching project during the previous year. As a result of his research, Tough (1981) describes teaching tasks, which he calls major decisions or actions that can be performed by either the teacher or the learner. Though they are listed in a sequential order, both the teacher and the learner can take circuitous routes and could totally eliminate some steps: (a) choosing the goal; (b) deciding which activities are appropriate; (c) obtaining the printed materials and other resources; (d) estimating the current level of knowledge and skill; (e) dealing with difficulty in grasping parts; (f) deciding when and where to learn; (g) deciding how much money to spend; (h) dealing with lack of desire for achieving the goal; (i) dislike of the activities necessary for learning and doubts about success; and (j) deciding whether to continue (p. 4). Modeling the natural and human behaviors of learners who are involved in self-directed learning projects may be an effective way to create an Internet learning experience.

When creating an Internet learning protocol, it may be important to not only include all the above decisions or actions described by Tough but also build in flexibility to allow the learner to go back and forth through the process in a more natural way. But, just as some people like to read the last chapter of a book first, some learners will want to jump ahead in an Internet learning program. It seems that it would be important to electronically disallow this behavior of jumping ahead only when it would create confusion or be illogical.

Tough believes that self-directed learning can also be called self-teaching and further, that the tasks listed above are performed by the self-teacher. What Tough has described is a learning process, one that adults have been observed doing naturally without guidance from a teacher. In light of Tough's research, a mechanism for addressing intangible barriers such as lack of motivation and confidence as well as those that are tangible (i.e., lack of knowledge, money) may give an Internet learning program more humanness. Tough (1979) replaces the term self-learning or self-teaching with the term, "self-planned learning project" (Intro, p. 2). He describes learner problems such as: (a) applying the knowledge to real-life situations; (b) finding and joining one or more fellow learners or experts who can provide companionship; (c) persuading one or more individuals to cooperate with the project, or at least to refrain from blocking it; (d) overcoming laziness or inertia; or (e) dealing with (or avoiding) unpleasant consequences of the learning, such as the smell after practicing a new recipe or aching muscles after practicing tennis (p. 69). In dealing with problems, the self-teacher might also decide which people could assist with one or more tasks (either directly or by offering advice) and then might obtain that assistance. Tough emphasizes that the above tasks related to problems in learning are strictly learner tasks, not teacher tasks, because the learner alone can do them.

Very early in the history of computers, Tough (1971) recognizes the value of nonhuman planners. He says that computers can present printed material (or even audio and visual material), evaluate responses, and use the learner's response history for choosing particular branches or sequences of material. Further, Tough (1971) sees the advantage of a good nonhuman resource for planning and, in fact, it "… may be the most efficient guide in a learning project. … [A nonhuman resource for planning] can bring to the learner the expertise, personality, and teaching style of experts and good teachers in any field" (p. 127). The learner does not have to travel or spend money for contact with experts.

Smith (1982) furthers the concept of learning without a teacher or learning how to learn by identifying the learner's learning characteristics. He says, adults who have learned how to learn know how to develop a personal learning plan based on strengths and weaknesses, how to cope with anticipated barriers, and they are aware of their preferred learning style. Further, Smith says adults who know how to learn, know: (a) how to negotiate the educational bureaucracy; (b) how to write sound learning objectives; (c) how to learn from life; (d) how to use intuition and dreams for learning; (e) how to learn from a mentor; and (f) how to help others learn (p. 16). Smith (1982) distinguishes those who have learned how to learn from those who have not, "The person who has learned how to learn ... can expect results from investments in learning and education—more knowledge acquired in less time for less money—and almost certainly will enjoy the learning process more than one who goes about it aimlessly" (p. 16). If Internet users have not learned how to learn, they too, may go about it aimlessly (Isenberg & Titus, 1999). It might be the case that a protocol for applying adult learning principles to Internet learning could be particularly helpful for adults who have not learned how to learn.

Piaget's theory of cognitive development supports the concept of learning without face-to-face teaching / learning. Piaget studied the developmental stages of children and concluded that the final stage called the formal operations stage of development is problem-solving when thinking is abstract (Ormrod, 1999). This occurs at age 12–15. According to his theory, children will learn if they are placed in an environment that is tailored to their stage of development. Further, he describes the attainment of each stage as achieving equilibrium. Arlin (1975) and Riegel (1973) build on Piaget's stage theory. Both support the notion that there is a fifth stage of development, which represents adulthood and is not a stable plateau equilibrium but instead one where the possibility for change remains (Long, 1983). According to Riegel (1973), significant changes take place when there is a state of disequilibrium. This statement seems to be a description of high-stakes learning or when the rewards and consequences for learning are significant.

Regarding children using computers without face-to-face teaching / learning, Papert (1993) said, "the idea of Piagetian learning has emerged as an important organizing principle ... and sets a research agenda concerned with creating conditions for children to explore naturally domains of knowledge that have previously required didactic teaching; that is, arranging for children to be in contact with the material—physical or abstract—they can use for Piagetian learning" (p. 187).

Many of the later researches on self-directed learning are based on earlier works by Gestalt who emphasized the importance of organizational processes in perception, learning, and problem-solving (Ormrod, 1999). The basic ideas of Gestalt psychology are that: (a) perception is often different from reality; (b) the whole is more than the sum of its parts; (c) the organism structures and organizes experience; (d) the organism is predisposed to organize experience in particular ways; (e) learning involves the formation of memory traces which, over time, become simpler, more concise, and more complete than the actual input; and (f) problem-solving involves restructuring and insight (Ormrod, 1999).

WHOLE-MIND LEARNING

Learning is a complicated process and there has been much written about the factors that are necessary for it to happen. Ormrod (1999) defines learning as "… the means through which we acquire not only skills and knowledge but values, attitudes, and emotional reactions as well." (p. 3). Ormrod recognizes that education psychologists have defined the concept of learning in two different ways. First, learning is a relatively permanent change in behavior due to experience and, second, learning is a relatively permanent change in mental associations due to experience. The difference between the two is what changes when learning occurs. One supports a change in behavior (behaviorism) and the other supports a change in thought processes (cognition). Ormrod's (1999) research resulted in her declaration, "I firmly believe that both the behaviorist and the cognitive perspectives have something important to say about human learning and that both provide useful suggestions for helping people learn more effectively" (p. 4).

Joseph LeDoux (2002), a neuroscientist, studied the physical mind, or the brain, and wrote about the three centers for thinking: cognition, motivation, and emotion. Learning is coordinated across all three centers at the level of the synapse. Learners' fears, hopes, and desires influence how they think, perceive, and remember. Though "emotional states are not typically acknowledged as associated with learning" (Taylor, 1986, p. 69), Taylor supports LeDoux when she describes experienced-based learning as the "orchestration of emotional states" (p. 69). Therefore, a behavior change program must account for and understand these complex processes (LeDoux, 2002, p. 24). Lindeman (1961) said, "… from the viewpoint of education, [that] emotions and intelligence are continuous and varying aspects of a single

Background

process and [that] the finest emotions are those which shine through intelligence ..." (p. 68). The question arises whether an Internet learning experience can address thinking, motivation, and emotions.

Mezirow (1991) refers to whole person learning in relation to transformational learning. Mezirow (1978) introduced the concept of transformative learning with a study of women going back to school after a long hiatus. From this study on re-entry women, Mezirow (1981) identified the following elements of perspective transformation: (a) a disorienting dilemma; (b) self-examination; (c) an assessment of role and alienation from traditional social expectations; (d) relating one's discontent to similar experiences; (e) exploring options for new ways of acting; (f) building competence and self-confidence in new roles; (g) planning a course of action; (h) acquiring knowledge and skills for implementing one's plans; (i) provisional efforts to try new roles and to assess feedback; and (j) a reintegration into society on the basis of conditions dictated by the new perspective (p. 7). Clearly, Mezirow is describing a learning process with ten parts that create a whole transforming experience. In 2000, Mezirow acknowledged the importance of the affective, emotional, and social context aspects of the learning process in the meaning-making process (Baumgartner cited in Merriam, 2001). Tennant and Pogson (1995) go beyond describing perspective transformation. They say, "the danger of omitting a social and historical critique when ... engaging in education for perspective transformation, is that, in the absence of such a critique, conventionally held views of what it means to be enlightened or developmentally more mature may dominate and subvert the process" (p. 119). The assumption here is that a life course is a product of history and culture and is socially constructed. And therefore, "individual development should be considered both a social and a personal phenomenon" (Tennant & Pogson, 1995, p. 118). In light of these authors' findings, a protocol for applying adult learning principles to Internet learning may benefit from including a social and historical critique.

From his research, Mezirow (1981) builds on Habermas' three domains of learning: learning for task-related competence, learning for interpersonal understanding, and learning for perspective transformation. Mezirow extends the concept of three domains of learning to say that the third domain, perspective transformation, involves all three domains and that they are intricately intertwined, terminology that reflects the wholeness of the experience. He sees the task of the adult educator as one of providing learners access to alternative meaning perspectives from old habits of seeing, thinking, or acting. The concept of perceptual transformation has relevance to the creation of a protocol for Internet learning. First, to be transformative, a learning experience should be process-oriented and second, the methodology should include elements that will provide a whole-mind experience.

THE FOUR PILLARS OF LEARNING

A small group of education experts from around the globe identified adult learning needs for the new century and are calling on practitioners to address them. The International Commission on Education for the Twenty-first Century is a group of fifteen culturally diverse individuals with a shared goal "to serve peace and international understanding by means of the preservation and expansion of education, science and culture for all of humanity" (Delores, 1998, preface). A resulting report identifies education as most important in confronting the challenges of the future, one of them being the tension between the explosion of knowledge and people's capacity to assimilate it. The Commission says that if education is to succeed at its tasks and overcome its challenges, it must be organized around four types of learning called pillars of learning—*learning to know*, that is acquiring the instruments of understanding; *learning to do*, so as to be able to act creatively on one's environment; *learning to live together*, so as to participate and co-operate with other people in all human activities; and *learning to be*, an essential progression which proceeds from the previous three" (Delors, 1998, p. 86).

Traditional education focuses on *learning to know* and to a lesser extent, *learning to do*. It is assumed that the other two just naturally follow. The Commission believes that equal attention should be paid to all four pillars of learning so that education is regarded as a total experience throughout life. Discussion of each of the four pillars of learning creates a framework for this century's practice of adult education.

Learning to Know

Learning to know assumes that the learner has already learned how to learn. Because it is impossible to know everything, emphasis must be placed on learning to learn. It is not enough to teach children a standard body of knowledge that will last a lifetime. Tools must be provided to enable every individual to learn throughout life. A basic childhood education provides instruments for learning like reading skills and an understanding of resources. However, the Commission believes that *learning to know* additionally requires skills that, for adults, may have been dulled over time—thought, concentration, and memory.

Thought is the deliberate use of the mind. Idealism theorists argue that the most important factor in education is to teach the learner how to think (Ozmon & Craver, 1995). The Commission promotes combining inductive and deductive methods of teaching thinking skills to provide a mix of the concrete and the abstract. "One may be more relevant than the other in particular disciplines, but in most cases, coherent thinking requires a combination of the two" (Ozman & Craver, 1995, p. 88).

Concentration skills are worrisome to the Commission because today's "information surfing could be harmful to the process of discovery, which takes time and involves going more deeply into the message received" (Ozman & Craver, 1995, p. 87). Quick-reads, information bytes, and headlines are popular in today's world where the volume of information far exceeds the time available to learn it. Educators of children and adults can create the conditions for learning concentration skills through such things as games, travel, training, and projects.

Lastly, the Commission is concerned that memory is becoming obsolete with the world's phenomenal ability to record, store, and transmit information. No longer is it even necessary to remember names at a time when everyone wears a nametag. Cell phones automatically dial phone numbers, coffeemakers automatically brew at 6 a.m., and computer software automatically sends meeting reminders. But, although one must be selective, it is still important to learn some things by heart. Delors (1998) states that, "all specialists agree that the memory must be trained from childhood and that it is inappropriate to eliminate from schools …" (p. 88).

Therefore, the first pillar of learning involves thought, concentration, and memory. The Commission believes that adults who learned these skills in childhood may be at risk for losing them due to information overload in combination with media crutches that enable information surfers (Isenberg & Titus, 1999) to function in their personal and professional lives without knowing too much about any one thing.

Learning to Do

The Commission believes that applying knowledge is more complicated than ever before. Physical work is being replaced by more mental work. With smarter machines that can do the physical labor of jobs, people are left to do the service part of jobs. "The development of services therefore makes it essential to cultivate human qualities that are not necessarily inculcated by traditional training and which amount to the ability to establish stable, effective relationships between individuals" (Delors, 1998, p. 90). It could be, then, that work competencies are changing from a focus on knowledge and skill to a focus on attitude, interest, and value. As a result, *learning to do* may be raised to a new level requiring the additional competencies of attitude, interest, and value (Ormrod, 1999). LeDoux's (2002) statement succinctly describes the situation: "A purely cognitive view of the mind, one that overlooks the role of emotions, simply won't do" (p. 200). Emotions may therefore be another important aspect of learning to do to be considered when creating an Internet learning protocol.

Learning to Live Together

The Commission believes that *learning to live together* is one of the major issues for education in the new century. Conflict and violence at home, at work, and among and between societies can be barriers to learning. There has been conflict in the world since the beginning of time but the capacity for human destruction is greater than ever before. As media observers, people around the world feel powerless in stopping the escalation of conflict. The Commission asks, "Is it possible to devise a form of education which might make it possible to avoid conflicts or resolve them peacefully by developing respect for other people, their customs, and their spiritual values?" (p. 92). The Commission suggests that this can be done in two ways, through discovering self and others and through working together toward common goals. Discovering the unique contribution of others by getting to know them leads to respect. Working together toward a common goal leads to putting aside differences. A learning process, with or without a teacher that can bring people together in these two ways may begin to address the issue of how we *learn to live together*.

Learning to be

Perhaps as a result of *learning to know, learining to do and learning to live together*, one would then naturally *learn to be*. Delors (1998) summarizes *learning to be* as giving people "the freedom of thought, judgment, feeling and imagination they need in order to develop their talents and remain as much as possible in control of their lives" (p. 94). This requires a holistic education (LeDoux, 2002; Mezirow, 1981) that addresses the mind, body, and spirit of every learner. Imagination and creativity blooms when there are opportunities to discover and experiment (Delors, 1998). Delors (1998) is concerned that both imagination and creativity are at risk due to a "certain standardization of individual behaviour [*sic*]" (p. 95). The twenty-first century needs individuals who are allowed to soar and become great contributors. This will only happen, according to Delors, when education provides the opportunities for discovery and experimentation.

Hence, the four pillars of learning succinctly describe both the Commission's concerns and the educational challenges for practitioners in the twenty-first century. To address the challenges, Delors (1998) recommends education practitioners: (a) foster the learner's thought, concentration, and memory skills; (b) improve the learner's ability to establish stable, effective relationships between individuals; (c) help the learner discover how to avoid conflicts or resolve them peacefully by developing respect for other people; and (d) provide the learner with opportunities to discover and experiment for optimal growth of imagination and creativity.

THE ROLE OF CREATIVITY IN INNOVATION

According to Csikszentmihalyi, professor of psychology at the University of Chicago, creativity never happens suddenly but instead comes after years of hard work. Csikszentmihalyi (1996) views creativity as a systematic process, not just the flash of a good idea. He says creativity can be observed only in the interrelations of a system made up of three main parts—the domain, which consists of a set of symbolic rules and procedures (like math or education), the field, which includes all the individuals who act as gatekeepers to the domain, and the individual person (pp. 27–28). "Creativity happens when a person, using the symbols of a given domain such as music ... or mathematics, has a new idea or sees a new pattern, and when this novelty is selected by the appropriate field for inclusion into the relevant domain" (p. 28). This author rejects the notion that creativity is an insular spontaneous event but instead, views it as the result of a systematic set of preconditions.

An engineer named David C. Morrison also thinks of creativity as a process. He founded a company called Involvement Systems in 1990, which helps large companies improve the thinking skills of their employees. Of interest is his description of creativity as an equation: "Creativity is knowledge times imagination times evaluation ... because if either knowledge, imagination, or evaluation is missing then there would be no creativity" (Fraley, 2003, ¶ 2). This businessman's view of creativity supports Csikszentmihalyi's (1996) view—creativity is a systematic process and without all the parts, there is no whole. Morrison further hones the definition by using a math equation metaphor to demonstrate the sequential nature and multiplicity of the three components.

Albert Einstein once declared, "Imagination is more important than knowledge" (ThinkExist, 2004, ¶ 10). Einstein's statement supports Morrison's statement that puts imagination after knowledge in the linear equation. And, with humor, Einstein also said, "The secret to creativity is knowing how to hide your sources" (ThinkExist, 2004, ¶ 22). Here, Einstein demonstrates his understanding that there is no spontaneous magic to creativity, but instead hard work. Lindeman (1961), the spiritual father of adult education, also thinks of creativity as a process, "creativeness is less dependent upon its ends than its means: the creative process, not the created object, is of supreme importance" (p. 59).

The results of creativity improve the world and enrich lives. Yet, some think that creativity is a luxury to be reserved for good times when problems are few. For example, schools are more apt to support music and art when the budget has excess than when the budget is slim. With budget cuts and downsizing, education as well as business seem to be going back to basics—looking for immediate practical solutions to short-term problems. Yet, Csikszentmihalyi (1996) believes that exactly the opposite strategy is needed—creativity and risk taking provide the innovation to create solutions to long-term problems. Csikszentmihalyi (1996) summarizes creativity:

> Creativity is any act, idea, or product that changes an existing domain, or that transforms an existing domain into a new one. And the definition of a creative person is: someone whose thoughts or actions change a domain, or establish a new domain ... however, ... a domain cannot be changed without the explicit or implicit consent of a field responsible for it (p. 28).

INTERNET LEARNING

To meet present day educational goals, there is a shift away from traditional classroom learning. In recent years, adult learning stakeholders have invested greatly in Internet learning because it addresses the goals by making learning of all kinds and at all levels possible anytime, anywhere, and at any pace. Corporations routinely use Internet programs to train, teach, and educate employees. Universities and colleges offer Internet degree programs to widen their reach. A membership organization called Software & Information Industry Association (SIIA) predicts trends based on member business experiences: "Most now recognize the power of technology to transform learning into the more flexible, personalized and accountable endeavor required by today's knowledge-based economy." (Trends, 2001, ¶ 1). As a result, learning technologies are both driving the vision for today's knowledge-based educational paradigm and providing the engine for its delivery" (Trends, 2001, ¶ 4).

A recent SIIA report states that economics is driving an increasing demand for continuous update and upgrade of one's abilities. Sloan Management Review estimates that 50% of all employees' skills become outdated within 3–5 years (Trends, 2001). Twentieth century educational traditions and nineteenth century infrastructure cannot meet twenty-first century demands. The report summarizes the areas in which technology addresses educational goals for the twenty-first century: (a) personalized learning; (b) software that enables computer-based education that is customized to the individual's unique learning needs, styles, and pace; (c) instructional management to efficiently collect, manage, and analyze data; (d) distributed learning, which enables real-time, flexible access to engaging instruction and content that can be provided both synchronously or asynchronously to allow for the student's learning needs and pace; and (e) enhanced communication to ensure critical interaction between and among students, educators, and communities (Trends, 2001, ¶ 5–8).

The SIIA report positions Internet learning more as a product than a process or function. The report's list of features in the previous paragraph reads like a commercial advertisement, similar to an automobile commercial—comfortable adjustable seats, a variety of colors and styles, and a dashboard alert system to let you know when the car needs service. The Internet is like an automobile, it gets you from one place to another. Both are vehicles for movement. However, it could be said that both the driver of the automobile and the driver of the Internet may each need two things to get where they want to go. Drivers of the automobile may need an operator's manual (function) for how to use the car and a roadmap (process) for how to get where they want to go. Drivers of the Internet may need a protocol (function) for how to use the Internet and adult learning (process) for how to get where they want to go.

Further, the SIIA report defines areas that must be fully addressed before Internet learning can realize its potential for meeting educational goals: (a) 21st century skills that include the ability to access and analyze information, draw and communicate conclusions, collaborate to solve problems, be self-directed learners, and implement technology literacy; (b) life-long learning skills; (c) equity and access; (d) instructor support; (e) modern regulations (the shift to a learner-based e-time model requires that long-standing rules be updated to remove barriers to education technology); (f) research and development; and (g) accessibility (Trends Report, 2001). In other words, the report suggests that supporting structures be in place for Internet learning to be successful.

The report concludes that computer learning indeed empowers learners to take control of, and responsibility for, their own learning. And, further, educators and technology providers must work together on implementation and integration in order to improve the efficiency and effectiveness of teaching and learning. Like Isenberg and Titus (1999), the SIIA understands the tremendous potential of the computer as a tool to facilitate the learning process and empower learners but warns practitioners of the need for more work in this area. To date, authors have discussed what needs to be done, but not how to do it with a computer. Recall Isenberg and Titus' (1999) dynamic model (Figure 1, p. 7) describing the practitioner concern that the practice of Internet learning has leaped ahead of research on adult learning. The model depicts what needs to be done—apply the adult learning process (theoretical) to Internet learning (practical). Further, the model suggests the methodology to get the answer to what needs to be done—action research. Perhaps, through action research, "researching what you are doing while you are doing it" (Isenberg & Titus, 1999, p. 4), the how question could be answered with a protocol that clearly directs practitioners how to do it (how to construct an Internet learning program on any topic).

Perhaps, Papert (1993) thought of the best metaphor for the potential of computers. In his early writings, he compares computers to simple gears, which he uses to illustrate how models are the basis for all learning. The learner can be the gear, taking the place of the moving part and turning with it, which creates a double relationship—both abstract and sensory. The image he portrays is that the gear has the power, for example, to carry powerful mathematics into the mind. The gears, he says, act as a transitional object, just as does a learning model. Papert (1993) says, "The computer is the Proteus of machines. Its essence is its universality, its power to simulate" (preface, p. xxi). "What an individual can learn, and how he learns it, depends on what models he has available" (preface, p. xix). Tough (1971) supported nonhuman planners as models for how to learn it. Papert seems to say that learning is about how structures grow out of one another to create a logical and emotional form. Hence, the necessity for a learning process that addresses emotion is reinforced (LeDoux, 2002; Mezirow, 1981; Taylor, 1986).

Researchers outside the field of adult learning have studied the pros and cons of Internet learning. In one study, Internet learning was found to be more effective than a traditional classroom experience. Radhakrishnan and Bailey (1997) studied a group of college engineering students. Half were exposed to a prototype Internet learning system and the other half experienced traditional classroom learning. The researchers concluded that an Internet-based system resulted in significantly better learning as measured by an average of ten or more points on a 75-point quiz. They also found that students working with the Internet-based system spent more time studying the subject, which did affect their performance.

Field (1997) sees a potential problem with computer learning. He is concerned that computers, as learning tools, are treated by adults as they treat televisions—as background noise, usually on but rarely watched intensely. He is also concerned that computer technology tends to treat the learner as passive, "as a recipient who absorbs the correct messages in a largely straightforward manner" (p. 36). Further, he recognizes that this passive model of the learner is at odds with everything we know about how adults learn. Field suggests that practitioners "make learning how to learn a priority across all forms of adult learning so that adults can exploit the learning potential of the new communications technologies to the full" (p. 42). Smith (1982) also supports the importance of learning how to learn.

Kraut et al. (1998), at Carnegie Mellon University found an untoward effect of the Internet use on participants' social involvement and psychological well-being. They found that "greater use of the Internet was associated with declines in participant's communication with family members in the household, declines in the size of their social circle, and increases in their depression and loneliness" (p. 1017). The authors believe that these results have the following implications for the design of computer technology: (a) encourage real-world friendships and tangible help; (b) include information and communication services that are geographically based and designed to support people who already know and care about each other; and (c) develop and deploy services that support pre-existing communities and strong relationships. The importance of this research is that a protocol for an Internet learning experience may benefit by somehow fostering real-world personal and community relationships.

Bier, Gallo, Nucklos, Sherblom, and Pennick (2001) found positive psychological effects of the Internet. They studied home Internet use by low-income families and found that Internet access enabled the study subjects to "experience powerful emotional and psychological transformations of identity, education, and community, transformations contributing to what has popularly become known as empowerment" (p. 1). Additionally, results led the researchers to conclude that although access to the Internet among the study group is not equal to that of higher income groups, they are the most enthusiastic of user groups for the Internet's potential to empower and enrich their lives.

Agarwal and Day (1998) studied graduate students who took an economics course online and found that "Internet use significantly enhances economic education by increasing the communication between student and teacher, and by the use of economic data and real-world applications to enhance the teaching of theory" (p. 108). Cavalier and Klein (1998) found that orienting activities, goals, and objectives enhance learning of Internet-based intentional content. So, in this study, learning was enhanced when the teacher provided the students with a learning process while the Internet provided the content. Also noteworthy is the importance of communication between teacher and student, which could be real-world or electronic.

Researchers have studied the relationship between computers and pedagogy. Education reformer Larry Cuban (1993) describes his future vision of technology's role in school reform:

> To make teaching and learning self-directed, active, engaged, and community-enhancing. The prized values here are in teaching for understanding, cultivating student autonomy, and creating adult-child learning communities. Students will be self-directed, thoughtful, independent, and able to work well with others (p. 204).

Hornbeck (1991), as a former superintendent of schools in Maryland, describes the role of computers in learning:

> The computer motivates. It is non-judgmental. It will inform a student of success or failure without saying by word or deed that the student is good or bad. The computer individualizes

learning, permitting mastery at one's own pace. In most instances, the learner has far more autonomy than in many other teacher directed settings ... Such generic qualities allow the learner more often than not to be in charge (pp. 1–2).

The goals for youth engaged in computer learning are similar to those for adults. Hornbeck, like Taylor (1986) and LeDoux (2002), understands the value of addressing emotions in learning but he takes it a step further by applying that understanding to computer learning potential.

Researchers Stites, Hopey, and Ginsburg (1998) see the great potential of integrating Internet and adult learning. They believe that educational technology can: (a) improve both educational attainment and skill acquisition; (b) bridge the gap between educational disparities of race, income, and region; (c) contribute to accountability; (d) provide a relevant and appropriate context for adult learning; (e) accommodate learning differences; (f) motivate and sustain adult learning; (g) provide greater access to adult learning; (h) empower adult learners; (i) facilitate institutional change; (j) redefine relationships and roles; and (k) reconcile the gaps between learning in the workplace and learning in school. In an effort to move from theory to practice or from goals to strategies, a how-to protocol could be created as a proof-of-concept.

INTERNET LEARNING AND ANDRAGOGY: MAKING THE CONNECTION

The Internet has both advantages and drawbacks to adult education practitioners. To make the connection between Internet learning and andragogy, practitioners must find ways to cash in on the advantages while minimizing the effects of the drawbacks. The advantages are the Internet's ubiquity and its great popularity. It is the fastest growing technology ever known. Creating a protocol for how to integrate andragogy and the Internet will help practitioners cash in on the Internet's advantages.

Presently, Internet drawbacks outnumber its advantages for adult education practitioners. The following is a discussion of the drawbacks and how to minimize their effects. Stites et al. (1998) see two drawbacks in making the connection between Internet learning and andragogy: "... [1] the Internet is not all that easy to use and [2] it requires learners and teachers to be engaged" (p. 16).

First, it could be argued that if Internet learning was more meaningful, it would be perceived as easier to use. A comparison could be made to how rote learning is made more meaningful. Ausubel (1967) describes the difference between meaningful learning and rote learning. He describes meaningful learning as learning that can be related to concepts that already exist in one's cognitive structure. Merriam and Caffarella (1999) describe rote learning as "learning that does not become linked to a person's cognitive structure and hence is easily forgotten" (p. 255). Ausubel (1968) suggests that advance organizers prepare a person for new learning by providing the cognitive structure. Thus, including an advance organizer that links new learning to a person's cognitive structure might make Internet learning more meaningful and therefore, easier to use.

Second, Stites et al. (1998) say that Internet learning requires learners and teachers to be engaged. According to a dictionary definition, engaged means geared together. Therefore, one could say that the Internet requires that the learners and the teachers be geared together with the Internet. Papert (1993) proposes that computers do have the potential to engage learners and teachers, knowing that the teachers are learners. He compares computers to simple gears describing the learner as taking the place of the moving part and turning with it. Therefore, the mechanism of Internet learning makes it possible to have all learners (teachers and students) equally engaged.

A third drawback is that the Internet, as an example of artificial intelligence, has no culture. A parallel to making the connection between Andragogy and Internet learning is Bruner's (1990) discussion of the connection between human learning and artificial intelligence (the use of computers to model the behavioral aspects of human reasoning and learning). He says, "human beings do not terminate at their own skins; they are expressions of a culture. To treat the world as an indifferent flow of information to be processed by individuals each on his or her own terms is to lose sight of how individuals are formed and how they function" (p. 12). Artificial intelligence has no culture. But, one could install elements of a culture (the sum total of the attainments and learned behavior patterns) into artificial intelligence (Internet learning) by extracting it from the learner through questions and answers.

Applying Andragogical Principles to Internet Learning

A fourth drawback is the effects of stereotyping. The term schema is used by Ormrod (1999) to refer to an organized body of knowledge about a specific topic. Important to the concept of making a connection between andragogy and Internet learning is that "schemas ... influence how learners process, store, and remember new information" (p. 255). Stereotype schemas that come from past unsuccessful Internet learning may be a barrier to new Internet learning and must be overcome. By surprising the computer learner with an andragogical experience on the Internet, adult education practitioners will create a new schema for the learner that could improve learning.

To restate, the Internet has both advantages and drawbacks to adult education practitioners. Practitioners could cash in on the popularity of the Internet by using a protocol to apply andragogy to Internet learning experiences. Four drawbacks were addressed: (a) advance organizers could make the Internet easier to use; (b) engaging the teachers and the learners is already possible as a result of the mechanism of Internet learning; (c) elements of a culture can be added by extracting them from the learners by the questions asked; and (d) surprising the learner with a positive experience for Internet learning will create a new schema that will minimize the negative effects of the old one. Focusing on the advantages and minimizing the drawbacks will naturally strengthen the connection between andragogy and Internet learning.

Conclusion

In this chapter, several topics were explored in the literature that would seemingly relate to a study that examines the application of andragogical principles to computer Internet technology. A scaffold of logic was built, upon which suggestions for a protocol will be based. The topics reviewed were: (a) principles of adult learning; (b) technology of adult learning; (c) issues with face-to-face teaching / learning; (d) issues without face-to-face teaching / learning; (e) whole-mind learning; (f) the four pillars of learning; (g) the role of creativity in innovation; (h) Internet learning; and (i) making the connection between Internet learning and adult learning principles.

Learning is composed of process elements, which are systematic and comprehensive and the process is more important than the content. Setting a physical and psychological climate that is conducive to learning is beneficial. Stimulating dialog is an effective methodology that should be tailored to the learner's style and readiness. Self-directedness should be fostered and could be accomplished with an action-oriented learning contract that includes praxis. Learning and changing are synonymous and both require a whole-mind approach that addresses cognition, motivation, and emotion. Though teachers manage the learning process, learning happens without teachers, as well, because there is an inherent natural process for learning. For individuals who have never learned how to learn (a prerequisite for learning to know), nonhuman planners have value.

The four pillars of learning describe the educational challenges for practitioners. To address the challenges, the Commission recommends that education practitioners help learners: (a) improve thought, concentration, and memory skills; (b) establish effective relationships; (c) avoid conflicts by developing respect for others; and (d) discover and experiment for optimal growth of imagination and creativity.

Challenges and future-oriented problems are solved through innovation. Creativity leads to innovation. Just as learning is a process, so is creativity. And, just as the process in learning is more important than the content, so too is the creative process more important than the created object. Therefore, understanding the process (protocol) for creating a problem-solving innovation that integrates adult learning principles and computer Internet technology is more important than the created object (proof-of-concept). And finally, though the drawbacks in making the connection between andragogy and Internet learning outnumber the advantages, the potential effect of the advantages is far greater than the effect of the drawbacks.

To this end, the phenomenon of integrating andragogy and Internet technology can be better understood through the use of interpretive inquiry. This looks in depth at lived experience. The thoughts, feelings, and motivations of the individuals are studied in depth through interviews. In the following chapter, values and belief systems such as andragogy will be explored as they relate to Internet learning.

CHAPTER THREE

RESEARCH METHODOLOGY

As computer learning grows, there is a concern that adults are not getting their learning needs met using computer Internet technology. From this concern, the research question arises, "Is it possible to support the principles and technology of adult learning, while creating an Internet learning experience?"

Sub-questions will be:

1. What are the issues with face-to-face teaching / learning during the development of the program?
2. What are the issues without face-to-face teaching / learning during the development of the program?
3. Can an Internet program stimulate whole-mind thinking (cognition, emotion, and motivation) to learn?
4. How does the design meet the goal of the International Commission on Education for the Twenty-First Century (UNESCO) for learning throughout life as described by the four pillars of learning: learning to know, learning to do, learning to live together, and learning to be?

The byproduct of this research on how to integrate andragogy, the art and science of helping adults learn, and Internet technology is an interactive Internet-based program called Virtual Health Coach, designed to help adults learn how to make lifestyle behavior changes to improve their health. I have knowledge on this topic from interest and work experience, thus allowing a focused effort on the learning process instead of the content. From this proof-of-concept, I developed a protocol for how to apply andragogical principles to any Internet learning experience.

Qualitative researchers say that there are no value-free or bias-free designs and that the values and beliefs of both the researcher and the phenomena studied are important variables. Therefore, my effort to design the Virtual Health Coach program so that it follows the literature guidelines summarized in chapter two resulted in a how-to design protocol that reflected my bias. Yet, separate from the how-to design protocol was the other important variable—the phenomenon of how it came to happen that the product was actually built. And, it was the description of this variable that increased the understanding of the people and the events that impacted the outcome. Qualitative research is holistic and process-oriented and answers general questions, not specific (Gay, 1996). There was one general story here with two specific parts: one was designing an Internet-based andragogical learning experience to match what the literature recommends; and the other was building it so that it works, while satisfying the needs and wants of all the stakeholders. The link between one story and the other was made through interpretive inquiry.

INTERPRETIVE INQUIRY

Interpretive inquiry seemed to be the qualitative methodology that best answered the research question, "Is it possible to support the principles and technology of adult learning, while creating an Internet learning experience?" This methodology was best for this study because it is "not just concerned with describing the way things are, but also with gaining insights into how things got to be the way they are, how people feel about the way things are, what they believe, [and] what meanings they attach to various activities" (Gay, 1996, p. 13). Hultgren (1989) believes that interpretive inquiry methodology is used to explore, understand, and reveal the meaning of lived experience. "Every lived experience ... occurs within historical social reality. It also lies beyond the immediate awareness of mind but, nonetheless, can be brought to consciousness" (Dilthey cited in Ermath, 1978, p. 219). To write about the sometimes bumpy-road lived experience of integrating andragogy and computer Internet technology from the perspective of not only an observer author / researcher but as a participant, revealed lessons that created insight, which can lead to further research in the area. Besides interpretive inquiry, the other approaches to research that were considered are phenomenology, grounded theory, case study, and action research.

PHENOMENOLOGY

Phenomenology seemed to be a possible approach because such a study describes the meaning of the lived experiences for several individuals about a concept or a phenomenon (Creswell, 1998). The problem with this approach is that the phenomenon of integrating adult learning and Internet technology is not already happening and commonplace. The end result of a phenomenological study is that readers come away with the feeling that "I better understand what it is like for someone to experience that" (Polkinghorne, 1989, p. 46). The stakeholders of the project to integrate adult learning principles and Internet technology (including the author / researcher) are not "without presuppositions" (Creswell, 1998, p. 52) and therefore do not meet Creswell's criteria for a phenomenological study.

GROUNDED THEORY

One might see an argument for using grounded theory as the inquiry method because this study's desired outcome is to result in a protocol for how to integrate adult learning principles and Internet technology. "The intent of a grounded theory study is to generate or discover a theory, an abstract analytical schema of a phenomenon, that relates to a particular situation" (Creswell, 1998, pp. 55–56). "It refers to any approach to developing theoretical ideas (concepts, models, formal theories) that somehow begins with data" (Schwandt, 1997, p. 61). The problem with using the grounded theory inquiry method for this study is that in grounded theory, the "participants interviewed are theoretically chosen to help the researcher best form the theory" (Creswell, 1998, p. 57). Or, to say it another way, in grounded theory, "the testing of the emergent theory is guided by theoretical sampling" (Schwandt, 1997, p. 61). I did not theoretically choose the participants for interview in this study. The interviewees included all of the major stakeholders of the project.

The first step in grounded theory is to tease apart the different elements of the experience (Glaser & Strauss, 1967). A theory then results from the arranging and rearranging of the elements until relationships emerge. The intent of the study is to identify the elements of the experience but not to formulate a theory.

CASE STUDY

Case study is another methodology that was considered. There may be overlap between interpretive inquiry and case study methodology. When a research question asks *what*, "it is justifiable rationale for conducting an exploratory [case] study, the goal being to develop pertinent hypotheses and propositions for further inquiry" (Yin, 2003, p. 6). "A case study is an exploration of a 'bounded system' [bounded by time and place] or a case (or multiple cases) over time through detailed, in-depth data collection involving multiple sources of information rich in content" (Creswell, 1998, p. 61). This study explores a definable event bounded by time and place and will draw from multiple sources of information. "The case study's unique strength is its ability to deal with a full variety of evidence—documents, artifacts, interviews, and observations" (Yin, 2003, p. 8). Yin, however, says that a case study should be used when exploring "a contemporary set of events, over which the investigator has little or no control" (p. 9). The investigator in this study *did* have influential control over the event of integrating adult learning and Internet technology. Establishing partnerships with the stakeholders was essential to the building of Virtual Health Coach, but I was always in control of the product development (My intellectual property) and held the title, project leader, even though I was not always in control of the process (meetings, budgets, timelines, implementation, evaluation, etc.). In light of this, case study methodology was eliminated.

ACTION RESEARCH

There is another category of research called action research that could reflect another way knowledge was obtained in this study. Lewin (1997) said this about action research:

> The research needed for social practice can best be characterized as research for social management or social engineering. It is a type of action-research, a comparative research on the conditions and effects of various forms of social action, and research leading to social action. Research that produces nothing but books will not suffice (Lewin, 1946, reproduced in Lewin, 1948, pp. 202–203).

I was not only the content author of the Virtual Health Coach program but also played a strong role in the production of the final product—a social management program to help people make changes to improve health. It was not sufficient to simply write about how to integrate adult learning and Internet technology. I felt compelled to actually do it.

The lieutenant colonel referred to me as the Big Toe during the two-year production time. The Big Toe was the leader of the development team and was responsible for final approvals of every team member's work. The back-and-forth production work during the two-year time could be called action research by Kenny and Harnisch (cited in Deshler & Hagan, 1989) as "researching what you are doing while you are doing it for the purpose of solving a problem" (p. 152). Kenny and Harnish (cited in Deshler & Hagen, 1989) believe that the experience of creating the program is a blending of deductive (premises lead to conclusions) and inductive (conclusions lead to premises) approaches—a definition of action research. However, for this look back at that two years of action research, interpretive inquiry seemed to be the methodology that was the best fit for the research questions.

In summary, phenomenology was not chosen because the stakeholders of the project, whose job was to integrate adult learning principles and

Internet technology (including myself), are not "without presuppositions" (Creswell, 1998, p. 52) and therefore do not meet the criteria. Grounded theory, the testing of the emergent theory guided by theoretical sampling (Schwandt, 1997), was not chosen because I did not theoretically choose the participants for interview in this study. Case study was not chosen because Yin (2003) states that a case study should be used when exploring "a contemporary set of events, over which the investigator has little or no control" (p. 9) and as the investigator in this study, I *did* have control. Action research was not chosen because although the experience of creating the program defines action research, the action research already happened. Interpretive inquiry seemed to be the methodology that was the best fit for the research questions because the methodology allows the participants to have presuppositions, it allows the researcher to have control over the event that is studied, and it allows the researcher to probe, describe, and make sense out of a unique event that happened in the past. Hultgren (1989) summarizes interpretive inquiry as a method that is used to explore, understand, and reveal the meaning of lived experience.

SUBJECTS

All of the major stakeholders of the project were interviewed. According to Rossi, Freeman, and Lipsey (1999), stakeholders are "individuals, groups, or organizations having a significant interest in how well a program functions, for instance, those with decision-making authority over it, funders and sponsors, administrators and personnel, and clients or intended beneficiaries" (p. 2). Subjects who met these criteria included: (a) myself as researcher; (b) the programmer who built the electronic platform and the program's interactivity; (c) the graphic artist who designed the visual and audio elements of the program; (d) the United States Air Force lieutenant colonel who championed the idea, found funding, and gave direction to Virtual Health Coach; and (e) the regional account manager for a large global pharmaceutical company that provided funding for the program's development.

First, I was also the researcher of this study. The collaboration with the other stakeholders had the potential to solve my problem. As researcher,

I now had a means for turning sixty-six pages of content and logic into a product. I had a bias toward Internet technology because I saw it as key to the future of lifelong learning. But, "without theory, researchers don't know where to begin" (Ethnographic Research, 2002, ¶ 11). I supported the reconstructionist education theory. "Reconstructionists would like to link thought with action, theory with practice, and intellect with activism" (Ozmon & Craver, 1995, p. 187). Further, "reconstructionists advocate an attitude toward change that encourages individuals to try to make life better than it was or is" (p. 171). As a result of my self-proclaimed biases and preferred ideologies, the study results are subjective rather than objective, which is expected in inquiry studies. Interpretive inquiry is "suspicious of any form [of inquiry] that can inform judgments about the human condition ... that claims to be 'objective', [and] to transcend human subjectivity" (Fazzaro, n.d., p. 3).

As the teller of my own story, the truth of memories may be doubted, as well. Bruner (1990) discusses the difference between recovering the past versus creating a new one as the storyteller of one's own story. Bruner (1990) refers to the work of Donald Spencer who wrote about psychoanalysis:

> Speaking from within psychoanalysis, Spence addressed the question of whether a patient in analysis recovered the past from memory in the sense, in which an archaeologist digs up artifacts of a buried civilization, or whether, rather, analysis enabled one to create a new narrative that, though it might be only a screen memory or even a fiction, was still close enough to the real thing to start a reconstructive process going. The truth that mattered, so went his argument, was not the historical truth but something he chose to call the narrative truth (p. 111).

From this argument, it could be said that my memories as the researcher were the truth, as I knew it.

Second was the programmer stakeholder, a man in his thirties who gave the program functionality and made it work. His stake in the project was related to not only his role as programmer but also his position as president of the Internet technology company. He saw the potential for a contract (money and security) as well as an opportunity to gain new skill—professional development on the client's dollar. New learning used to solve one problem can usually be applied to another. Attractive to him was financial support for trying new technology in creative ways. The end product, in turn, could then be used as a sample work to sell to other potential customers.

Third, the graphic artist was a man in his thirties employed by the programmer and received a salary, but had no other financial stake in Virtual Health Coach. However, artists are known for their work, not their riches. It might be said that an artist for hire has his or her professional reputation at stake when putting a piece of artwork in front of the public eye. Just as actors choose roles carefully, so must artists. If either fails to communicate the right look, feel, or attitude, both run the risk of jeopardizing future work. If the look and the feel of an Internet program are not right (i.e., appealing, engaging, communicating the right message), users may move on before reading the content or testing the functionality. The researcher, the programmer, and the artist could perhaps have been thought of as a troika of talent needed to build an Internet program, each with a unique contribution and a unique stake in its success.

Fourth was the Air Force lieutenant colonel (intended beneficiary), a man in his fifties. Historically, the military solves problems through innovation. "For a *specific* military, innovation is manifested by the development of new warfighting concepts and / or new means of integrating technology. New means of integrating technology might include revised doctrine, tactics, training, or support" (RAND, 1999, ¶ 3). Virtual Health Coach could be considered as a form of military support. The lieutenant colonel was the director of the Medical Defense Partnership for Reinvention (MDPR), a health division of the Department of Defense. He sought partnerships for successful collaborations that produced the most innovative products. Partnering with me for the development of Virtual Health Coach was a worthy objective for the lieutenant colonel because: (a) it aligned with the goals of MDPR; (b) it had the potential to solve a military problem that being unhealthy lifestyle habits among military personnel and their families that lead to high medical costs; and (c) it had the potential to bring him recognition. The potential of the concept was obvious to him, partially if not entirely, due to the fact that he has a doctoral degree in adult education.

The fifth and remaining stakeholder was a major global pharmaceutical company's regional account manager, a man in his fifties. Military physicians, who practiced medicine at the Air Force base where the MDPR was located, were a large group of his customers. When asked by the lieutenant colonel for education grant money for the Virtual Health Coach project, he championed the idea and found the money proposed to complete the project. His return on investment was threefold: (a) fulfillment of his company's goal, which is to develop products that not only manage disease but also promote health; (b) have a new reason to talk to physicians other than just selling drugs; and (c) have a behavior modification program that promotes categories of drugs that his company manufactures (i.e., nicotine replacement products).

To restate the important stakeholders of this project, there were five: (a) myself as the researcher, (b) the programmer, (c) the graphic artist, (d) the lieutenant colonel who was the director of MDPR, and (e) the regional manager of a large global pharmaceutical company. All had an investment of time, talent, or money and all expected a return on their investment. The members of this stakeholders project became development partners for a two-year period of time. "Development partners can equal more than the sum of their parts" (Solberg, 1999, Intro). "Challenging is a business partnership that joins two industries [health care education and technology] to create a product so innovative that it deserves praise from both sides" (Solberg, 1999, ¶ 1). Rossi et al. (1999) describe the complexity of the partnership, "Every program is a nexus in a set of political and social relationships among those with an association or interest in the program" (p. 55).

INSTRUMENTATION

Roth (2001) says that interpretive inquiry cannot be learned by talking about it or by reading about it, but, instead, requires participation. "Thus, even the slightest description of how to collect data or interpret data inherently underdetermines just what you have to do" (Roth, 2001, ¶ 1). Qualitative design requires the researcher to become the research instrument (Denzin & Lincoln, 1994, p. 212). And further, Denzin and Lincoln remind the reader that the qualitative researcher is ideologically driven by biases and values. Therefore, as the researcher of this study, I incorporated a description of my role as a participant in the development of the product and as a researcher in reflecting how the product was developed that includes my own biases and ideological preferences. As both a participant and a researcher, I used the following techniques to gather data: structured interviews, literature review, email correspondence, draft versions of the program, personal notes, and meeting minutes. I relied on historical material and memory for part of the information base that supplemented observations and interviewing data. A decision-making chart was created to describe the educational and political situational constraints that were encountered along the way, the decisions that were made as a result of the constraints, and then the consequences of the decisions. A comparison can be made between my perspective and that of Ron Casella, who studied the history of educational travel as part of his dissertation research. Casella (1997) described himself as studying historical materials from a symbolic interactionist perspective. As both author / researcher and participant during the study's two-year period of time, the role mix enabled me to "reexamine, over time, the content of the daily lesson" (Pike, 1992, pp. 36–37). From Pike's (1992) understanding of Mills (1959), Pike believed that blending the "inner life and external career" would help in developing an "intellectual craft" (Mills cited in Pike, 1992, p. 38). Claywell (2003) believes that "the insider approach adds insight and understanding that outsiders could not begin to achieve" (p. 63).

There are two sets of interview questions for the five stakeholders (see Appendices A and B). The list of questions for the researcher, the programmer, and the graphic artist was three times longer than the list of questions for the lieutenant colonel and the regional account manager because the first three stakeholders were considered the "troika of talent needed to build an Internet program." These three people did the physical work of building the program, while the other two stakeholders (the lieutenant colonel and the regional account manager) could be thought of as the supporters of the builders, providing: (a) a Memorandum of Understanding between MDPR project office and myself as the researcher to provide a structure for getting the work done over a defined period of time; (b) securing development money in the form of an education grant; (c) providing logistics leadership for the project such as setting deadlines, calling meetings, and providing secretarial support; (d) providing expert feedback from the MDPR staff during the program's development (staff included the lieutenant colonel with a Ph.D in adult education, a nurse, a physician, and a health promotion expert called a preventionist); and (e) the pharmaceutical company providing a market for the product and marketing materials.

The study specifically explored the experience of integrating adult learning principles and computer Internet technology. It did not seek to understand in detail the experience of supporting the development of such a product, though the relationships between all the stakeholders were very important to the study. Hence, the experience of creating the program was of most interest to me and required more interview questions.

Procedure

Open-ended, informal, yet structured interviews were the primary means of collecting new data. "It has become common in qualitative studies to view the interview as a form of discourse between two or more speakers or as a linguistic event in which the meanings of questions and responses are contextually grounded and jointly constructed by interviewer and respondent" (Schwandt, 1997, p. 75). Equally important were my memories of the two-year-old project and the documents that reflected reality at the time (i.e., project notes, draft versions of the programs, and emails between the stakeholders).

One-on-one interviews were scheduled with each of the individual stakeholders with the exception of the Air Force lieutenant colonel, who preferred to write the answers to his interview questions and send them as an electronic file. "Writing forces the person into a more reflective attitude, which may make it more difficult to stay close to an experience as it is immediately lived" (Van Manen, 1990, p. 67). It might be that the lieutenant colonel preferred a writing assignment to an interview because he may have felt that he had more control over what he wrote, and perceived that he may *not* have had as much control over what is said in an interview. My past experience with the lieutenant colonel is that he wrote emotionally charged messages rather than spoke them (e.g., his retirement speech was a quiet PowerPoint presentation without his voice commentary). "The interviewing procedure [was] informal, and designed to encourage meaning-making by narrative recounting rather than the more categorical responses one obtains in standard interviews" (Bruner, 1990, p. 123). The list of prompt questions (Bruner, 1990) is longer for me, the programmer, and the graphic artist with eighteen questions. The lieutenant colonel and the regional account manager had a list of six questions.

A tape recorder was used to audio record the interviews (all but the lieutenant colonel's interview). "Tape recorders can create the illusion that research is effortless" (Bogdan & Biklen, 1998, p. 130). Interviews lasted a maximum of 120 minutes per session, per participant. Interviews were scheduled no more than two weeks apart. All interview recordings were transcribed. Transcriptions took approximately 6–8 hours per interview. Transcriptions helped me critically analyze statements made during an interview, and improved my interviewing skills. Transcriptions were done using a computer as a word processor and a transcription machine with finger-toggle control.

The interview transcription was emailed to each research participant after the interview. Interviewees were asked to edit their content as they wished. This step provided intersubjectivity to improve objectivity by increasing interviewee participation with the intent to correct any perceived errors and add additional information that may not have been given during the interview.

After appropriate human subject approval, and after receiving the signed informed consent of each participant (see Appendix C), the five stakeholders including myself were interviewed one at a time in a place convenient and comfortable for them. The sequence of the interviews was as follows: lieutenant colonel, programmer, graphic artist, myself as the researcher, and regional manager. Conducting interviews before and after my self-interview allowed me to compare them and discover any subtle nuances in awareness after interviewing myself. "Sometimes it is easier to talk than to write about a personal experience" (Van Manen, 1990, p. 67). In 2004, Henschke describes a difference in his awareness of a topic after interviewing himself and said, "Stuff rose to the top in me and flowed out that I had not thought of before."

The interview questions that were developed were open-ended and designed by me to trigger critical reflection in the stakeholders of the two-year time span during which the development of the product occurred. On the one hand, the sequence of the eighteen questions for the three major stakeholders was ordered in a way that led the interviewee through the emotional aspects of the learning / changing process. The interviewee required time to answer the questions, to reflect back or dream about spent emotions, struggles, barriers, driving forces, disappointments, and successes. On the other hand, the sequence of the five questions for the two supporting stakeholders was designed more to elicit facts than emotions.

Beyond the interviews, facts about the two-year-old project were retrieved through my memory and documents related to the project (i.e., personal notes, emails between stakeholders, and draft versions of the program). Using multiple methods is called triangulation and is a means of checking the integrity of the inferences that are drawn (Chelimsky, 1987; Rossi et al., 1999; Schwandt, 1997). Rather than rich fieldnotes described by Bogdan and Biklen (1998) as "well endowed with good description and dialogue relevant to what occurs at the setting and its meaning for the participants" (p. 123), the documents related to the project (mentioned earlier) provided: (a) a means of evaluating discrepant interview data, (b) additional data not included in the other sources, or (c) corroboration of data from the other sources.

DATA ANALYSIS

An inductive process was used to analyze the data, which allowed for categories and patterns to emerge from the data. First, the interview segments of data were coded by topic and by interviewee. A segment of data is a data element that is understandable by itself because it contains an idea or a piece of information. The topics of the segments were derived from the data itself. The literature was explored to explain how it compared with the observations. Next, to get a sense of the whole, the topics were classified into categories by looking for relationships that connected statements and events. Then, I identified recurring patterns that became themes. "Having a scheme is crucial; the particular scheme you chose is not" (Bogdan &

Bilken, 1998, p. 181). I wrote down notes, which included lists of ideas and diagrams that sketched out relationships noticed (Miles & Huberman, 1994). Next, the project notes, emails between stakeholders, and draft versions of the program were reviewed to evaluate any discrepancies, add to, or corroborate patterns or themes that emerged from the interview data. My memories evaluated discrepancies, added to, or corroborated patterns or themes and were called memories in the text and were woven into the results of the analysis as the third perspective.

Van Manen (1990) refers to data analysis of the lived experience as the phenomenological method of analysis. It differs from traditional content analysis in that content analysis specifies beforehand what it wants to know from a text. In contrast, "phenomenological human science is discovery oriented" (Van Manen, 1990, p. 29). The research attempted to capture the unique nature of this lived experience. By hearing this voice, it was the hope that the findings will help other practitioners who are facing similar issues related to the development of non-face-to-face educational experiences.

Chapter Four

Presentation of Data

"Information is indifferent with respect to meaning" (Bruner, p. 4). The information gathered for this study is "indifferent" without a structure of meaning. "The meaning or essence of a phenomenon is never simple or one-dimensional" (Van Manen, 1990, p. 78). It is a complex mix of events and emotions over a period of time. Though the break down of data elements into categories could be described as mechanistic, analysis of emerging themes is a human activity. "Making something of a text or of a lived experience by interpreting its meaning is more accurately a process of insightful invention, discovery or disclosure—grasping and formulating a thematic understanding is not a rule-bound process but a free act of "seeing meaning" (Van Manen, 1990, p. 79). In this chapter, I present and explore meaning in the data.

Making the Connection Between Research and Interview Questions

Analysis of the text from five interviews (myself as the researcher, the programmer, the graphic artist, the sponsoring Air Force lieutenant colonel, and the regional account manager of the pharmaceutical company) is presented. Out of the main research question, come the four research sub-questions. The 24 interview questions (18 questions for the programmer, graphic artist, and researcher, and six questions for the lieutenant colonel and the regional account manager) represent topics generated by me prior to the study (see Appendices A and B). Applying the Isenberg and Titus model (Figure 1, p. 6), the 24 interview questions represent a practical theme. The four research sub-questions represent a theoretical theme. Each of the 24 practical theme interview questions was placed with one of the four theoretical theme research sub-questions.

The method used for placing each of the interview questions under one of the four research sub-questions was nonscientific but process driven. I thoughtfully and systematically looked for a connection between each research sub-question and each interview question based on the literature review and on my intuition. For example, under the research sub-question—What are the issues with face-to-face teaching / learning during the development of the program, I placed interview question A13—Describe your relationships with the other stakeholders and how they affected your work (author / researcher, lieutenant colonel, and regional account manager). I did this because relationships between the stakeholders were issues of face-to-face teaching / learning. A second example is, under research sub-question—What are the issues without a face-to-face teacher, I placed interview question A5—What one problem was hardest to solve? I did this because the development team did most of their individual work without face-to-face teaching / learning.

Through this thoughtful and deliberate process, a theoretical–practical or theory–practice connection was made between each research question and its corresponding interview questions. The Isenberg and Titus model (Figure 1, p. 6) of a new dynamic three-dimensional research / practice model depicts the overlap and interchange of practice and research that is necessary in dealing with the technologies of today and in the future. According to the Isenberg and Titus model, practice and research are perpetual, as are technology and the learning process (the overlapping circles behind the practice–research overlapping circles). Therefore, it could be said that the 24 interview questions are from the practical perspective and represent the practice or technology of adult learning. On the other hand, the research question and sub-questions are from the theoretical perspective and represent the research or the learning process of adult learning.

ALIGNING THE INTERVIEW QUESTIONS WITH THE APPROPRIATE RESEARCH SUB-QUESTION

The interview questions listed in Appendices A and B, are lettered and numbered accordingly: A = programmer, graphic artist, and author / researcher questions; and B = lieutenant colonel and regional account manager questions (see Appendices A and B). The number after the letter represents the number of the question within the set of questions. This is depicted in Table 2.

MERGING THE RESEARCH QUESTIONS WITH THE INTERVIEW QUESTIONS

To get a sense of the whole experience of creating an Internet learning experience while attempting to support the principles and technology of adult learning, all the data were reviewed. Out of the 24 interview questions that were placed with the four research sub-questions came the responses of those interviewed. The interviews were all face-to-face audio-taped conversations except the lieutenant colonel's interview, which was written. All interviews took place between November and December 2003 and each was no longer than 120 minutes in length. I transcribed the interviews verbatim (see Appendix D).

Capsules of stakeholder answers to each of the interview questions are provided in this section of the paper. Interview questions A1–18 were asked of the researcher, programmer, and graphic artist. Interview questions B1–6 were asked of the lieutenant colonel and the pharmaceutical company regional account manager.

Issues with face-to-face teaching / learning

Research sub-question: What are the issues with face-to-face teaching / learning during the development of the program?

TABLE 2. Aligning Interview Questions with Research Sub-Questions

Main Research Question:
Is it possible to support the principles and technology of adult learning, while creating an Internet learning experience?

Sub-Research Questions:

What are the issues with face-to-face teaching / learning during the development of the program?	Can an Internet program stimulate whole-mind thinking (cognitive, emotion, motivation) to learn?	How does the design meet the goal of the International Commission on Education for the Twenty-first Century (UNESCO) for learning throughout life as described by the four pillars of learning: learning to know, learning to do, learning to live together, and learning to be?

Interview Questions:

What are the issues without face-to-face teaching / learning during the development of the program?	A1. How did the thinking and planning process for this project differ from other Internet-based learning projects you have created?	A2. Describe in detail your tangible and intangible goals for this project.
A4. What new learning did you come away with from the experience?	A5. What one problem was hardest to solve?	A3. What did you do differently with this project than with previous projects?
A10. Discuss barriers to the project's progress and how you coped with them.	A8. What one piece of the development was most important to get right?	A7. Were there any surprises or ah-ha experiences during or after the development?
A13. Describe your relationships with the other stakeholders and how they affected your work.		A12. With the same budget and time restrictions, what would you have done differently?
		A6. In your thinking, is this system for Internet-based learning more appropriate for a particular type of learning and why?
		A14. List 3–4 guidelines you could give to future technology companies partnering with an educator of adults to create an Internet-based learning program.

(Continued)

Table 2. (Continued)

A17. Did this project ever seem to drift from a serious vein that should have been more prominent?	A9. Discuss the difference between the process and the content of Virtual Health Coach.	A15. Was there ever a time during your work on this project that you wanted to quit and walk away from it? If so, why? And, if so, how did you stop yourself from quitting?
B2. Discuss the return on your investment of time, money, or intellectual contribution.	A11. If there had been no budget or time restrictions, what would you have done differently?	A16. Compared to other projects you have been involved in, how would you rate the perceived value of this project on a scale of 1–10 with 1 representing least value and 10 most value. Explain your answer.
	B5. Does the program integrate adult learning principles and computer technology?	B1. Describe your initial interest in participating in the development of this program.
	A18. What other questions do I need to ask that you think would provide important information for this process?	B3. What are your plans and goals for using the program?
		B4. How does the program fill a void, add value, or accomplish a goal for you?
		B6. Are there other appropriate applications for this learning system? If so, what are they?

Note. A1–18, interview question set for the author / researcher, programmer, and graphic artist; B1–6, interview question set for the lieutenant colonel and the pharmaceutical company regional account manager.

Interview question: A4. What new learning did you come away with from the experience?

The programmer, graphic artist and I all learned something new that relates to issues with face-to-face teaching / learning. The programmer learned the importance of implementation. He learned that just providing the program is not enough, but instead, a live teacher must implement or facilitate the program. He said,

> This is new, this whole merging of technology and adult education and that you have to have a plan to implement it. ... you need to implement it rather than just handing it over ... it was a stepping stone for certain individuals to move on in their lives and they had no intention of using it, we found out much later. ... there's nobody in charge of it. ... nobody to head it up, nobody to implement it ... it's just out there (programmer, A4).
>
> It's like giving someone a textbook (author / researcher, A4).
>
> Without giving instructions on how to use it (programmer, A4).

The graphic artist learned the importance of not making the program too big or too long in order to keep the learner interested. He said,

> When you add audio, you're automatically making this a big, big file. So, that meant that I couldn't go too crazy with the animation because then we would run the risk of making it too big to download or taking such a really long time that people wouldn't hang out (graphic artist, A4).

I also learned to value each stakeholder's unique contribution to the project, and that success was only possible when the stakeholders used each other as expert resources.

> I learned that they all had value and a unique contribution to this thing that was different from mine and was going to be the reason for its success. And I think I learned that just

because you have the process doesn't mean you have all the answers. Having the process and the content, I thought, well, I'm the Big Cheese, I don't need them in order to finish this but I truly needed them and could not have done it without them (author / researcher, A4).

To restate the new learning related to the issue of face-to-face teaching / learning: facilitating or implementing the program is just as important as the program itself, managing the program's size and length will help avoid disinterest among the learner, and learning to use the unique contributions of others will lead to the success of a program.

Research sub-question: What are the issues with face-to-face teaching / learning during the development of the program?

Interview question: A10. Discuss barriers to the project's progress and how you coped with them.

The programmer, the graphic artist, and I all described barriers to the project's progress. The programmer said the barriers to the project's progress were time, money, staff, and the military's conservatism. "First and foremost ... time and money" (programmer, A10). Not having enough staff was also a problem, for the programmer lost his programmer business partner soon after work started on the project. "We *had* the staff but then we *lost* the staff right when the project started" (programmer, A10). The programmer coped with the barriers by working extended hours and shifting deadlines and responsibilities to buy time. He said,

> All the animation was done at midnight and on weekends for [the graphic artist]. ... We did a lot of shifting of deadlines and responsibility back to the military for items that bought us time on others (programmer, A10).

Lastly, the programmer coped with the military's conservatism by working toward a compromising solution. The programmer said,

> I think one of the barriers was the military and their conservatism. We had to pull out some pieces that they didn't

> like ... They had us dumb it down. I thought that what we had originally was right on. And, the fact that we had the real term and we included a description. ... We insisted. That was something we stood up for because people need to know these (programmer, A10).

The graphic artist listed time, money, staff, and the military as barriers.

> "Money, time. It was a staffing thing, too. It was just [the programmer] and I that did this whole thing (laugh)" (graphic artist, A10). Regarding the military's conservatism, the graphic artist said that negotiation was the coping strategy. "... there wasn't much we could do about the Air Force. I mean all we could really do was negotiate that" (graphic artist, A10).

As researcher, I found that money and time were barriers.

> it was money. They didn't want to give us the money that it would take to build it. ... I'd allow myself a little bit of time every morning to do the work and I'd set a goal for myself and made sure I accomplished that before time was up to get ready for this other work of mine (author / researcher, A10).

Another barrier for me was the lack of agreement over issues related to the product's development. I used assertive communication skills to cope with the lack of agreement to create a win–win situation. I worked hard to:

> make sure that it was always a win–win situation. They would always feel like they were winning even when I was winning as well. And, that's the only way I figured out how to get around the lack of agreement on something was just to somehow turn it into a win–win situation. ... I really worked *hard* to communicate assertively and not aggressively (author / researcher, A10).

To summarize the barriers to the project's progress as described by the programmer, graphic artist, and me as the researcher and how we coped with them: (a) they coped with lack of time, money, and staff by working extended hours and shifting deadlines and responsibilities; and (b) I coped with the military's conservatism by using assertive communication skills to negotiate win–win solutions.

Research sub-question: What are the issues with face-to-face teaching / learning during the development of the program?

Interview question: A13. Describe your relationships with the other stakeholders and how they affected your work?

The programmer, myself as the researcher, and the graphic artist all described relationships with the other stakeholders as valuable but each described the value in a different way. The programmer valued his working relationship with me as open and crucial to the project's progress because it fostered creativity and a pleasant working environment. He said,

> You [the researcher] were crucial every step of the way from beginning to end. I think our relationship was a perfect open working relationship ... You were open to ideas and I was open to trying to do things you wanted to do and I think it made it a very pleasant project. It wasn't so rigidly defined that we couldn't go outside the boundaries of it from time to time and do something (programmer, A13).

The graphic artist's animation was affected by his relationship with all four of the other stakeholders because their feedback gave him direction and determined the final product. He understood the importance to him and to the project that all the stakeholders be involved in the planning when he said,

> I think my relationship and how you guys affected me was mainly in developing the character because that went in front of everyone. And everyone had to make a determination on that. ... I liked having that feedback. I liked the fact that everyone was involved. I think it helped the project. It affected me in a good way. If one person developed this whole thing without say from anybody, it would have just been that one person's ... (graphic artist, A13).

As researcher, I valued my relationships with each of the stakeholders because each offered a unique contribution to the project. I learned from each of them, and I also learned to not ask unless I was ready to listen and respect their answers.

> They're all very unique characters. All with their special contributions and their special talents and different personalities. The relationships were very good with all of them. ... I learned from every single one of them. ... And, don't ask unless you want an answer and you're ready to act on that answer (author / researcher, A13).

Research sub-question: What are the issues with face-to-face teaching / learning during the development of the program?

Interview question: A17. Did this project ever seem to drift from a serious vein that should have been more prominent? In other words, were important aspects of this project ever at risk of being lost in the midst of the fun?

The programmer, graphic artist, and I all thought that the project benefited from having fun. Without exception, none of us thought that the seriousness of the project was ever jeopardized by fun. We all felt that having fun was important to accomplishing the project's goals. The programmer thought that having fun built fun into the program. He said,

> I don't think so because I don't think any aspects were lost in it. It *was* fun. We always knew that there was something serious behind this. ... there was something important to this. ... It had to help people. And that was an important goal even though we were having fun with it. ... if anything, we gained. ... the fact that we were having fun built fun into it (programmer, A17).

The graphic artist admitted to having too much fun recording the voice.

Presentation of Data 73

However, my prewritten content kept the project from drifting too far off course. The graphic artist said,

> They [certain aspects of the project] were [at risk of being lost in the midst of fun] when we were recording it! There were a lot of things that didn't make the cut that were pretty entertaining. I think because you wrote it before we ever started planning ... Your words are what we had this character say. So really, the only way we could have messed that up and pulled away was to get a little cartoony with it sometimes or a little cluttered up with props and goofy things like that (graphic artist, A17).

And further, the graphic artist believes that though it pulls away from the serious vein, a fun approach to learning helps people relax. He said,

> So, I think at times maybe it pulls away from the serious vein because of the make-up of the character ... being a whistle. I think anytime you do that, it's going to somewhat make it less serious. ... In a way, it's very good because people relax and it seems like more of a fun approach to things (graphic artist, A17).

I adamantly denied that the project drifted from a serious vein because of too much fun. Instead, I defended the need to have fun in order to release energy and creativity.

> There's never too much fun (pause) at all, especially with a project like this. It was like theater. ... if you can't have fun, then you lose the energy and the creativity and so we *absolutely* had fun in every possible term. Never, ever, ever ... never too much fun (author / researcher, A17).

To summarize the responses to interview question A17: (a) the programmer thought having fun built fun into the program, (b) the graphic artist said that the prewritten content kept the animation and voice recording fun in a serious vein but that a fun approach to learning helps people relax, and

(c) as researcher, I believed that having too much fun working on a project like Virtual Health Coach was not possible because having fun created energy and creativity.

Research sub-question: What are the issues with face-to-face teaching / learning during the development of the program?

Interview question: B2. Discuss the return on your investment of time, money, or intellectual contribution.

When asked to discuss return on investment, the lieutenant colonel and the regional account manager both claimed their return was high but for different reasons. The lieutenant colonel was pleased that the program met the goals of the project or, in other words, the project did what it said it would do. He said his return on investment was high with a substantial bang-for-the-buck as compared to other programs. The lieutenant colonel said,

> The return on investment (ROI) was, in my estimation, exceptional. Given the dollars, person hours and intellectual capital invested, the VHC [Virtual Health Coach] product is of high technical and professional quality and fulfills the spirit and intent of the virtual coaching agenda. When compared to other products I have had experience with, the bang for the buck is substantial in terms of the quality of content, appearance, usability and comprehensiveness (lieutenant colonel, B2).

The regional account manager was surprised to find an unexpected return on investment—a way to build relationships with potential customers as he explains below.

> traditionally, people expect a return on investment and a lot of times it's measured in dollars or some type of value. In this particular instance, it was being set up in a way that return on investment could really not be measured with any dollars or potential for a contract or things like that but really the value that I was attaching to it was it was allowing me to build a new environment to create in the minds of the customer a different level of interaction with the pharmaceutical

industry, something they had not been accustomed to before (regional account manager, B2).

And, the regional account manager credits his work with Virtual Health Coach as the reason for his promotion to national account manager when he said, "a key component of me going to a national account manager was Virtual Health Coach" (regional account manager, B2). Further, he said that the physician on the lieutenant colonel's team was also promoted as a result of Virtual Health Coach. The regional account manager explained,

> And, at that time, I came up for national account manager and because of the types of programs I had been doing like Virtual Health Coach, which was a really new way of working in that federal field, that was really what positioned me and set me apart from the rest of the group in order to get the job as national account manager. ... As a matter of fact, every time I see [the Air Force physician who worked on the Virtual Health Coach project under the lieutenant colonel], I pat him on the back and he pats me on the back because we were responsible for each other's promotions (regional account manager, B2).

In summary of interview question B2, both the lieutenant colonel and the regional account manager thought their return on investment of time, money and intellectual contribution was high—the lieutenant colonel's rating of high (in comparison to other such projects he had been involved in) was because it allowed him to reach his goal for the project and the regional account manager's rating was high because it exceeded his expectations as a new innovative way for his company to build relationships with potential customers.

Issues without face-to-face teaching / learning

Research sub-question: What are the issues without face-to-face teaching / learning during the development of the program?

Interview question: A1. How did the thinking and planning process for this project differ from other Internet-based learning projects you have created?

Regarding the thinking and planning process, the programmer, graphic artist and the researcher all thought of how the Virtual Coach project was different from past work they had done. The programmer was familiar with the planning process but the difference with Virtual Health Coach was that the script was already written. He had never built an Internet-based learning project before Virtual Health Coach but thought the process was the same as others except that the project started from my script. The programmer said,

> This was like our first Internet-based learning project. We've never had a learning project per se. The planning process is not real different from others. We plan, structure, organize, outline, and then scope out the project following your diagram of the project. So, that's all basically the same. The difference here is the fact that we started from the script (programmer, A1).

The graphic artist said this project was different for him because he was involved in thinking and planning for the first time and not just doing the work. He said,

> I *did* work with a company that did this sort of thing briefly and I was pretty much just involved in the animation / illustration side of *that* project. And really didn't have much to do with the overall look, navigation or any of those things. So, this one I actually did get to think about laying this thing out. How people will navigate through it and how it will flow and how to make those links easy to find and kind of walk people through. ... Planning for the animation was a lot more in depth ... it required me to think a lot more (graphic artist, A1).

I had no previous experience to compare to this project. In fact, I mentioned, "I have never created an Internet-based learning project. So this really doesn't apply" (author / researcher, A1). Therefore, this experience was new for me and not comparable to anything I had done before.

Research sub-question: What are the issues without face-to-face teaching / learning during the development of the program?

Interview question: A5. What one problem was hardest to solve?

The programmer, the graphic artist, and I each expressed our one problem hardest to solve. Each described a different problem. The programmer and graphic artist solved their biggest problems by adding an innovative process.

The biggest problem for the programmer was that computer software technology was not yet sophisticated enough to do what he wanted it to do. He was forced to be innovative and make it work for him by inventing middleware. He said,

> Flash technology wasn't up-to-date yet. ... We had to build an external program that was kind of middleware to communicate with the computer and with Flash. Well, now they *have* that. It's built in. If we built [Virtual Health Coach] today, it would be a lot easier (programmer, A5).

The graphic artist struggled with throughput, or how to get people in and out in a natural way. When asked what problem was hardest to solve, the graphic artist said,

> how to step people through. The way we did it was the sections were almost like arrows, they all had a point at the end that kind of walks you through it, forces you through it, kind of like reading a sentence word by word. There was only one way to do it and you had to go through these processes (graphic artist, A5).

For me as the researcher, the biggest problem was giving up some of my content in exchange for process in order to facilitate learning. I said,

> It was so hard to not put everything in that I had written. But, when you're trying to get a certain affect, and you think you've created that affect through writing, to say you can't do it that way, you have to do it another way, that was the

> hardest problem. It was kind of like the author of a book when the editor says you have to rewrite the whole first chapter, or we're going to take Chapter Three out or we're going to change your title, or write out a character. Wait a minute! This is my treasure, this is my creation, don't mess with it. But, it got messed with a lot (author / researcher, A5.)

Research sub-question: What are the issues without face-to-face teaching / learning during the development of the program?

Interview question: A8. What one piece of the development was most important to get right?

The answers to interview question A8 varied among the three development team stakeholders. The graphic artist and I both agreed that the climate (the look and feel) of the program was very important to make the learner want to stay long enough to get into the content. Not surprising, the programmer thought the navigational flow was most important to get right. The programmer said,

> I'm going to say flow ... the whole flow of the thing. It was so important to get it right. I think if we had structured it any other way than it is right now, I don't think it would be as effective (programmer, A8).

> And, the programmer said that having the right flow and structure was more important than the content to create the right feelings in the learner. He said, that people felt what they were supposed to feel when we wanted them to feel that way. ... I think if you strip out the content, the basic structure and flow is perfect (programmer, A8).

The graphic artist thought the character was most important to get right so that any learner could relate to it. He said,

> It was very important to get that character right. It will turn people on or turn people off. And so, you had to be more mindful ... you didn't want to alienate anybody. It had to be one size fits all so people could relate to it. So, for me, that was the most important part (graphic artist, A8).

The graphic artist also thought it was important to achieve simplicity in order to free the mind for learning the content by using simple primary colors and uncluttered pages. He said,

> we wanted them to learn something so we didn't want to clutter it up with too much craziness that would take away from the content. I think solid color ... that solid blue ... is calming. It kind of helps you. If it were warm colors, I think it would have been too much for the eye and it would have taken away. The colors that we used were simple. Well, I think it frees your mind and let's you focus on what it is you really need to be focusing, which is the content. And, if we got too crazy and had some funky lines, and some curves and some weird angles and all sorts of hip artistic high dollar ad firm kind of stuff and we just went crazy, you would lose that attention to the content. ... It wasn't meant to be a creative juggernaut piece. It was meant to instruct people and I figured the best way we could do that was to keep it simple and not cluttered up with all that stuff. Because with people's short attention span, if they're looking at all of that, they might just decide, Aw, it's just too much and there's just too much going on for me to focus. So, Keep It Simple Stupid was the theme there (graphic artist, A8).

As the researcher, I thought the most important thing to get right was the look and the feel of it, or setting the climate. First impressions will determine whether the learner sticks around or moves on.

> The look and the feel are most important to get right. ... the initial character, if he turns you off, then you're not going to go back and you're not even going to look, wait around long enough to know what the process is all about, much less the content (author / researcher, A8).

Research sub-question: What are the issues without face-to-face teaching / learning during the development of the program?

Interview question: A11. If there had been no budget or time restrictions, what would you have done differently?

Regarding what would have been done differently if there had been no budget or time restrictions, the programmer said, "More [name of animated character]" (programmer, A11). The graphic artist said, "… more characters like we're talking about now to give people an option" (graphic artist, A11). As researcher, I said, "I don't think I would have done anything differently" (author / researcher, A11). Therefore, I was the only one of the three stakeholders who would not have done things differently.

Research sub-question: What are the issues without face-to-face teaching / learning during the development of the program?

Interview question: B5. Does the program integrate adult learning principles and computer technology?

When the lieutenant colonel was asked if the program integrates adult learning principles and computer technology, he wrote the following, which included a cartoon:

> It is obvious the VHC integrates adult learning principles. This is apparent if one considers the six characteristics of adult learners enumerated below and as outlined by Malcolm Knowles, a pioneer in adult learning who popularized the term andragogy.

In pedagogy, the concern is with transmitting the content, while in andragogy, the concern is with facilitating the acquisition of the content.

1. Adults are *autonomous* and *self-directed.*
2. Adults have accumulated a foundation of *life experiences* and *knowledge* that may include work-related activities, family responsibilities, and previous education.
3. Adults are *goal-oriented.*
4. Adults are *relevancy-oriented.*
5. Adults are *practical*, focusing on the aspects of a lesson most useful to them in their work. They may not be interested in knowledge for its own sake. Instructors must tell participants explicitly how the lesson will be useful to them on the job.
6. As do all learners, adults need to be shown *respect*.

The VHC design accommodates these six characteristics very nicely, and does so within the context of an Internet-based delivery system. The Internet technology has been astutely leveraged to incorporate adult learning principles and the VHC goal of helping to "coach" individuals who are interested in changing their lifestyles and seeking assistance in doing so (lieutenant colonel, B5).

When asked the same question, the regional account manager also said yes and added that the program is well suited for the military because of the distance learning needed for deployed military staff. The regional account manager said,

Absolutely! Oh, excellent! You couldn't ask for a better group to work with because the Department of Defense and the VA [Veteran's Administration] are probably the most technical groups you'll find out there in the health care system. But also where I see, (maybe I'm getting ahead of myself), it really lends itself well to the military because of the deployments (regional account manager, B5).

Can an Internet program stimulate whole-mind thinking?

Research sub-question: Can an Internet program stimulate whole-mind thinking (cognitive, emotion, motivation) to learn?
Interview question: A3. What did you do differently with this project than with previous projects?

The programmer, graphic artist, and I all found it easy to think of how this project was different from previous projects. The programmer found collaboration to be a new way to work. He said,

> I think what was different for me was, when we put this thing together. It was a collaboration rather than me just telling you how it was going to be. Rather than me dictating. ... You and I went back and forth with this idea until we slowly started to put it together. I think that was different ... to have someone to collaborate in the structure and assembly, which is usually not the case (programmer, A3).

The programmer was accustomed to telling his customers how it was going to be done. But, this time I was involved in the mutual planning of the program.

The graphic artist animated to match a voice for the first time, which was a new skill for him. Just talking about it made him smile and laugh when he started to answer the question. The graphic artist said,

> (Laugh) I animated a whole lot, a whole lot more! I was doing a little bit of it but not to this level, which you know I always wanted to do anyway. I aspired in my youth to be a cartoonist when I was growing up so it's something I wanted to do anyway (graphic artist, A3).

Had you ever animated to match a voice (author / researcher, A3)?

> No. No. That was the first time I ... I've known we could do it. And you know the theories involved and you know what it would take to do it but had there been a call to do it? No, so this gave me the opportunity to actually do it (graphic artist, A3).

When I asked myself the question, What did I do differently with this project, my answer was that collaborative teamwork that required patience and respect for my team members' contributions.

> So, if I could just relate that experience to any other project I've done, on my own, outside of work, it truly was a joint effort team process collaborative approach where one piece doesn't move ahead without the other without complete understanding and agreement. I had to learn patience and

Presentation of Data 83

> I had to learn to say it a different way, write it a different way, do it a different way when it wasn't satisfactory the first time, because, my first time out of the chute was not always accepted by all (author / researcher, A3).

Research sub-question: Can an Internet program stimulate whole-mind thinking (cognitive, emotion, motivation) to learn?

Interview question: A7. Were there any surprises or ah-ha experiences during or after the development?

Perhaps the best way to collectively describe the development team's surprises or ah-ha experiences is to call them fun. The development team's ah-ha experiences were all good, not bad. Starting with the programmer, it took some time for him to really understand what I was trying to accomplish with the program. The concept was new to him and he had no experience from which to draw. The programmer said,

> For me there was. I read that script. I read it 3, 4, 5, 6 times. Then we extracted what we thought would be good monologue for [the animated character] without really understanding the whole process and program. Without understanding the Susan Isenberg concept (little laugh). And, it clicked one day. And I remember, I was working on an idea for structure and tossing some things back and forth and I think I came to you, I called you and it just all started pouring out, how to plan this whole thing. And you said, That's it, that's it! You had nothing bad to say. Just all of the sudden everything clicked all at once. ... I think at that point, I became such a champion or co-champion of the project. It was like I get it, I could argue it. I could sit at the military meetings and argue this program and process and *effectively* because I understood it that well (programmer, A7).

Initially, the graphic artist said there wasn't a lot of room for ah-ha experiences in his work because it was repetitive and tedious. He said,

> I think there were probably more [ah-has] for [the programmer] than for me because he really knew this new technology.

> ... My end was just pretty tedious. I took a recorded wave file and brought it to Flash and just started basically lining up body movements and mouth movements with the audio ... And, there wasn't a lot of room for ah-has (graphic artist, A7).

But, as he talked further, the graphic artist admitted to surprising himself with his own creativity and he called the creative results happy accidents. He said,

> Some of the surprises were those happy accidents like the buttons and the arrows. Some of them made me step back and say, oh, that works! ... That'd be great if we could throw that in there ... and we did (graphic artist, A7).

The biggest ah-ha for me as the researcher was the programmer's ah-ha.

> Well, I think [programmer] was my only surprise. It was a funny thing because it was as if overnight he figured it out. He read and read and read this program and tried to analyze the process to decide how best to create this program. And literally, overnight figured out what this was all about and the magic of it. And, once he got it, he's been the biggest supporter of it. So, he was able to problem solve in the creation of it and thereafter around how to sell it, how to add new features to the program ... (author / researcher, A7).

Because it was a different approach from that which the programmer was accustomed, he went through a learning process before he really understood it—a learning process that included reflection and critical inquiry. And when he finally did master the concept, he achieved flow in his work on the project and the teamwork improved between the programmer and me.

As a summary of interview question A7, the programmer's ah-ha moment was when he finally understood the concept of Virtual Health Coach, the graphic artist described his development work ah-has as happy accidents, and my ah-ha was observing the programmer's ah-ha, which validated my work as understandable.

Research sub-question: Can an Internet program stimulate whole-mind thinking (cognitive, emotion, motivation) to learn?

Interview question: A12. With the same budget and time restrictions, what would you have done differently?

Reflecting back, the troika of talent would not have done anything differently, with the same budget and time restrictions. Our responses were as follows: "I don't think there's anything I would have done different" (programmer, A12). "I don't think there's anything I would have changed" (graphic artist, A12). And, "Nothing" (author / researcher, A12).

Research sub-question: Can an Internet program stimulate whole-mind thinking (cognitive, emotion, motivation) to learn?

Interview question: A9. Discuss the difference between the process and the content of VHC.

Each member of the development team articulated the difference between the content and the process. The programmer distinguishes process from content by describing the process as a constant and the content as something that can change. He said,

> I think we already talked about [how] the flow and structure [are] the process. And the content, you can strip it all out or change it. The content can change completely but the structure and flow always remain the same (programmer, A9).

The graphic artist was less clear in his description of the difference between process and content. But, he talked himself into the fact that the process, which has a beginning and an end, is more important than the content. But, he was clear to say that the content must be right, as well. The graphic artist said,

> [Regarding Virtual Health Coach] I think the process is what's really good about it. You set people up, you explain things to them, you entertain a little bit up front, you

> have [the animated character] kind of telling them some things, you know ... Then, you move on to the next section where you start to learn how people learn, [how to] make these changes ... So, I think that *that* step-by-step type of deal is good. You kind of feel like you've read a book or something or you've accomplished something at the end. You've gone through all these stages and then at the end, you get your reward, which is this plan to do all this. That process is probably the most important thing (graphic artist, A9).

As researcher, I made the distinction clear—the process is constant and the content changes. I said,

> The process will remain the same. That way, as I hope to describe in the paper, this is a process that can be applied to any ... content that is a piece of intentional learning and the content changes according to the curriculum, what it is you want to learn, whether it's finishing your GED, whether it's how to build a house, learning to manage your stress or getting your finances in order. All that content changes but the process remains the same. What do you do first, what do you do second, what do you do third (author / researcher, A9).

In summary of interview question A9, the programmer and I both easily distinguished the process from the content. The difference was less clear to the graphic artist but he finished answering the question saying that the process was not only different from the content but it was more important.

Research sub-question: Can an Internet program stimulate whole-mind thinking (cognitive, emotion, motivation) to learn?

Interview question: A18. What other questions do I need to ask that you think would provide important information for this process?

The programmer and the graphic artist quickly moved on for they could not think of other questions. They said, "I can't think of anything else" (programmer, A18). "Not really. I don't think so" (graphic artist, A18). But as the researcher, I took the open question opportunity to express my feelings and emotions about the project.

> I don't think there's additional information other than the fact that it was about the most impactful thing I've ever done in my life, meaning it was all-consuming. It's become a part of who I am. To be able to tell the story of how that happened, how it came to be that I was working as a one-woman company, had a contract with the military to create a piece of software and ... I got to pick my own development company and I thought I was just the most fortunate person in the world. I got an education grant, $70,000, from the biggest pharmaceutical company around and I'm just blessed. And, I think because I felt that way, I wanted to give it everything I had. I somehow understood, Susan, this is a once-in-a-lifetime opportunity. Don't blow it! I don't care if you're tired, I don't care if it doesn't make any sense right now, just keep working at it, keep talking, keep working, keep problem-solving, keep creating face-to-face meetings and it will happen. And, there's no option to fail (author / researcher, A18).

In summary of interview question A18, the programmer and graphic artist had nothing to say and seemed to be ready to end the interview. However, my answer was one of the longest. I took the opportunity to emote.

How does the design meet the goal of the International Commission on Education for the Twenty-first Century?

Research sub-question: How does the design meet the goal of the International Commission on Education for the Twenty-first Century (UNESCO) for learning throughout life as described by the four pillars of learning: *learning to know, learning to do, learning to live together, and learning to be*?

Interview question: A2. Describe in detail your tangible and intangible goals for this project.

Making money was a tangible goal for everyone but the intangible goals part of the question seemed to solicit more weighty answers from the programmer, the graphic artist, and me. First, the programmer wanted the right personality for the character—one that was fun and appealing. He said,

> Well ... there was money. Intangibles I guess were the right ... personality for the health coach. ... Nothing you could taste or feel. ... It had to be fun, it had to appeal to a certain audience (programmer, A2).

The intangible goals of the graphic artist were similar to the programmer's goal—the character had to be engaging and appealing. The graphic artist seemed sensitive to the perception of the learner. He said,

> My goal for this was for it to be engaging ... to get something that would appeal to a mass audience and that wouldn't alienate anyone and would get the point across and not overly entertain because you had to learn something too. I didn't want it to get lost with the bells and whistles (graphic artist, A2).

And finally, as researcher, I simply wanted Virtual Health Coach to do what I said it would do—help people make behavior changes to improve lifestyle habits. Additionally, I was anxious to know if it was possible to integrate adult learning principles with Internet computer technology.

> My goal was to have a program that worked yet engaged people, kept them there long enough so that they went through the process and hopefully that they would then change behaviors ... So, those are my tangible goals. The intangible goals were to make a success. I really wanted to create something that would work based on what I've learned about adult learning and what I knew about behavior change ... (author / researcher, A2).

And, so it was that the programmer's and graphic artist's goals were intangible success measurements of the program like appealing and engaging while my goal was efficacy, which is tangible.

Research sub-question: How does the design meet the goal of the International Commission on Education for the Twenty-first Century

(UNESCO) for learning throughout life as described by the four pillars of learning: *learning to know, learning to do, learning to live together, and learning to be?*

Interview question: A6. In your thinking, is this system for Internet-based learning more appropriate for a particular type of learning and why?

This interview question was not immediately clear to two of the three interviewees. The programmer and the graphic artist struggled to come up with answers only after having me clarify the question.

After he understood the question, the programmer thought this system for learning could be used for any kind of Internet-based learning because it helped combat information overload. The programmer said,

> I think you could use it for anything. ... It's a great format, structure to apply to just about anything. ... There are three million websites to go find information. ... So, what you're going to do is skip around. And then, you don't know if you're getting the best information or the right information or the information that's right for you. ... it's a big benefit when you can decide what you're going to do and how you're going to do it. And, then you have it detailed enough to look for information on very specific things you want to do in your plan. You're not just looking at everything in general. It's much quicker to get the information you need ... and not get overwhelmed and give up because of information overload (programmer, A6).

The graphic artist thought that this system for Internet-based learning would work for any kind of learning that does not require physical props. He used the example of learning to use a bow and arrow, which additionally requires guided practice. The graphic artist said,

> this way will work for just about any system that you don't really need physical props to learn to do it. If it's just learning something and all you need is your brain to learn it, then sitting in front of a computer to do it is a very good way (graphic artist, A6).

And finally, I thought that this system for Internet-based learning was most valuable for intentional learning that is difficult or has an emotional component.

> I *do* think that it's more appropriate for intentional learning, learning that happens not by chance but because you need to learn something now for some particular reason. That's why I think it would be particularly good for not only behavior changes to improve healthy lifestyle habits but also like preparing for a GED class, course, test. Getting your financial affairs in order, something that you know you need to do but you just can't figure out how to do it. You need to learn a system for accomplishing it ... The answer is anything that is particularly difficult, has an emotional component, and you know you have to do it. You know you have to learn it (author / researcher, A6).

In summary, the answers to interview question A6 varied. The programmer thought it was a good way to learn anything. The graphic artist explained his affirmative answer by adding that it is a good way to learn things that do not require hands-on practice. But I was most explanative. I said this system of learning is best for intentional difficult learning that has an emotional component.

Research sub-question: How does the design meet the goal of the International Commission on Education for the Twenty-first Century (UNESCO) for learning throughout life as described by the four pillars of learning: *learning to know, learning to do, learning to live together, and learning to be*? *Interview question*: A14. List 3–4 guidelines you could give to future technology companies partnering with an educator of adults to create an Internet-based learning program.

From the perspective of the technology company, the programmer thought it was important to either have a person like himself, who is both technologically savvy and creative or alternately, have two people, each with one of those competencies who work as one. The programmer said,

> If I was going to tell another company like us, just have somebody like me there. ... I've always had the ability to

see other people's visions and be able to translate it into technology and design. ... I always see creativity, especially in programming, with how it functions but not how it looks and feels. And [conversely], if you have a graphic designer, or someone who is very creative, they don't understand the technology, therefore, they're going to do things that you really can't make work. ... You either need somebody like me that has a little of both or you need two people. You have a very creative person working side-by-side with a technology person (a programmer who understands it) working side-by-side throughout the entire project. And they have to work as one building it (programmer, A14).

When the graphic artist was asked the same question, he recommended keeping it simple and to make sure it does what it is supposed to do. He said,

Keep it simple, don't clutter it up to take away from the message, make it entertaining but not too entertaining, and make sure that it actually functions the way that it needs to function (graphic artist, A14).

However, my perspective was different from those of the programmer and the graphic artist.

If you, as an adult educator, go to work with a technology company, it would be best to not try to run their show. You only have one show and that is the content and the process. The process more than anything. So stick to your guns about the process and let a few other things go ... Don't try to tell them how to do their work. ... Be open-minded to possibilities or you won't let in all the good creativity and the possibilities ... So be sure and keep your mind open and not your ears closed to new ideas (author / researcher, A14).

To summarize interview question A14, the programmer recommended having a person like himself with both technology skill and creativity. And, if there is no such person available, have two people that work as one—each with one of those skills. The graphic artist said to keep it simple and make sure that it does what it is supposed to do. As researcher, I recommended the adult educator focus on managing the process but not the people for fear of stifling creativity.

Research sub-question: How does the design meet the goal of the International Commission on Education for the Twenty-first Century (UNESCO) for learning throughout life as described by the four pillars of learning: *learning to know, learning to do, learning to live together, and learning to be*?

Interview question: A15. Was there ever a time during your work on this project that you wanted to quit and walk away from it? If so, why? And, if so, how did you stop yourself from quitting?

Interview question A15 brought forth a resounding no reply from the development stakeholders. Though none would have walked away, two of the three interviewees admitted to negative feelings along the way. It was the programmer who kept a cheerful optimistic attitude throughout the two-year project, which kept the rest of the group doing the same.

When asked this question, the programmer quickly said, no because it was fun and exciting. He said,

> No, not this project. There have been projects like that. Not this one. We knew we were doing something different, it was fun, it was a challenge, but it was a fun challenge along the way. And, I was always excited to work on it rather than not. I couldn't wait to do the next thing (programmer, A15).

The programmer also said he would not have walked away but admitted to the agony of tedious animation. He said,

> Only when I was in the full-on animation ... when I had the headphones on going frame-by-frame trying to sync up vowel sounds with the right mouth on [the animated character]. That gets real tedious (laugh). It gets really agonizing after awhile. And I think at that point I was just, Awww ... tired of even looking at it. I wouldn't have quit so that wasn't the question. But, that was one thing that got me ready to pull my hair out (graphic artist, A15).

However, I struggled with feelings of disappointment and depression over the barriers of production. However, I received clarity and energy from the programmer and the graphic artist when they, as a group, would take time to process what they learned from each difficult episode.

> No, there really wasn't a time. And I was the biggest stakeholder of all in this because this was my life and it wasn't just a contract to keep the pay coming in. This is my life's work so I had the biggest stake in it and I was never ... I was disappointed at times and I was tired, and I was kind of depressed about the progress and about stumbles along the way. I had a discussion with [the technology company] kind of chewing it over after-the-fact especially when it came to the Air Force issues, especially with [the programmer], I would get clarity and get new energy based on us processing each time something would happen—the good and the bad of it, what are the possibilities based on what we just heard. So, I would get energy from the group any time I would feel like I wanted to quit. I'd just *say* anything at all, they would just jump right in and we'd boost each other (author / researcher, A15).

As it was, none of the three developers of Virtual Health Coach came close to walking away from the project. However, the graphic artist and I admitted to negative feelings about the work using emotionally charged words like tedious, agonizing, disappointed, and depressed. But, walking away was not an option for the graphic artist. I gained energy from the group by just talking about what happened. The programmer sustained an optimistic attitude about the project because he found it fun and challenging. His positive attitude throughout the entire project sustained the development team through times of personal and group doubt.

Research sub-question: How does the design meet the goal of the International Commission on Education for the Twenty-first Century (UNESCO) for learning throughout life as described by the four pillars of learning: *learning to know, learning to do, learning to live together, and learning to be*?

Interview question: A16. Compared to other projects you have been involved in, how would you rate the perceived value of this project on a scale of 1–10 with 1 representing least value and 10 most value. Explain your answer.

Not surprising, all three interviewees rated the project as a 10 in perceived value. The programmer gave it a 10 because of its uniqueness. He said,

> I would give it a 10 for experience, for personal experience. We were able to do something unique, so it's value was very high in that respect (programmer, A16).

The graphic artist gave it a 10 because his colleague from another company said it was far above what he had seen in the industry. He said,

> Compared to other things I've done, I'd have to value this at a 10 because the only other thing I ever did that was even close to this was a project with [an Internet-based learning company in central Missouri]. I did some stuff with them before I moved back to St. Louis and when they found out … I talked to [a Web-based learning company employee] on an email once and he had said that it was far above what he had seen in the industry. And he's in that industry. Web-based learning and stuff like that. He said it was very much beyond what he had seen before. And so that made me feel that this really is a step above (graphic artist, A16).

I gave it a 10 because I know the learning system works in my life. I model it every day in every way. Hence, one might say, I *am* the Virtual Health Coach and to down rate the project, would down rate my life.

> Well, 10 obviously. It's my life work and it's going to be my doctoral dissertation. It's really how I live my life. It's what it's all about. And, I do live the lessons that I teach and I live the process of learning everyday in my own life with my children and how I coach them and with my communications with my husband and with my job at work. I'm a manager of an education department at a hospital. With my staff, I use all that I know every day and it never fails me! The process

never fails me. So, it is absolutely a 10. Because it's kind of a fulfillment of everything I do and everything that I am (author / researcher, A16).

In summary of interview question A16, the programmer, the graphic artist, and the author / researcher all had a strong interest in the project because of our passion for the work.

Research sub-question: How does the design meet the goal of the International Commission on Education for the Twenty-first Century (UNESCO) for learning throughout life as described by the four pillars of learning: *learning to know, learning to do, learning to live together, and learning to be*?

Interview question: B1. Describe your initial interest in participating in the development of this program.

When asked the above question, both the lieutenant colonel and the regional account manager were interested in helping others. The lieutenant colonel was initially interested in helping military personnel with a program that was high quality with a far reach and a low cost. He wrote,

> My interest was born of a long-standing belief in the value of health risk appraisal and the provision of assistance for individuals interested in reducing their level of risk. Additionally, I was motivated by a desire to capitalize on available technology to provide health coaching to a large number of people without investing substantial human resources. Another motivating factor was a desire to demonstrate that quality educationally and technologically sound products could be developed quickly and at a modest cost (lieutenant colonel, B1).

The regional account manager was initially most of all interested in benefiting patients by working with physicians in a new way. He said,

> There were a number of things that came together all at the same time. [The Air Force doctor] and I had just met. He had just taken his new position there at the MDPR

[Medical Defense Partnership for Reinvention] at [the Air Force base]. I had just taken the new position as regional account manager for the federal group and they had just met you at the same time. In our discussions, we were trying to find some common ground where we could really work together to benefit patients in a new way that they had not been used to working with pharmaceutical companies before. And so, when I presented them with a test or the challenge to present to me a number of needs that they felt [the pharmaceutical company] could have an interest in and that would be a benefit to the Air Force and a benefit to patients most of all, I gave them that challenge and one of their first responses was the Virtual Health Coach and that was the one that they really seemed most interested in. So, that was how I got interested in it (regional account manager, B1).

So it was that, both the lieutenant colonel and the regional account manager were initially interested in Virtual Health Coach because they saw the program's value in helping others.

Research sub-question: How does the design meet the goal of the International Commission on Education for the Twenty-first Century (UNESCO) for learning throughout life as described by the four pillars of learning: *learning to know, learning to do, learning to live together, and learning to be?*

Interview question: B3. What are your plans and goals for using the product?

Both the lieutenant colonel's and the regional account manager's plans and goals for the product were not aligned with their initial interest. More than his initial interest in helping military personnel, the lieutenant colonel planned to use Virtual Health Coach at his new job as faculty member of a state university. He said,

Having retired from the military and accepted a position in academia, I am presently negotiating an arrangement for the use of the VHC to serve university faculty and staff through the office of human resources (lieutenant colonel, B3).

And more than his initial interest in helping patients, the regional account manager planned to use Virtual Health Coach as a way to find out more about the needs of his customers. He said,

> For me, more than just being able to talk to physicians, it was one way to find out a little more about the customer, find out what their needs were. So that when we were *in* a position to talk to physicians, we would have a better message that was more in sync with what their needs actually were. That's kind of what we were looking like there. That and being a new team, not knowing a lot a people within the federal sector, it was also a way to introduce ourselves in a nontraditional way (regional account manager, B3).

To summarize interview question B3, the lieutenant colonel and the regional account manager's plans and goals for the program were self-serving as compared to their initial interest, which was to serve others.

Research sub-question: How does the design meet the goal of the International Commission on Education for the Twenty-first Century (UNESCO) for learning throughout life as described by the four pillars of learning: *learning to know, learning to do, learning to live together, and learning to be*?

Interview question: B4. How does the program fill a void, add value, or accomplish a goal for you?

Regarding interview question B4, goals were met for both the lieutenant colonel and for the regional account manager. Most of all, the lieutenant colonel thought the program added value because work on the project resulted in a rewarding experience for the team members. But, the program also achieved a goal for the lieutenant colonel, which was to provide a product that could be utilized by the Health and Wellness Center (HAWC) managers to extend the reach of their staff. The lieutenant colonel said,

> First and foremost, the VHC demonstrated the merits of close, collegial collaboration between the product's technical

developers, the product's originator and intellectual property owner, the project funder, and the end user community representatives (MDPR). The shared responsibility and accountability that emerged was efficient, effective and rewarding to the team members. The goal of providing a product that Health and Wellness Center (HAWC) managers throughout the military health system could utilize to extend the reach of their staff was realized (lieutenant colonel, B4).

The void the product filled for the regional account manager was its ability to be offered as a solution by a pharmaceutical company that wanted to be known by its physician customers for more than just drugs. The regional account manager said,

> There was a very vague concept being presented by our department at that time, our Managed Markets Division. Very vague in terms of account management style, where you were able to meet with the customer to really present [the pharmaceutical company] as a solutions-oriented company so that you're not just pharmaceuticals but you had more than the drug. You've got the education materials. So we were trying to develop that as a solutions orientation. Really good when you're standing in a meeting in Philadelphia and people start talking about that, but had never seen anything concrete that was really like that (regional account manager, B4).

To summarize interview question B4, goals were met for both the lieutenant colonel and the regional account manager—a product that *could be* utilized by HAWC managers to help others and a product that *could be* a solution for physicians trying to help patients. However, both the lieutenant colonel's and the regional account manager's initial interest in helping end users was never validated.

Research sub-question: How does the design meet the goal of the International Commission on Education for the Twenty-first Century (UNESCO) for learning throughout life as described by the four pillars of learning: *learning to know, learning to do, learning to live together, and learning to be*?

Interview question: B6. Are there other appropriate applications for this learning system? If so, what are they?

Neither the lieutenant colonel nor the regional account manager had difficulty listing other appropriate applications for this learning system. The lieutenant colonel described the process as applicable to almost any arena. His discussions were centered around the perceived needs of others related to his world of work and family life. He said,

> The basic premise behind the VHC was to provide a product that permitted individuals to assess their health status and address specific behavior change opportunities by developing a plan for doing so. The VHC model is applicable to most any arena wherein the objective is to coach, to plan, and to act. A good example would be coaching individuals wishing to address their financial planning (or lack thereof). Another would be career planning, especially for adults seeking to make a career change. A third might be to facilitate various forms of mental health counseling to include depression counseling and marriage and family counseling. Yet another might be guidance counseling for high school students (lieutenant colonel, B6).

The regional account manager thought of personal applications related to his own perceived needs such as retirement planning as well as family-related needs such as his daughter's need to eventually go back to work. Lastly, he thought of a need related to the world of work—personal development of highly skilled workers who lack people skills. He said,

> It didn't take me very long to come up with a couple totally unrelated to pharmaceuticals. The one I have a very high level of interest in is preparing for retirement. I was presented with an opportunity for early retirement [little laugh] six months ago and so it started me thinking. I really need to spend some time thinking about what I want to do and I can think of using a tool that would help me do a review of where I've been and what are my strengths, what do I really care about and do an analysis there and start to develop opportunities

from that. Right now, we're doing it by the seat of our pants because my wife and I are moving to a retirement community—an active adult community. And that's why it's on the top of my head because I see people are moving into this ... Actually it's a new place down there ... They're going to have 6,000 homes. More and more of the people I met ... Some know they want to play golf all the time and some don't. I'm seeing a need out there for developing a plan for change for retirement. And, I can even see the tools in my head that you could put together to do that. ... [Another is] return to the work force. Right now, my daughter would need to use it, for example. Right now she's bringing up the kids. At some point, she may want to return to the work force. You see this all the time. ... [Another is] career development, career or personal development, not medical development. I'm talking more along the lines of ... You know, I've been in enough management positions now that I know there're people who just don't have a clue how to relate to other people. They may be top-notch scientists but they just *do* not have a clue. It's not to say that can't be changed. It's a whole concept of first identifying steps necessary to do it. And, I spend a lot of time on the Internet and I've never seen anything again like Virtual Health Coach, that type of concept (regional account manager, B6).

To restate the answers to interview question B6, both the lieutenant colonel and the regional account manager suggested other applications of this learning system that related to their worlds of work and family. The regional account manager seemed to express himself on this topic with more emotion than the lieutenant colonel.

This section has provided a capsule of stakeholder answers to the interview questions aligned with each research sub-question for the purpose of merging the research questions with the interview questions. Interview questions A1–18 were asked of myself as researcher, the programmer, and the graphic artist. Interview questions B1–6 were asked of the lieutenant colonel and the pharmaceutical company regional account manager. Again, the verbatim responses to the interview questions are in complete form in Appendix D.

EMERGING THEMES

The verbatim interview transcripts and the supporting data (personal notes, emails, documents, and drafts of the program) were read and reread by me. Thoughts and reflections were handwritten in the margins. This activity was compelling because the real story of what happened was different from the story as I remembered it. New details learned from the regional account manager's interview brought forth a new understanding of the lived experience. Just as predicted by the foreshadowing in Chapter One, side stories emerged that enlightened the central story. When handwritten notes in the margins of the data pages were reviewed, repetitive use of thirteen descriptive words or phrases was noted. The repeating thirteen words or phrases emerged as themes and are listed in Table 3. Data elements were then coded with one of the thirteen theme names and its source (interviewee, the question set and number, or the supporting source such as electronic mail, personal note, program draft, document or memory).

The following is an analysis of the interview and supporting data by theme. At the end of each data element, identification of the data source is found in parentheses—the stakeholder and the interview question's letter and number (A1–18 or B1–6) from which the data element was extracted. To better understand the greater context of the data elements, all of the verbatim interview quotes can be found in Appendix D.

Emerging theme: Interest

Among the stakeholders, there were varying interests in the project. The military expressed an interest in the idea of a Virtual Health Coach at

TABLE 3. Emerging Themes

Interest	Trust
Legalities	Fun
Money	Leadership
Skill	Getting it right
Relationships	Educational constraints
Doubt	Situational constraints
	Evaluation

the Society of Prospective Medicine Conference in Colorado Springs, Colorado, September 1999. I presented a poster on the concept. An Air Force physician was in attendance and engaged me in a meaningful dialogue about his interest in bringing the idea back to his Medical Defense Partnership for Reinvention (MDPR) team (of which, he was a member) at a large Air Force base in the Midwest. He saw the potential health and cost saving benefit of such a program for the military population. Upon invitation, I presented the idea to the MDPR, which included the lieutenant colonel, in October 1999.

The project was of interest to all the stakeholders because it had a potential for personal return (i.e., money, recognition) on investment (i.e., time, money, talent). The stakeholders all perceived a need for such a product. And, all seemed to see the project as a challenge. Stakeholders, in turn, describe their return on investment. The programmer said, "… there was money. That was always a big [factor], you know." (programmer, A2). As for me as the researcher, "I really wanted to create something that had impact to get academic attention, would earn money, and would work based on what I've learned about adult learning and what I knew about behavior change modification in the area of health" (author / researcher, A2). And, the lieutenant colonel said,

> My interest was born of a long-standing belief in the value of health risk appraisal and the provision of assistance for individuals interested in reducing their level of risk. Additionally, I was motivated by a desire to capitalize on available technology to provide health coaching to a large number of people without investing substantial human resources. Another motivating factor was a desire to demonstrate that quality, educationally and technologically sound products could be developed quickly and at a modest cost (lieutenant colonel, B1).

Additionally, the military calculated a savings with Virtual Health Coach related to a resulting decreased need for live coaching. Their goal was to use the Internet-based / CD program to reach 100% of beneficiaries with four or more modifiable health risks (bad health habits that are controllable, like smoking). They planned to save greater than $50,000 compared to live coaching of this population.

The regional account manager had a different interest in Virtual Health Coach. He saw the program as a way for him to build relationships with potential buyers of his pharmaceutical products while, at the same time, benefiting his customers and the patients. The regional account manager said,

> I had just taken the new position as regional account manager for the federal group [military] and they had just met you at the same time. In our discussions, we were trying to find some common ground where we could really work together to benefit patients in a new way that they had not been used to working with pharmaceutical companies before (regional account manager, B1).

Furthermore, he said,

> Traditionally, people expect a return on investment and a lot of times it's measured in dollars or some type of value. In this particular instance, it was being set up in a way that return on investment could really not be measured with any dollars or potential for a [drug] contract or things like that but really the value that I was attaching to it was it was allowing me to build a new environment to create in the minds of the customer, a different level of interaction with the pharmaceutical industry, something they had not been accustomed to before. And doing it in such a way that it was going to have a benefit to the customer as well as to the patient. My belief at that time was that we didn't have to have anything attached to a contract or any type of product or anything like that because I really felt that by using this type of system, introducing more people to like the Virtual Health Coach in terms of recognizing that they [the patient] perhaps had a problem that just by default we would start to see some benefit without any direct intervention [sale of a drug]. And, I think it's held true (regional account manager, B2).

Finally, the regional account manager said,

> But, it was truly a unique way to create an interest on the part of the pharmacy staff or the medical staff we were working

> with to show that we're doing things just a little bit different. And it did pay off very well. Excellent. Extremely high profile contacts (little laugh). And again, not tied to anything in specific but just that we were able to demonstrate that we were looking for different ways to do things (regional account manager, B3).

The lieutenant colonel announced his retirement from the military in November 2002. He accepted an associate professor position at a university in the school's new Doctor of Health Administration program. At his retirement, the lieutenant colonel offered me the opportunity to use the university that hired him as a testing site for Virtual Health Coach. He said that he wanted to make Virtual Health Coach available first to the university faculty and then to university students at no cost to the school. In contrast, his offer to me was that instead of a cost in dollars, there was the value of collecting data for testing purposes. The lieutenant colonel said,

> Having retired from the military and accepted a position in academia, I am presently negotiating an arrangement for the use of the Virtual Health Coach to serve university faculty and staff through the office of human resources (lieutenant colonel, B3).

The school's human resource department was very interested in the program for faculty and employees. When I issued a proposal with an associated price the university declined due to lack of budget.

Two of the key stakeholders described interest in the Virtual Health Coach project as a challenge. The programmer said,

> We knew we were doing something different, it was fun, it was a challenge, but it was a fun challenge along the way (programmer, A15).

The graphic artist said,

> I aspired in my youth to be a cartoonist when I was growing up so it's something I wanted to do anyway. But, I don't

do a lot of that. It's only when we get projects like this that I really get the opportunity to use that (graphic artist, A3).

The programmer also was interested in the project because he saw a need for the product as a way to manage Internet information overload. The programmer said,

> It's a great format, structure to apply to just about anything ... There were computers around way back when, but it was so far away from people's minds to actually have a computer that could access that kind of information and was something only smart people do. ... At some point, the personal computer came into play and people started to feel more comfortable with it. And then, when they opened up the Internet, and you could access this information, we ran with it. Ran blind! And still are! ... There have been a lot of attempts by search engines to try to organize that information the best way possible. A lot of portal sites popped up like WebMD, Goggle, Ask Jeeves, to try to organize that information. Even then, it isn't enough. Because, you can still overload on information. You can search on any subject like weight loss. There are three million websites to go find information. ... So, what you're going to do is skip around. And then, you don't know if you're getting the best information or the right information or the information that's right for you. ... And that's why you need someone to organize your thoughts before you even get in there and start doing the research for certain things. And that's why I think it's a big benefit when you can decide what you're going to do and how you're going to do it. ... It's much quicker to get the information you need and get started on your plan and not get overwhelmed and give up because of information overload (programmer, A6).

Emerging theme: Legalities

The first legal matter that was addressed was protection of intellectual property, which is an essential part of invention. The military required it before even considering investing in the project. Fortunately, I had applied for a United States patent and a copyrighted trademark before the idea was presented at the 35th Annual Meeting of the Society of Prospective Medicine Conference in Colorado Springs, September 1999. Since then, the name and trademark Virtual Health Coach received registration status, while the product patent is still pending. The average amount of time it takes to receive a patent is two to three years.

In spite of the patent-pending status of the intellectual property, the lieutenant colonel expected to have ownership of the source code (the behind-the-scene design formula that allows programmers to make changes in the program or replicate it) as evidenced by his electronic mail to me during Memorandum of Understanding (MOU) negotiations in the year 2000. The lieutenant colonel said, "I would think we co-own the code and each has a copy" (lieutenant colonel, electronic mail, 2000). The military did not receive a copy of the code because the source code is patent protected. The MOU gave them the right to have the product but not the source code.

The second legal issue was a concern of all the stakeholders about collecting personal health information (referred to as PHI by the health care and insurance industries) because of the new HIPAA (Health Insurance Portability and Accountability Act) Privacy Rule that became effective in April 2003. "HIPAA's main objectives include improving portability and continuity of health insurance coverage, reducing fraud and abuse, simplification of health care administration, and protecting patient information" (HIPAA Compliance Regulation Training, 2002, ¶ 1). My memory is that the military expressed a legal concern over the security of personal health information that could potentially be collected by Virtual Health Coach. The programmer guaranteed there would be firewall and inscription protection at the highest level, even though the program does not really collect any personal health information (i.e., blood pressure, health history, current health status), only lifestyle behavior information (i.e., plan for managing weight, barriers to quitting smoking, self rewards for carrying out plan). But, even if it was *perceived* that Virtual Health Coach was collecting personal health information, then, all the stakeholders agreed that it was important to take precautions to protect personal health information from being discovered.

Late in the planning, the key stakeholders made a decision not to collect demographic data upfront in the program that would allow the military to link lifestyle behaviors with individual military personnel. Collecting anonymous lifestyle information for aggregate reporting purposes eliminated the second legal concern. The programmer discusses the decision not to collect personal health information. He said,

> We made a very critical decision early on that probably saved that whole technology thing and it was that we made this thing totally, *totally* anonymous. When [the lieutenant colonel] used it, he didn't ask for anything specific. I think that's what saved us. If we would have attempted to get their name and address, phone number and everything else, *that* would have changed the whole scope of it. And we would have had to do some military encryption technology that nobody has access to. We, as a [technology] company would have had to go through some kind of an approval process because we were getting access to military encryption (programmer, A13).

The programmer believed that not collecting personal health information was a good decision. He said,

> I thought that was just a brilliant move on our part. Because, I think that saved us on a lot of things. We basically put it on them. That's why the final decision was, well, here's what you can do. You set up your Website, let them log in and you can collect all that information and then you can provide a link to our program. But, we're not going to collect all that information. We're just not going to do that. That was a wise decision on our part. That saved us from a lot of that (hesitation) meddling (little laugh) (programmer, A13).

My concern over getting paid was the third legal issue. To receive legal vendor status with the military, it was my responsibility to register my company with the military's General Services Administration (GSA)—a necessity for receiving the grant money from the MDPR. A number known as a GSA number issued to my company in 2000 remains in effect at the writing of this paper for future opportunities to do business with the military.

The fourth legal issue was related to my concern that once the terms of the MOU were met, the military would use and promote Virtual Health Coach without giving me credit, the programmer, or the graphic artist. So, to ensure that each party would give recognition to the others involved in the development of the program for the purpose of mutual benefit, in April 2000, I amended the MOU by adding the following statement under the Mutual Benefit section. The MOU was changed to read:

> The Department of Defense and [the author / researcher's company] will mutually support each other after this project is completed by recognizing the collaborative and supportive contributions of each other as an appropriate occasion arises (MOU, April, 2000).

Also, an acknowledgments section was added to the front of the program that cannot be separated from the program and gives credit to each of the stakeholders and their role in the project.

The last legal issue was the military's unauthorized public offerings of Virtual Health Coach in the winter of 2003. "Such public offering exceeds the scope of permissible usage allowed under the Memorandum of Understanding" (attorney representing my company in a letter to MDPR, December 2003). In the fall of 2003, I stumbled upon four Navy websites that were giving away Virtual Health Coach without password protection. This was a violation of the MOU, which states that the military has full rights to the product within the military population only and no rights in the public sector. A member of the MDPR team was called and I asked him to close down the websites. It is my memory that the conversation was disagreeable. On the call, the MDPR team member argued for the military's right to have the public sites for maximal use of the program. Then, when challenged with the terms of the MOU, the MDPR team member denied being at fault using the argument that he issued Virtual Health Coach to all the bases with a cover letter written by me warning of the limitations of its use to military populations only. He did what he said he would do. But, he was not holding himself accountable for the outcomes. The lieutenant colonel concurred, "... I do not see that MDPR has violated the agreement, but it does appear that the Navy has" (electronic mail, December, 2003). My lawyer was contacted and within a month after no response from the MDPR member, and after the lawyer threatened a lawsuit, all four publicly accessible Virtual Health Coach programs were taken down from the military websites.

Emerging theme: Money

Lack of money was the first and most consistent topic of the project. The first concern was getting the money needed to build the program as planned. The programmer proposed an initial amount that was not accepted by the military. A much lower price was eventually agreed upon. "There were whole pieces we took out—the email portion, the pull up, the stuff we just removed altogether to try to fit within the budget" (programmer, A1). The project required more labor than was budgeted for in the proposal. The programmer said,

> we put a lot of hours into it. It was not done during normal working hours. It was done with a lot of 12-hour, 16-hour days including weekends. All the animation was done at midnight and on weekends for [the graphic artist] (programmer, A10).

Second, a lack of success in finding development money caused the military to seek another way of promoting the Virtual Health Coach idea—from a health promotion program to a disease management tool. The initial proposal, which was unsuccessful in getting funded, was the result of a collaborative effort between the lieutenant colonel and his team along with the programmer and me. The first proposal focused on the potential large cost saving benefit of population health management through disease prevention. The first draft MDPR grant proposal said,

> The Military Health System (MHS) is moving toward a population health management philosophy, deeply rooted in prevention that will never be able to match needs with available or foreseeable resources. Technology in the form

of a computer-based interactive multimedia virtual health coach, offers a value-priced tool as a way to greatly multiply a health and wellness staff's ability to service a large number of customers quickly and efficiently. It is proposed that technology offers a faster response to the problem of high-risk populations [defined by the military as those military personnel with four or more modifiable health risks such as smoking, obesity, or excessive alcohol use] and, for that reason, the focus of this application will be to create an electronic virtual health coach for that population segment. Human energy can be focused on low-risk populations where the sense of urgency in terms of health improvement and cost savings is not as time critical (first draft MDPR grant proposal, 2000).

The cost savings was projected to be more in the first year than the entire cost of the program's development. According to the proposal, the military's goal was "100 percent of beneficiaries with four or more modifiable health risks to receive and use Virtual Health Coach CDs or Web Virtual Health Coach alternative" (first draft MDPR grant proposal).

But the military did not find development money with the first proposal. An MDPR team member's electronic mail revealed the military's frustration in finding funding, "Still no patron saint. We are still in consideration for funding by an Air Force group ... I'll keep probing" (MDPR team member, electronic mail, August, 2000).

Then, in an effort to find a funding source, the military suggested a modified grant proposal that would be a means for "more closely meeting their organizations business focus" (MDPR team member, electronic mail, August 2000). It was an effort to fit the program into an existing disease management plan.

The United States Air Force (USAF) is attempting to reengineer clinical medicine delivery so it centers on the primary care manager (military physician) and his support staff. As part of that, they are trying to get each primary care manager team member (med techs, nurses, and admin) specialists to all who participate in patient care delivery to the extent possible by their training. All I tried to do was emphasize the versatility of the Virtual Health Coach (CD and Web) that it could be implemented at the clinic level as well as by an organization as the Health and Wellness Centers (MDPR team member, electronic mail, June 2000).

So it was that, when the military changed the proposal from a disease prevention program to a disease management program, they were successful in securing a grant from the pharmaceutical company, which was communicated to the programmer, the graphic artist, and me as an education grant. In fact, it was much later (December, 2003) discovered to be a charitable grant rather than an education grant. The pharmaceutical company's regional account manager said,

> I had a new pretty impressive boss. Here, I'm asking for a significant chunk of change to get this thing going. I was surprised. At first, there was no rolling of the eyes but just some frustration because there wasn't enough detail. So we went back and got some additional detail. And, another good learning experience was—put 30 pounds of paper on your boss' desk about a week before Christmas ... Timing is everything. So, another critical lesson learned. And, by doing that, we were able to really demonstrate what the value of the program would be in very general terms and you can get the charitable grant to do that (regional account manager, B4).

> It's a charitable grant and that's why I have to go through great lengths to make sure that when I'm talking to any of my customers about it, they know they own it, not me. I just help facilitate and when I also introduce this through my regional account managers, to make sure *they* understand it. This isn't tied into anything. This is *theirs*. But it's a good way for you to show that there are other ways for us to work together. And, that's what we've been doing (regional account manager, B4).

Therefore, to receive funding, the argument for Virtual Health Coach changed from cost saving disease prevention to charitable gift giving.

A third money issue was that there was not enough grant money to implement the program once it was finished. In the place of an implementation plan, there was a distribution plan. The programmer discusses the lack of an implementation plan.

> One of the problems with the military is that we satisfied the terms of the contract and then we had no more say in it. The terms of the contract according to the military were, We'll help you get it built and then it's ours and it's also yours in the public. And so there really was a stopping point and they would have had to pay for me, for you, to help them implement. It was a lack of commitment to take that project all the way through to the end because that would have taken more money. Clearly, they didn't have enough money. They didn't have the foresight to really create a plan from beginning to end. Their goal was completion of the program and to get it out to physicians and that was it (programmer, A4).

The last money issue involved the programmer and graphic artist's concern that Virtual Health Coach could have been better if there had been more money and time budgeted for the project. The graphic artist was concerned over the voice that was used for the animated character. The sanguine graphic artist describes how he, the programmer, and I overcame the lack of money needed to get the voice right. He said,

> Money? Like I said, going back to the talent, I thought [the voice actor] was good for it. But, we could have used other people if we had the money that those other people wanted. If you go through some of those agencies, they charge you an arm and a leg. We could have put it in front of focus groups. But we didn't have that ability. So, what we really did to overcome that was that we just kind of went somewhere in the middle. He had some extreme voices and some not extreme voices. We just kind of went somewhere in the middle and hoped for the best. And that's really all we could do with what we had and hoped for the best and hoped that it appealed to enough people and hoped enough people got it, hoped enough people were not offended or turned off by it (graphic artist, A10).

When asked what he would have done differently if there had been more money, the programmer said, "More [name of animated character]. More animation" (programmer, A11).

Emerging theme: Skill

Each stakeholder contributed to the project in a unique way. The programmer was skilled in applying technology to my ideas. When asked to list guidelines for future technology companies partnering with an educator of adults to create an Internet-based learning program, the programmer thought that a visionary like himself was vital to the project's success. He said,

> If I was going to tell another company like us, just have somebody like me there. I'm not bragging on myself but ... I've always had the ability to see other people's visions and be able to translate it into technology and design. ... I don't know it that's unique or just that ... There are a lot of people who can't see the big picture and I think that if you had a lead programmer who wasn't a real big visionary, I don't know if that person could pull off a project like this (programmer, A14).

The graphic artist described the programmer's visionary skill as a big grasp and as one of the biggest guidelines for others attempting to do similar projects. The graphic artist said,

> I think [the programmer] really understood what it had to do. That would be one of the biggest guidelines. Make sure you really know what this needs to do and what the user needs to walk away with once they've viewed this. I think they really need to have a big grasp of that (graphic artist, A14).

Further, the programmer had the technological skill to use a program called Flash beyond its maximum capability. "We made it a desktop application that we imported over to the Web, which is what it was never intended to do", said the programmer (A5).

Creativity was included among necessary skills. The programmer said, "We can offer a basic plan, the basic structure, and apply any content to it but it involves some human intervention and creative work" (A16).

However, the graphic artist had the skill to know that too much creativity causes the message to be lost. He said,

> Nine times out of ten, they [graphic artists] miss the message by being really, really creative. And, I didn't want to do that. It [Virtual Health Coach] wasn't meant to be a creative juggernaut piece. It was meant to instruct people and I figured the best way we could do that was to keep it simple and not cluttered up with all that stuff. ... Because with people's short attention span, if they're looking at all of that, they might just decide, Aw, it's just too much and there's just too much going on for me to focus (graphic artist, A8).

The programmer described my unique contribution as the researcher when he said to me, "You were crucial every step of the way from beginning to end" (programmer, A13).

The lieutenant colonel demonstrated skill in four areas—foresight, leadership, technology, and problem-solving. Based on a memory of conversations and on an electronic mail, the lieutenant colonel demonstrated foresight very early in the planning (November, 1999, before the technology company was hired) when he advised me to find a vendor that could support Web capability. "The Web product should be your primary focus! Depending on timing to market, a CD-ROM could prove a *very* short-lived tool" (lieutenant colonel, electronic mail, November 1999). It is the opinion of the author / researcher that he was correct in his thinking.

The lieutenant colonel had the leadership skill to keep the project moving forward by playing the role of taskmaster—setting deadlines and assigning tasks. As researcher, I found the value of someone in this role.

> we had the military pushing us. I think that's the part they played best. That was the reason why we had to keep moving, because they kept us going. We had deadlines. They gave us money. We had to give them that return on their investment (author / researcher, A17).

The pharmaceutical regional account manager perceived the military as technologically skilled. He said,

> You couldn't ask for a better group to work with because the Department of Defense and the VA [Veteran's Administration] are probably the most technical groups you'll find out there in the health care system (regional account manager, B5).

The programmer touted the military's problem-solving skill in finding a solution to one of the flow problems, which was that users lost their place in the program if they were interrupted and would then have to start over when they returned. The lieutenant colonel wanted the program to remember the users' place if they had to leave the program before finishing, so that upon returning, they could proceed from where they left off. The programmer said,

> One thing that the military *did* contribute during that process was that we were under the assumption that people would sit down and spend a half hour or forty-five minutes and go through the whole program or maybe not. That was the way it was set up. When we went to present it, they said, What if we leave, what if we stop and come back to it later? We said, Uh, well, you'll have to find your place. So, that was one big thing that they brought to the project that we built into the program the ability to remember where you left off. So that makes it easier to complete at your leisure (programmer, A5).

Emerging theme: Relationships

Collaborative, open and collegial relationships between stakeholders moved the project forward. Five uniquely skilled stakeholders worked separately and in teams to accomplish a common goal. The perceived value of the relationships varied among stakeholders.

The programmer valued my collaborative and open nature to new ideas from all the stakeholders during the development of Virtual Health Coach. The programmer said,

> If you look at the beginning of the project, from the script or [from] your whole concept, to the script, to our original scope, if we wrote a detailed scope of how to build this thing to where it is today, there's a lot of things in between that changed, a lot of back and forth, a lot of things we didn't do, a lot of things we added because of that close collaboration along the way. I don't know that this project could have ever been defined that perfectly up front. And the fact that you were open to change and to let's try this and here's something that someone else is doing or somebody might suggest something, even the military. And you were open enough to do it (programmer, A13).

As researcher, I found the importance of taking a collaborative approach to move the project forward.

> The partnership with the Air Force required that I dance with the Air Force as well as the development company all at the same time. And, I was kind of the go-between. So, if I could just relate that experience to any other project I've done, on my own outside of work, it truly was a joint effort team process collaborative approach where one piece doesn't move ahead without the other without complete understanding and agreement. I had to learn patience and I had to learn to say it a different way, write it a different way, do it a different way when it wasn't satisfactory the first time because, my first time out of the shoot was not always accepted by all (author / researcher, A3).

The programmer offered evidence of my efforts to create a climate of collaboration. He said,

> It could have been horrible. It could have been you in the middle, military demanding things from you, you having to communicate with us, then we'd get back to you and you go back to the military. But it never happened that way. I think it's because of the way *you* approached it. It had nothing to do with us, or the military necessarily. It's the fact that you made it a partnership right from the beginning and you

> dragged us to the meetings ... not kicking and screaming but whenever there was a meeting or anything, no matter what it was, we were always present and part of it. Just by creating that climate up front (little laugh), we avoided a lot of that stuff (programmer, A13).

Feedback was a result of the collaborative relationships between all the stakeholders, which the graphic artist valued during the developmental process. The graphic artist said,

> I liked having that feedback. I liked the fact that everyone was involved. I think it helped the project. It affected me in a good way. I think that it was good. If one person developed this whole thing without say from anybody, it would have just been that one person's (graphic artist, A13).

The work assignment quickly forced the programmer, the graphic artist, and I to be collegial and to function as a team. The programmer valued our relationship because it allowed them to speak with one voice in meetings with the military. Solidarity gave the team power. As researcher, I stated,

> I think the project really forced us to be collegial real quick. We had to do this and we had to do in a short amount of time and we were kind of forced to be a team. And I thought we got to that point really quick because a lot of people couldn't do that (author / researcher).

> Right. Real quick. When we went to meet military, we always spoke with one voice. It was clear from their point of view that we were on the same page all the time (programmer, A13).

The programmer saw the importance of having either one person with a mix of skills or two people with different skills working as one as he described the programmer and graphic artist team relationship. The programmer said,

> I always see creativity, especially in programming, with how it functions but not how it looks and feels. And on the other side of the thing, if you have a graphic designer, or someone who is very creative, they don't understand the

technology, therefore, they're going to do things that you really can't make work. You either have to have somebody like me that has a little of both or you have two people. You have a very creative person working side-by-side with a technology person, a programmer who understands it working side-by-side throughout the entire project. And they have to work as one building it (programmer, A14).

The lieutenant colonel saw the collegial collaboration as beneficial not only to the process, but also rewarding to the people. He wrote,

First, and foremost, the VHC demonstrated the merits of close, collegial collaboration between the product's technical developers, the product's originator and intellectual property owner, the project funder, and the end user community representatives (MDPR). The shared responsibility and accountability that emerged was efficient, effective and rewarding to the team members (lieutenant colonel, B4).

The regional account manager believed that the relationship that resulted from the process of working so close with the military on the product was more important than the product itself. The regional account manager said,

It was not the tool itself. For me, it was the process. It was the process of working so close with [the lieutenant colonel], [the Air Force physician] and some of the other support staff (regional account manager, B3).

The Virtual Health Coach project gave the regional account manager and the military a common language, through which to dialogue.

Of interest is the programmer's perception of the value of his relationship with the Air Force and the pharmaceutical company, which he described as "useless" except for the money. The programmer said,

So, with the Air Force, I think that relationship was not critical to the project except for the financial situation. The Air Force and [pharmaceutical company] can be lumped together because [pharmaceutical company] was completely useless to the project except the finance (programmer, A13).

To the programmer, his relationship with the military was much less important than his relationship with the graphic artist and me.

Emerging theme: Doubt

Doubt was a way of searching for certainty as the stakeholders tried to move the project forward. Initially, there was doubt about ability to work together and there was doubt about talent. The project was completed only because stakeholder interest exceeded stakeholder doubt.

Early in the process, there was doubt about working together. The MOU (Memorandum of Agreement) financial negotiations planted seeds of doubt in the minds of both the lieutenant colonel and me. The lieutenant colonel doubted his ability to work with me because of my stubborn insistence on intellectual property compensation. I doubted my ability to work with the lieutenant colonel because of his stubborn resistance to pay for it. The lieutenant colonel's language took on a less cordial tone. "Your intellectual property is the intellectual capital you bring to the table as your skin in the game for the proposed project. This is your contribution to the collective seed money for launching the Virtual Health Coach" (lieutenant colonel, electronic mail, February 2000). I capitulated and received no short-term reward (intellectual property compensation) to ensure what I perceived to be the greater long-term reward (a completed program).

Adding to the uncertainty was my doubt about the quality of product the military was willing to build. After agreeing on the concept and the proposal plan, the proposed cost was rejected by the military due to not only a refusal to pay for the intellectual property but also a desire for simpler animation. As the proposed cost lowered, so did the expectations for the product as described by the lieutenant colonel in an electronic mail document, "This is a prototype / proof-of-concept, not a real, full-blown development effort" (March 2000). And, the "Bottom Line" (actual subtitle) of the proposal rejection read, "Please offer a budget that incorporates the feedback provided above. If that is not deemed a desirable or plausible notion, we will say thanks, but no thanks and will be friends but not business partners" (lieutenant colonel, electronic document, 2000).

I considered walking away at this point. Not only did I have doubts about working effectively with the military but I also doubted the proposal would yield a quality product. Because the project required more labor than was budgeted for in the proposal, it cost more than twice the amount of the education grant award. "Our initial budget was almost triple what we ended up getting" (programmer, A1). Though it was considered a proof-of-concept, it took a full-blown development effort to complete it. And it happened that the programmer and graphic artist put more time into the project than was paid for only because that's what they wanted to do. "We ended up saying, we'll do it for whatever money you can get us" (programmer, A1). They had no doubts they could pull it off. The programmer said,

> I knew we could pull it off. There was worry, anxiety about certain deadlines. But, I think we handled it correctly. We did a lot of shifting of deadlines and responsibility back to the military for items that bought us time on others (programmer A10).

The graphic artist said, "My goal for this was for it to be engaging and I knew we could pull that off ..." (A2).

Doubt about talent arose in the programmer very early in the production process. He doubted the talent of a co-programmer who was also his business partner at the time. Though the partner left the partnership very early in the project, he had completed some preliminary work that the programmer doubted would lead to a unique learning experience. The programmer said,

> I worked with somebody who was heavily a programmer and didn't have a creative bone in his body. The way [the previous partner] structured it [Virtual Health Coach] originally was as a big giant database program, where you go in and create the questions, and it would display each question on each page. But it would be no unique experience. Everything's exactly the same. That was the opposite of what we needed to create here. We needed to create an experience

Presentation of Data 121

and climate rather than a program to just gather information (programmer, A14).

Further, the programmer was able to distinguish the critical difference between creating an experience and climate and just gathering information by referring to them as opposites. Doubt about working together and doubt about talent fostered a search for certainty that eventually moved the project forward.

Emerging theme: Trust

Establishing trust was an important goal of the program as well as an important aspect in the process of building the program. The programmer and graphic artist used images of past learning such as an old-style blackboard and chalk in Virtual Health Coach to create a physical and psychological environment of trust among users of this new learning process. The programmer and I discussed the topic,

> The goal was to create a new climate for learning with some traditional aspects. We threw in things like graphics of clipboards, and chalkboards, and things that people are familiar with (programmer, A8).
>
> A link to past experiences (author / researcher).
>
> We created a virtual traditional classroom (laugh) if that makes any sense. And the reason is that we wanted them to realize that it is a learning climate. So, we had to flash things in front of them that they remember as part of the learning climate. That's what makes it a learning climate. It's those bits of history. ... What looks like a game plan for a football team ... to try to create the climate of being on a team or working with a coach, working with someone other than yourself so you felt you aren't doing this by yourself (programmer, A8).
>
> But in reality, you really are. You're out there. It's all you. The coach is just to cheer you on, to motivate, build confidence, check in with you, [to] show you the process, to show you the plan (author / researcher).

> So, all those elements are there, which create the right environment for learning on both physical, I guess in the individual sense and psychological because you're seeing these past school references and stuff flash in front of you (programmer, A8).

Establishing a climate of trust for Virtual Health Coach builders was just as important as establishing a climate of trust for Virtual Health Coach users. The programmer felt safe going outside the boundaries because I was open to new ideas, as described by the programmer. He said,

> You [the author / researcher] were open to ideas and I was open to trying to do things you wanted to do and I think it made it a very pleasant project. It wasn't so rigidly defined that we couldn't go outside the boundaries of it from time to time and do something (programmer, A13).

Events related to intellectual property rights resulted in a loss of trust between the military and me. It was my practice to have people or organizations who were interested in looking at the Virtual Health Coach content to sign a mutual nondisclosure agreement that disallowed them to share or use the idea for their own purposes as well as disallowing me to share or use any military secrets that I may learn during the exchange of ideas and intellectual property. When I asked the military to sign such an agreement, I recall that the lieutenant colonel replied that the military does not sign mutual nondisclosure agreements because the military, by its very nature is trustworthy. Therefore, it was to be understood that the military could be trusted to not disclose my proprietary work without signing an agreement to not disclose.

Early in the process, military personnel earned my trust through their words and later lost my trust through their actions. The military's violation of the terms of the MOU resulted in my distrust of them. The military did not do what they said they would do, thus they modeled behavior that was different from what they taught as evidenced by the discovery of Virtual Health Coach on four military public websites (see Legalities section, pp. 88–89).

Emerging theme: Fun

The project was fun for the programmer, graphic artist, and me. The programmer said, "It was a very fun project. All three of us [author / researcher, programmer, and graphic artist] were enthusiastic all along the way" (programmer, A10). I said that, "It was fun" (author / researcher). The programmer continued,

> We knew we were doing something different, it was fun, it was a challenge, but it was a fun challenge along the way. And, I was always excited to work on it rather than not. I couldn't wait to do the next thing. ... It was real exciting (programmer, A15).

I also added,

> There was always so much energy. It was always fun to come over here [the technology company office] in the middle of all your mess because you were churning ... Particularly when you had [the voice actor] come in (author / researcher, A15).

The programmer and I saw fun as an important part of creativity.

> We always knew that there was something serious behind this. We were very conscious of it all along the way, that there was something important to this, [and] that we had to reach these people. It had to help people. And that was an important goal even though we were having fun with it ... We got to hear [voice actor] and all his out-takes were just hilarious. I think that we always kept that in mind. I don't think we lost anything. I think if anything, we gained because the fact that we were having fun built fun into it. If we hadn't built fun into it, then it would be very, very dry (programmer, A17).

> And that's the nature of creative people. You have to have fun, too (author / researcher).

The last thing I said on this subject was,

> There's never too much fun ... at all, especially with a project like this. It was like theatre. You know if you can't have fun, then you lose the energy and the creativity and so we *absolutely* had fun in every possible term. Never, ever, ever ... never too much fun (author / researcher, A17).

Discovery was part of the creative fun, which the graphic artist described as happy accidents. He said,

> Working on it, you get those happy accidents that you happen upon something and you go, Just keep that, don't lose it, don't touch it! (graphic artist, A5).

The graphic artist thought that the program's fun approach would relax and entertain the learners. The animated whistle character was animated to speak my serious words. Care was taken to avoid cluttering the screens and being too cartoony, which could have made the character not believable. The graphic artist said,

> There were a lot of things that didn't make the cut that were pretty entertaining. I think because you wrote it before we ever started planning ... This was already done before we did anything on our part, which was good in that we had a complete script to pull from. Your words are what we had this character say. So really, the only way we could have messed that up and pulled away was to get a little cartoony with it sometimes or a little cluttered up with props and goofy things like that. So, I think at times maybe it pulls away from the serious vein because of the make-up of the character ... being a whistle. I think anytime you do that, it's going to somewhat make it less serious. You don't watch Bugs Bunny and think of that very seriously. In a way, it's very good because people relax and it seems like more of a fun approach to things. The message is very serious and everything you wrote is very serious so the only way I could have

screwed it up was to have the character, have [voice actor] read a voice that was like very Mickey Mouse that was not believable and not stern in any sense and totally way out there. We tried some of those and it didn't work (graphic artist A17).

Emerging theme: Leadership

Two leaders emerged among the five stakeholders, I did as the leader of the production effort and the lieutenant colonel as the leader of the funding effort. The lieutenant colonel was engaged and collaborative through the completion of VHC, which was celebrated at an Air Force base open house in October 2001 with high-ranking military personnel in attendance. Afterwards, implementation of the product was left to an MDPR team member. The lieutenant colonel seemed to disengage after the product was completed as he looked forward to promotion and retirement. The timetable of events was as follows:

Virtual Health Coach finished	May 2001
Virtual Health Coach implementation kits finished	August 2001
MDPR open house promoting VHC	Early October 2001
Lieutenant colonel promoted to colonel	Late October 2001
Lieutenant colonel retired	November 2002

With additional unbudgeted money found by the pharmaceutical company, Virtual Health Coach implementation kits were created and produced. They were colorfully designed cardboard boxes that each held ten VHC CD ROMs, a CD to reprint a doctor's brochure and a user's brochure, and a letter written by me to those in receipt of the VHC implementation kits (see Appendix E) explaining the terms of the program's use. A total of 5,000 CD ROMs were produced and 200 implementation kits were assembled. The plan was to distribute the kits to 200 military physician offices. This was to be accomplished by the regional account manager of the pharmaceutical company. The kits were both never picked up and never delivered by the regional account manager. Large stacks of the kits remain at the technology company at the writing of this report. However, the regional account manager began using single VHC CDs as physician gifts to build one-on-one relationships with potential customers. The following is his explanation of why the product was never implemented as planned. The regional account manager said,

> I really felt that by using this type of system, introducing more people to like the Virtual Health Coach in terms of recognizing that they perhaps had a problem that just by default we would start to see some benefit without any direct intervention. And, I think it's held true (regional account manager, B2).
>
> So, that was the return on investment that you anticipated? What was your return? Did you actually ... If I recall, the packets didn't actually get out like you expected them to get out. What was the end result of all of that? Did it actually happen the way you thought it would (author / researcher)?
>
> Not quite the way I thought it would. I was hoping that it would be embraced a little bit more. No fault of the program, but with [pharmaceutical company] (regional manager, B2).

It is my memory that I, too, became disengaged after the product was completed as I focused on the future of VHC in the public sector. Satisfying the terms of the MOU seemed to signal an ending before all the implementation work was done. As a result of the military not managing the implementation of VHC, the implementation happened in an unplanned way and the impact of the program is not known.

Emerging theme: Getting it right

My first task was to pick the right technology company. Once I chose the technology company, energy was high among stakeholders as the work began and everyone knew that to produce a quality program, things had to be done right. There were many things to get right after getting the right people—the right look, the right feel, and flow: (a) creating a climate for learning, (b) getting the character right, (c) creating flow, and (d) making sure it did what it was suppose to do. The last important thing to get right was deciding not to collect personal health information.

First, it was important to choose the right technology company. Another local computer program development company was asked by me to submit a proposal for the work of building Virtual Health Coach. The winning company was picked to do the work of building an electronic platform for the program because of their humanness and their proclaimed ability to integrate technology and human touch—their tag line. They delivered a clearly written proposal in a short time and in a nice way—cover page, plastic folder, etc. And, the winning company delivered and presented the proposal in person and made a follow up phone call to me within a week. The competing company electronically mailed their proposal and I received no follow-up phone call from them. I felt confident that the chosen technology company could turn my idea into a program that would provide whole-mind learning.

The programmer and I spoke on the most important parts to get right—the people, the look, the feel, and the flow. He said,

> So, that would be my number one ... My guidelines are that: You get the right people, build the look and feel and the flow first, and worry about all the functionality second (programmer, A14).

As researcher, I said,

> The look and the feel, not necessarily just the character. But, the look and the feel of it. The flow of it, I think more than anything. How it could be navigated. But, I have to agree with [the graphic artist] though, that the initial character, if he turns you off, then you're not going to go back and you're not even going to look, wait around long enough to know what the process is all about, much less the content. So, truly, the look and the feel are most important to get right (author / researcher, A8).

Next, the programmer, the graphic artist, and I described different aspects of the program to get right. First, creating a climate for learning. The graphic artist found it hard to set the stage. When asked what problem was hardest to solve, he said,

> Probably setting the stage. I look at it like we set up a scene on a theatre stage, so to speak. And where we positioned

everything because we knew that [the anonymous animated character] would be popping up occasionally and would be saying things. We didn't want him to just POOF, show up with a cloud of smoke or something and he's there. So we kind of had to make space for him, but how do you make space for him and still not get in the way of the content (graphic artist, A5).

Regarding the importance of establishing a climate for learning, the graphic artist talked with me about the importance of color. We said,

I think color was involved as well (author / researcher).
Yes (graphic artist, A8).
There are a lot of emotions with color (author / researcher).
Yes (graphic artist, A8).

You picked primary versus pastels. Is there a reason for that (author / researcher, A8)?
I think simplicity. In this case, if you want to entertain somebody and just entertain them, well then, you can flash all kinds of pretty colors and all kinds of pretty images in front of them and it will spark something in their brain and it will get their brains going ... they're seeing pretty things, but will they retain anything from that? Probably not. I think with this, we were kind of walking a two edge sword and we wanted it to be ... We wanted them to learn something so we didn't want to clutter it up with too much craziness that would take away from the content. That would distract ... I think solid color ... that solid blue ... is calming. It kind of helps you. If it were warm colors, I think it would have been too much for the eye and it would have taken away. The colors that were used are simple. I think it frees your mind and let's you focus on what it is you really need to be focusing, which is the content. And, if we got too crazy and had some funky lines, and some curves and some weird angles and all sorts of hip artistic high dollar ad firm kind of stuff and we just went crazy, you would lose that attention to the content (graphic artist, A8).

The programmer thought that including reminders of childhood school was important to getting the learning climate right. He said,

The goal was to create a new climate for learning with some traditional aspects. We threw in things like graphics of clipboards, and chalkboards, and things that people are familiar with. Almost a link to past experiences. We created a virtual traditional classroom (laugh) if that makes any sense. And the reason is that we wanted them to realize that it is a learning climate. So, we had to flash things in front of them that they remember as part of the learning climate. That's what makes it a learning climate. It's those bits of history. Even the chalkboard we used was very old. I don't know if you noticed that. It wasn't a white board. It was the traditional chalkboard on wheels, which is even older so that it reaches a wider audience. So that people who are familiar with the old learning stuff ... So, I think that helped create that, establish that up front (programmer, A8).

The programmer wanted to get the right character. The coach personality and voice had to be just right. The graphic artist said,

It was very important to get that character right. It will turn people on or turn people off (graphic artist, A8).

The programmer said,

[We had to] create a personality that didn't exist. Trying to get it even down to the voice I think was, I mean, it was intangible. Nothing you could taste or feel. ... It had to be fun, it had to appeal to a certain audience. And we had to try to determine what that personality would be and create that ...

And there was science behind it. I pulled up some studies and some research on the type of people that would use this product and tried to get an age range, gender, and everything, and try to figure out who'd be the most likely people to use it and what would appeal to them the most. So, we read what was there, we tried a voice that sounded like an authority figure but wouldn't sound like you were being preached at. We realized that most people don't listen to their doctors, why would they listen to this. We realized that people ask their best friends ...

So, we thought, well let's ... someone has to be ... sounds like they've lived it before ... they've lived this whole experience. They're not preaching at us, they're just teaching us from experience. And, so, with several different versions of a voice we ended up with kind of a Bronx New York accent that sounds like this person lived a hard life and learned by making every mistake there was. And, was a better authority than the people who read it from books or try to teach you how to be better (programmer, A2).

Creating flow was important to get right. The programmer thought flow was the *most* important thing to get right. He said,

I'm going to say flow. I'm going to say the whole flow of the thing. It was so important to get it right. I think if we had structured it any other way than it is right now, I don't think it would be as effective. I've had personal experience with it. I just think that was the most critical thing. That it flowed properly. That people felt what they were supposed to feel when we wanted them to feel that way. So people knew when they got past the science and theory, looking at their past and that they really did feel encouraged after they finished section four. They really do feel it. They feel even more confident after they get through [section] 5 and they get through 6. Because, they've answered a lot of questions and read through a lot of information but at that point they really do feel, I have a chance at this, I have a chance to change. And, I think they're looking forward to making a plan at this point. We succeeded there. I think if we had done it any other way, I don't know if it would have worked (programmer, A8).

The programmer continues to talk about the importance of flow. He said,

I think if you strip out the content, the basic structure and flow is perfect. Now, I can see all kinds of improvements in content. I can see a ton of that. I think if you strip all that away, you could fit the health coach on a single sheet of paper—it's structure and flow. And that's what's so unique about it and nobody else is doing it (programmer, A8).

But, the graphic artist warned that all of the important aspects mentioned above are useless if the program does not do what it is supposed to do. He recommends taking the time to understand the program. The graphic artist said,

> Make sure you really know what this needs to do and what the user needs to walk away with once they've viewed this. I think they really need to have a big grasp of that. If they don't have it, you're going to get a useless program out of them (graphic artist, A14).

> In other words, take the time to understand it (author / researcher).

> Really understand it from all sides and really take your time with that because if you don't, it doesn't matter how you animate it, how it looks, if the function's not right and it's not doing what it really needs to do, then it's useless (graphic artist, A14).

The last important thing to get right was the decision not to collect personal information from the learners. We development stakeholders never wavered from our collective right decision to not collect demographic and / or information from the users. The programmer said,

> We made a very critical decision early on that probably saved that whole technology thing and it was that we made this thing totally, *totally* anonymous (programmer, A13).

Emerging theme: Educational constraints

There were three educational constraints creativity, intellectual, and evaluation. The first educational constraint was creativity, which may have been due to traditional macho military thinking. Three issues of creativity were significant. The first creativity issue was the military's rejection of a weight management lesson in Virtual Health Coach titled, Fluffy Floater and Slimy Sinkers. It read as follows:

> A healthy way to achieve a normal weight is to decrease the fat and increase the fiber in our diet. If your diet is too low in fiber and too high in fat, your bowel movements will sink in the water and be solid and slimy looking. If you're eating

a high-fiber, low-fat diet, your bowel movements will float on top of the water and look airy and fluffy (draft version, Virtual Health Coach program).

After the objection to the original title, the title was changed to "Monitor the Fat and Fiber in Your Diet" in an attempt to reverse the decision but to no avail. Fluffy Floaters and Slimy Sinkers was taken out. I said,

I think one of the barriers was the military and their conservatism. We had to pull out some pieces that they didn't like. Remember the fluffy floaters? (Ardell, 2003, ¶ 10).

The second creativity issue was related to the perceptual learning style inventory (James & Galbraith, 1985) included in the program with permission from the authors. One leading member of the lieutenant colonel's team who reviewed the first draft of VHC wanted the olfactory learning preference taken out of the inventory. I received the following e-mail from him.

Even though there were positive indications on several learning styles, only one (smelling) came through in the summary and subsequent functions. I think it should list learning styles where there's some positive there. Smelling as a stand-alone just doesn't fit (or smells, so to speak) (electronic mail, lieutenant colonel's team member, 1999).

The lieutenant colonel's team member told me that when he took the assessment, it revealed that his *only* preferred learning style was olfactory learning and he was embarrassed about it. I reassured the over-age-50 team member that research on the James and Galbraith (1985) perceptual learning style inventory tool shows that for his age category (50 years of age and up), lower scores overall on all learning style preferences are common. James and Galbraith (1985) found that the "mean score between two age groups, 20 through 49 years and 50 years and over, were significantly higher for the younger age group in all seven subtests [preferred learning styles—print, aural, interactive, visual, haptic, kinesthetic, and olfactory]" (p. 22). And further, I told him that the least low score among all low scores was probably an insignificant finding (author / researcher, memory). After that explanation, the team member changed his mind and the olfactory learning style was allowed to remain in the inventory.

The third creativity issue was the controversial voice of the animated character. Upon the military's review of the first program draft and after all the voice and animation was completed, the lieutenant colonel did not like the voice and he wanted it changed. I recall my memory that he thought the voice of the animated male character sounded too feminine. In a face-to-face meeting between the developers and the military about the concern over the voice, the lieutenant colonel indicated that the voice may not align with the military's Don't Ask, Don't Tell policy regarding gays in the military. The programmer discussed with me the matter of the animated character's voice.

> There was science behind it. I pulled up some studies and some research on the type of people that would use this product and tried to get an age range, gender, and everything, and try to figure out who'd be the most likely people to use it and what would appeal to them the most. ... And, so, with several different versions of a voice we ended up with kind of a Bronx New York accent that sounds like this person lived a hard life and learned by making every mistake there was. ... And to realize that at that point the voice was a little too harsh and was almost too comical. So we softened it by making it a little bit more feminine. By making it more feminine, it had just the right appeal. It didn't offend anybody but one person in the military (little laugh) (programmer, A2).
>
> And I think he was afraid of it being offensive (author / researcher).
>
> Right. I don't think it really offended him but he was afraid to put it forward (programmer, A2).

The cost of changing the voice was determined to be equal to one-fifth the original amount for the whole project and a very large amount of additional time. In an effort to keep the original voice and animation, the programmer educated the military team on the research findings behind the voice selection. Additionally, I used intuition and creativity to propose giving the animated character a name that is a slight variation of the lieutenant colonel's name. The lieutenant colonel liked the idea very much. From that point forward, there was full acceptance and support of the character and his voice by the entire military team.

The second educational constraint was intellectual due to the educational level of the general military population. The military requested that some original words and concepts be changed to words that were easier to understand. The original words / concepts and the substitute words / concepts are depicted below in Table 4.

The development team (researcher, programmer, and graphic artist) capitulated and substituted the simpler words for stages of change but compromised in the preferred learning style inventory leaving in the correct word but putting the simpler word in parentheses next to the original word. In a conversation with me, the programmer defends the original words.

> They had us dumb it down. I thought that what we had originally was right on. The fact that we had the real term and we included a description (programmer, A10).

> That was a compromise to keep those words in (author / researcher, A10).

TABLE 4. Military Word Substitutions

Original Word / Concept	Substitute Word / Concept
Pre-contemplative stage of change	Third choice
Contemplative stage of change	Second choice
Preparation stage of change	First choice
Print learning style	Reading and Writing
Aural learning style	Listening
Haptic learning style	Touching
Kinesthetic learning style	Moving
Olfactory learning style	Smelling
Visual	Seeing

> Right. That was because we insisted. That was something we stood up for because people need to know these. If they're taking this kind of a learning style assessment that's been around for several years and developed by a lot of other people who are involved in this. They may want to go back and read about it or may be exposed to it at a later time (programmer, A10).
>
> Well, it has to be the right information if it's going to have staying power (author / researcher, A10).
>
> And to be credible. I think if you dumb it down too much you start losing that. That's not where we want to go and I think we prevailed on that one (programmer, A10).

The programmer, the graphic artist, and I regretted substituting the stages of change words for simpler words because the stages of change concept is mentioned twice in the program and the word substitutions only appear in one of the two places. The programmer and I feared that the discrepancy would confuse the user.

The third educational constraint was inadequate program evaluation due to the MOU's limits on time and money. The programmer used one small focus group of approximately five people made up of his company's clients who walked through the door one day to evaluate VHC. User-group feedback was delivered to the stakeholder group as a verbal report from the programmer stating that the users all liked it. Because the user-group was made up of the programmer's satisfied customers, the feedback was considered biased.

When the lieutenant colonel was concerned with both the animation and the audio, he surveyed his work team of nine people "without predisposing anyone" (see Appendix F). Though he called the survey a focus group, I understood that the purpose of the survey was to gain support against the character's voice. The lieutenant colonel wrote,

> After looking at the VHC demo on the Web, I was concerned with both the animation and the audio. Without predisposing anyone, I had nine of our staff give their opinion (lieutenant colonel, electronic mail, May, 2001).

In an e-mail to me, the programmer's business partner at the time accused the military team of bias. The business partner at the time wrote,

> I would caution against these statistics from a purely scientific view. The survey seems to have been put together in a hurry and does not seem designed to meet any truly scientific purpose ... The initial email concerning the situation stated that 9 persons had been asked for their opinion. I have 10 surveys. Who was the tenth person, [the lieutenant colonel]? It would not be reasonable for a person with such a strong opinion to participate in a survey designed for them. In actuality, it is not reasonable for somebody of such a strong opinion to either design or implement the survey. It is for these reasons and others that I felt this information to be biased and will not perform any but the most cursory statistics (programmer's partner at the time, electronic mail, May 2001).

A comment on one of the ten surveys defends VHC, which is evidence that he or she *was* predisposed. When asked to rate the animation on a scale of 1–7 with 1 being poor and 7 being excellent, the responder rated Virtual Health Coach as a six and included the following comments.

> I think that it is a cute animation. I think that it is a whistle and appears friendly and excited. I do not find it annoying at all (survey, May 2001, Appendix F).

When asked to rate the voice on a scale of 1–7, the same responder rated VHC as a 5 and defended the voice and its understandability, which is further evidence that he or she was predisposed.

> The voice is very understandable, but it does have a strong New York accent. Some others might find it difficult to understand (survey, May 2001, Appendix F).

When the program was finished, no scientific data was obtained to understand the effectiveness of the program. The graphic artist said,

> I think if we had a bigger budget and no time constraints, we would have done those things. We would have taken more time working on the character and deciding on the voice and putting it in front of people, getting feedback from it. Just doing more upfront stuff to plan for this. Really, really plan for this. And get good numbers on what people like and what they don't like and adjust accordingly. We could have developed the character with more feedback, which would have been nice. We still don't really know if that was the best way to go (graphic artist, A11).

Table 5 depicts the educational constraints, decisions that were made as a result of the constraints, and the consequences of the decisions.

Emerging theme: Situational constraints

Most of the constraints were situational and were in the areas of development, power, information, and implementation. The first situational constraint was in the area of development, in which there were three issues: (a) lack of time, (b) a severe decrease in funding from the original proposed amount to less than half as discussed earlier in this chapter, and (c) the loss of the programmer's partner at the time in the technology company right after the MOU was signed. When asked about the project's barriers, the programmer answered time and staff. He said,

> Time, which was deadlines that seemed to be impossible because we didn't have the staff. We *had* the staff but then we *lost* the staff right when the project started (programmer, A10).

When the graphic artist was asked about the project's constraints, he answered time and financial. He said,

> We had time constraints and financial constraints. We had a very limited pool we could pull from in terms of talent ... So my goal was really just to get something as animated as we could get and flowing as we could get with the software, the technology, the time, the money, and the talent pool to pull from (graphic artist, A2).

TABLE 5. Educational Constraints, Decisions that were made as a Result of the Constraints, and the Consequences of the Decisions

Educational Constraints	Decisions that were made as a Result of the Constraints	Consequences of the Decisions
Creativity constraint due to traditional military thinking	Educated military on the research behind the program's content and animated character.	Two battles won—the animated voice was not changed and the olfactory learning was kept in.
	Used intuition, creativity, and flattery to cajole military into changing their hearts and minds.	One battle lost—Fluffy Floaters and Slimy Sinkers was removed (Ardell, 2003, ¶ 10).
Intellectual constraints due to the educational level of the general military population	Capitulated and changed the stages of change words to make them simpler in one of two areas where the concept is mentioned.	The inconsistent language creates confusion.
	Compromised by including in parentheses new simpler words for the learning styles but left original words in.	The learning style inventory section is understandable, while at the same time teaches the user new terminology.
Evaluation constraints due to MOU's time and money limitations	The technology company used one small focus group of their satisfied customers who walked through the door one day to evaluate Virtual Health Coach.	Virtual Health Coach was completed and delivered without any validation of effectiveness and with very limited and biased evaluation of user satisfaction.
	The lieutenant colonel surveyed the opinions of his work team of nine people.	

To restate the development constraints, there were three: (a) lack of time, (b) lack of money, and (c) lack of staff. The programmer and the graphic artist decided to work many hours of overtime to cope with lack of time, they worked the overtime without pay to cope with lack of money, and the programmer did the job of two people to cope with the lack of staff. The result of the above decisions was that the project was on time, within budget, but had less animation and voice than what was originally proposed and was undervalued.

The second situational constraint was my power constraints due to my gender amid two male-dominated arenas of work—military and computer technology. The male power was subtle and so it called for subtle counterbalance. I used communication assertiveness rather than aggressiveness to represent my interests. Examples were my use of the word *I* to describe my feelings instead of the word *you* to assign blame, my use of interpretive statements to seek understanding, and my ability to seek compromising win–win solutions to problems. Use of assertive communication created a climate of respect and kept the lines of communication open.

The following seven decisions I made leveled the playing field in the gender power struggle: (a) to consult a patent lawyer for intellectual property protection; (b) to consult a contract lawyer to ensure the MOU document represented my interests; (c) to consult with my Masters in Business Administration (MBA) son for expert business advice; (d) to consult with my military pilot son and my retired military officer husband for military language and culture advice; (e) to consult with my computer savvy husband for expert advice on technology issues; (f) to prepare well for joint meetings at the military base so the programmer, graphic artist, and I all spoke with one voice; and (g) to be on time and wear a conservative dark business suit when attending stakeholder meetings on the military base, which communicated respect and a confident professional appearance.

The results of the above decisions were: (a) the military had confidence that the program's legal protection was sufficient to warrant an investment in its development and the MOU was changed to ensure the source code ownership for me; (b) I developed a common language that increased my ability to communicate assertively in both the military and the computer technology arenas; (c) face-to-face meetings were *always* friendly, respectful, on time, and according to the agenda. Unfriendly, disrespectful, random expressions of displeasure or late communications were limited to the military and limited to electronic mail and phone calls (non-face-to-face communication).

The third situational constraint was information constraint due to withholding of information and competing stakeholder agendas. I made the decision to trust the military MOU to protect my interests and to trust the military to implement the program as planned. Therefore, I made no effort to find out if the military did was they said they would do. The consequence was that in December 2002 after the lieutenant colonel's promotion and retirement, the MOU was violated by the military and the implementation did not happen as planned. I accidentally discovered VHC to be open to the public on military websites across the world and a threat of legal action was required to close them down. I notified the already retired colonel of the violation and he acknowledged the problem. He wrote,

> I do not see that MDPR has violated the agreement, but it does appear that the Navy has. The MDPR folks need to revisit the correspondence that went out with the VHC [Virtual Health Coach] packages and make certain the guidance and prohibitions were clear. Once the root source is found, these documents may need to be shared. What may have happened is the VHC product got handed off to someone without the accompanying correspondence and guidance. ... I am not surprised that this happened, nor am I disappointed. Stuff Happens! Please don't get your lawyer too lathered up and give [the military team member] some time to sort this out (lieutenant colonel, electronic mail, December 2002).

I *did* give the lieutenant colonel's team member time to sort it out and the VHC public websites were eventually taken down only after a threat of legal action. Another consequence of information constraint was that the program was not implemented as planned. There was evidence that the military base HAWCs received VHC kits but the two hundred military physician VHC implementation kits were never delivered.

The fourth and final situational constraint was program implementation constraint due to a change from what was originally planned to what was done in order to satisfy the funder of the project, the pharmaceutical company's regional account manager. In August 2001, instead of planning to distribute the program to HAWC staff, who would know how to use VHC by means of an instructional letter in the kit, the military doctors were targeted for distribution of the program as gifts. There was no plan for training the physicians on how to use the program. Instead, the regional account manager gave a CD ROM copy of VHC without the accompanying implementation kit as a gift to any physician that he targeted for sales of his pharmaceutical products.

In February 2003, I spoke with the MDPR team member at the Air Force base, one of the key players during the product's development. Regarding current status of the product, I was told that the MDPR was closing April 19, 2003, due to lack of funds. He recommended contacting the state surgeon general. After several phone calls, I spoke with the state surgeon general who understood the military's right to use VHC, but had no one capable of taking it forward at the time. With the September 11, 2001, disaster, interest was less for wellness and more for national security. The military stakeholder (lieutenant colonel) was promoted and then retired, there was no money allocated in the project budget for implementation and the whole MDPR division was shut down. The pharmaceutical regional account manager was promoted to national account manager because of VHC but the implementation kits were never distributed to the military physicians in mass as planned. The programmer said,

> And we never got to that part. Because at our last meeting was, Well, [the lieutenant colonel] is retiring, the place is disbanding, and there's no money left in the military for that particular office. There was nobody to head it up, nobody to implement it. So, it's just out there (programmer, A4).

The programmer describes a lesson learned,

> Maybe that's something that we learned when we walked away. This is new, this whole merging of technology and adult education and that you have to have a plan to implement it. We actually have to do that. I think this is something that you and I are just going to have to learn. Ok, we just can't hand it over and have some instructions on the back of the CD. It's bigger than that and there has to be some promotion or instruction instead of just handing it to them. There has to be a method for how we get people involved in using this technology. I think that's something we discovered after the fact (programmer, A4).

142   APPLYING ANDRAGOGICAL PRINCIPLES TO INTERNET LEARNING

This was my perception of the problem,

> But, one of the problems with the military is that we satisfied the terms of the contract and then we had no more say in it. The terms of the contract according to the military were, We'll help you get it built and then it's ours and it's also yours in the public. And so there really was a stopping point and they would have had to pay for me [author / researcher], for you [programmer] to help them implement. ... They didn't have the foresight to really create a plan from beginning to end. Their goal was completion of the program and to get it out to physicians and that was it (author / researcher, A4).

Table 6 depicts the situational constraints, decisions that were made as a result of the constraints, and the consequences of the decisions.

Emerging theme: Evaluation

The word evaluation can be used to describe the project's outcomes—some intended and some unintended. An intended outcome was that the program was completed. In January 2002, the implementation kit material was finalized for production. The kits were assembled and ready for delivery by January 31, 2002. In a phone call with a MDPR team member on January 18th, I learned that two additional letters were written for inclusion in the VHC implementation kits to the HAWC staff—one from the lieutenant colonel and one from his boss, a brigadier general in the office of the state surgeon general. Both were letters of support to tell the packet recipients that the program is sanctioned by Air Force Headquarters (personal note, January 18, 2002).

There was evidence that VHC implementation kits, which included ten VHC CDs, a CD of the Internet version, physician and patient brochures, a CD of the reproducible marketing materials, sample provider and patient letters (see Appendix G), a page of health and wellness resources, a letter from the author / researcher (see Appendix E), and an enclosed printed list of National military resources for healthy behavior change were distributed to military bases throughout the nation and the world but the extent of the

Presentation of Data

TABLE 6. Situational Constraints, Decisions that were made as a Result of the Constraints, and the Consequences of the Decisions

Situational Constraints	Decisions that were made as a Result of the Constraints	Consequences of the Decisions
Development constraints due to limited time, a decrease in funding from original proposed amount, and one less programmer	The programmer and graphic artist worked many hours of overtime without pay. The programmer did a job originally proposed for two people.	The project was on time, within budget, had less animation and voice than was originally proposed and it was undervalued.
Author / researcher's power constraints due to female gender amid two male dominated arenas of work—military and computer technology	Author / researcher: -Invested in a patent and a copyright to protect intellectual property.	Military had confidence that the program was sufficiently protected to warrant an investment in its development.
	-Consulted a lawyer to review the MOU before signing.	MOU was changed to ensure Virtual Health Coach source code ownership for author / researcher.
	-Consulted regularly with her MBA son, military pilot son, and retired military husband for expert advice on face-to-face communication with the military. Consulted computer savvy husband regularly for expert advice on communication with the technology company.	Developed common language and an understanding of the different cultures that increased the author / researcher's ability to communicate effectively in both arenas.
	-Prepared well before joint meetings at military base. The development stakeholders spoke with one voice. -Dressed in conservative dark business suits for joint meeting on military base.	Face-to-face meetings were *always* friendly, respectful, on time, and according to the agenda. Unfriendly, disrespectful, random expressions of displeasure or late communications were limited to the military and limited to emails and phone calls (non face-to-face communication).

(Continued)

TABLE 6. (*Continued*)

Situational Constraints	Decisions that were made as a Result of the Constraints	Consequences of the Decisions
Information constraints due to withholding of information and competing stakeholder agendas	Author / researcher trusted that the stakeholders would do what they said they would do.	Military violated the MOU and the implementation was not carried out as planned.
Implementation constraints due to stakeholders leaving, the Iraq war, and MDPR closing down	Called the state surgeon general's office to find new stakeholder / sponsor.	State surgeon general's office acknowledged the military's right to use the program but he was not interested in going forward due to events of 9/11.

distribution is not known. The evidence that kits had been distributed was the calls and electronic mail that were regularly, though not frequently, received by the programmer and me throughout 2002 from military personnel asking questions about implementing VHC at their own facility. Because the terms of the MOU did not include implementation support, all calls and electronic mail received by the programmer and me were referred, at the military's request, to a MDPR team member. Those who called and electronically mailed were enthusiastic about receiving a VHC implementation kit but each had specific and detailed questions about how to implement the program at their military base. To me, it seemed that the programmer and I were receiving calls and e-mails because the military personnel had no one else to call. Though less frequent, the programmer and I continued, to receive similar calls and electronic mail. Again, an intended outcome was the completion of the project—the product was finished and implementation kits were mailed to the HAWCs. Simply finishing a project could be considered enough to merit a good evaluation. An unintended outcome of the project, though, was the later obvious confusion among the implementation kit recipients, which could be considered an unfavorable evaluation.

One other unintended outcome that could be thought of as unfavorable was the fact that the 200 targeted military physicians did not receive the

Presentation of Data 145

implementation kits as planned. The regional account manager evaluates the outcome as regrettable as he answers my interview question.

> If I recall, the packets didn't actually get out like you expected ... What was the end result of all of that? Did it actually happen the way you thought it would?" (author / researcher).

The regional account manager answered,

> Not quite the way I thought it would. I was hoping that it [Virtual Health Coach] would be embraced a little bit more. No fault of the program, but with [the pharmaceutical company]. Right at the end when we were trying to do that is when the merger took place and so the resources that we would have had to introduce it were really not there (regional account manager, B2).

So it happened that the regional account manager was promoted to national account manager and the pharmaceutical company lost the resources needed to introduce the program to 200 physicians as originally planned.

The programmer and I perceived that the regional account manager received no benefit from his company's investment. It seemed as if he had an unfavorable outcome from his work on the project. The intended outcome (delivery of the implementation kits to the military physician offices) did not happen. The programmer and I evaluated the pharmaceutical company's perceived lack of benefit. They discussed the topic,

> They [pharmaceutical company] received no benefit from it. They didn't take any benefit from it. They could have but they didn't even pick up the packets (author / researcher, A13).
>
> Yeah. They're [the Virtual Health Coach kits] still here. They never got involved at all. The only time they did is when it came down to ... well, just to pay for it (programmer, A13).

But, in fact, the pharmaceutical regional account manager *did* value VHC and *did* benefit from it. He valued VHC as a product that has application today more than ever in the Department of Defense, as evidenced by his account of the project's good intended outcome. The regional account manager said,

> I just want to congratulate you [the author / researcher] because the program *does* have tremendous value. And, I think that we've only just scratched the surface, even with the DoD [Department of Defense]. Even with version one ... But they're constantly undergoing change and then you throw in a few terrorist attacks and a war and it makes it harder but I wouldn't let that be a deterrent because those very events make the program even more important. Depression is much more a major player right now and when I'm talking about the military, I'm not talking about just GI Joe, I'm talking about the entire family. It's huge. In fact, I've had some documentation, some of the major military bases look at the communities surrounding them ... the incidence of depression has increased. And, being in the military, having depression, they sometimes don't want to go to a base physician. And everything else that goes along with the depression like smoking (regional account manager, B6).

It turned out that an unintended outcome of the project, working closely with the military, offered the biggest benefit of all to the regional account manager. He said,

> I'm probably the only one in the [pharmaceutical] industry that was able to sit in on ... just to learn. ... So, when I was talking with Product Management [about new pharmaceutical products], I could get them to think about things they needed to do perhaps different. Enlighten all the way around. It was the process (regional account manager, B3).

Individuals who worked on the project had good personal outcomes. The perception was that the military team and the regional account manager seemed to benefit more from the project than the military population, for which it was intended. One of the side stories that emerged from the interviews was the human story about how personal career benefits were realized by two of the project participants as a result of the project. The programmer opines on the events as they happened. He said, "... it [VHC] was a stepping stone for certain individuals to move on in their lives and they had no intention of using it, we found out much later" (programmer, A4). In the regional account manager's interview, which was conducted last, I learned that the regional account manager and the medical physician on the lieutenant colonel's team were both promoted because of their work on the VHC project. The regional account manager told how it happened that they were promoted. He said,

> I came up for national account manager and because of the types of programs I had been doing like Virtual Health Coach, which was a really new way of working in that federal field, that was really what positioned me and set me apart from the rest of the group in order to get the job as national account manager. ... As a matter of fact, every time I see [Air Force physician who worked on the Virtual Health Coach project under the lieutenant colonel], I pat him on the back and he pats me on the back because we were responsible for each other's promotions (regional account manager, before B1).

Despite the programmer's feeling that the military had no intention of using it, and that the program was merely a stepping stone for certain individuals to move on, the lieutenant colonel gave a surprising positive response to a question about his return on investment. He wrote,

> The return on investment (ROI) was, in my estimation, exceptional. Given the dollars, person hours and intellectual capital invested, the VHC [Virtual Health Coach] product is of high technical and professional quality and fulfills the spirit and intent of the virtual coaching agenda. When compared to other products I have had experience with, the bang for the buck is substantial in terms of the quality of content, appearance, usability and comprehensiveness (lieutenant colonel, B2).

Further, the lieutenant colonel said the project met its goal.

> The goal of providing a product that Health and Wellness Center (HAWC) managers throughout the military health system could utilize to extend the reach of their staff was realized (lieutenant colonel, B4).

And, recall, too, that the lieutenant colonel himself was promoted to colonel just after the program's launch. The lieutenant colonel, the military physician, and the regional account manager were all in receipt of good unintentional outcomes as a result of the VHC project—they all received promotions.

Lastly, the military used the project to show off the good things the MDPR does for the Department of Defense. This unintended benefit was described in the following electronic mail from a member of the lieutenant colonel's team. He wrote,

> We have some MDPR folks that are going to attend the annual Healthcare Information and Management Systems Society (HIMSS) Annual Conference Exhibition. It is the biggest healthcare trade show in the US. MDPR has been offered a corner in the [aerospace company]'s exhibit booth to show off what MDPR is all about. One of the things we will have running as a demo is the VHC so people can see the good things MDPR does for DoD [Department of Defense] (electronic mail, January 2003).

The unintentional outcomes that were unfavorable were (a) the confusion of the VHC kit recipients at the HAWCs, and (b) the targeted military physicians did not receive the 200 implementation packets.

In spite of all the issues and constraints, the programmer had no regrets as he evaluated the project's outcome. He said,

> No regrets. I thought what we came up with was just amazing with the time and budget restraints we had to deal with. ... I don't think there's anything I would have done different (programmer, A12).

> I think that the basic structure and flow is the key and it's perfect as it is. I can't imagine it could be any other way (programmer, A8).

The programmer was confident that the effort was worth it because the basic structure and flow are perfect. In other words, the process of how the user gets through the program is most important. The process is more important than the content.

The programmer, graphic artist and I learned the importance of ensuring that along with delivery of the Internet learning experience there should also be training of the personnel on how to use the program and how to receive benefit from it, and the training should be included in the implementation plan. The programmer and I understood the importance of implementation management. He said,

> This is something that we know when we go take it somewhere else. We already know up front. We'll tell them up front. And part of getting this package is that you get this front end consulting and all the materials you need to implement it rather than just handing it over. That's such a crucial part to get people into this. Because it's new and different (programmer, A4).

As researcher, I added,

> The advertising department and the understanding of what it is and how to use it. Also, how to use the data. They won't see the value of it unless they are able to use the data (author / researcher, A4).

The lieutenant colonel, the graphic artist, and I described possible applications of the Internet process for learning other than health coaching. The lieutenant colonel wrote,

> The VHC [Virtual Health Coach] model is applicable to most any arena wherein the objective is "to *coach*, to *plan*,

and to *act*." A good example would be coaching individuals wishing to address their financial planning (or lack thereof). Another would be career planning, especially for adults seeking to make a career change. A third might be to facilitate various forms of mental health counseling to include depression counseling and marriage and family counseling. Yet another might be guidance counseling for high school students (lieutenant colonel, B6).

The graphic artist said,

> If you're trying to teach someone with something, and you give them some knowledge, and give them whatever format, this way will work for just about any system that you don't really need physical props to learn to do it (graphic artist, A6).

As researcher, I said,

> I do think that it's more appropriate for intentional learning, learning that happens not by chance but because you need to learn something now for some particular reason. That's why I think it would be particularly good for not only behavior changes to improve healthy lifestyle habits but also like preparing for a GED class, course, test. Getting your financial affairs in order, something that you know you need to do but you just can't figure out how to do it. You need to learn a system for accomplishing it. I think that ... The answer is anything that is particularly difficult, has an emotional component, and you know you have to do it. You know you have to learn it (author / researcher, A6).

The regional manager had three application ideas for the learning process aside from health coaching. He said,

> I'm seeing a need out there for developing a plan for change for retirement. ... Return to the work force. Right now, my daughter would need to use it, for example. ... [And]

> career development, career or personal development, not medical development. I'm talking more along the lines of ... You know, I've been in enough management positions now that I know there're people who just don't have a clue how to relate to other people. They may be top-notch scientists but they just *do* not have a clue. It's a whole concept of first identifying steps necessary to do it. And, I spend a lot of time on the Internet and I've never seen anything again like Virtual Health Coach, that type of concept (regional account manager, B6).

Finally, the programmer thought that this process for learning could be used to learn anything. He said,

> I think you could use it for anything, especially when you're trying to achieve a goal. It creates a plan. I don't know if it helps you establish your goal because it doesn't do that. It provides you help in developing a plan to reach your goals. It doesn't really help you create the goals. You have to come into it with that. So, it could be applied to personal finance, to set goals and build a plan. It won't necessarily do the investments for you. But, it will help you plan for how you're going to deal with getting to that point. I can see it being applied to anything. It's a great format, structure to apply to just about anything (programmer, A6).

Though the story of how the product was built was not always about success and positive outcomes, the two leaders, the lieutenant colonel and I, both made a statement at the end of the interview to emote gratitude for the experience. In spite of his rigidity, the lieutenant colonel demonstrated a positive attitude toward the project as he reflected back on it. The lieutenant colonel evaluated the process as "more than the product people will see ..." when he added a personal note to the end of his interview. He wrote,

> Personal Note: It was indeed a pleasure to collaborate on the development of the Virtual Health Coach with a team of professionals who brought to the table an exceptional collection of health education, marketing, management and computer technology skills and experience. The VHC

> [Virtual Health Coach] represents more than the product people will see and use. It represents the outcome that can be achieved when people of intellect, experience and enthusiasm unselfishly join hands to accomplish a common goal (lieutenant colonel, after B6).

And in spite of my frustrations, I *also* demonstrated a positive attitude in my following personal note at the end of my interview.

> it [creating Virtual Health Coach] was about the most impactful thing I've ever done in my life, meaning it was all-consuming. It's become a part of who I am. To be able to tell the story of how that happened, how it came to be that I was working as a one-woman company, had a contract with the military to create a piece of software and ... got to pick my own development company and I thought I was just the most fortunate person in the world. I got an education grant, $70,000, from the biggest pharmaceutical company around and I'm just blessed. And I think because I felt that way, I wanted to give it everything I had. I somehow understood ... this is a once-in-a-lifetime opportunity. Don't blow it! I don't care if your tired, I don't care if it doesn't make any sense right now, just keep working at it, keep talking, ... keep problem-solving, keep creating face-to-face meetings and it will happen. And, there's no option to fail. And that's how I looked at it. There was no option to fail. And, I think *that* was the driving force (author / researcher, after A18).

CHAPTER FIVE

CONCLUSIONS AND RECOMMENDATIONS

Because of the ubiquitous Internet, the teacher of adult learners will benefit by seeking ways to apply andragogical principles to technology. Andragogy is the art and science of adult learning. Adults, more than ever, are using the Internet to meet their learning needs just to keep up with today's fast pace world. However, there is the concern over adults not being able to meet their learning needs on the Internet in the area of intentional learning. And, until adults learn how to learn, the Internet "may merely be an information box, not a tool for learning" (Isenberg & Titus, 1999, p. 1).

DISCUSSION

The following section provides a discussion of the linkage between the research sub-questions with the interview questions, by way of a thread-through of the literature review from chapter two.

Issues with face-to-face teaching / learning

Research sub-question #1: What are the issues with face-to-face teaching / learning during the development of the program?

Interview question: A4. What did you learn from this experience?

Related to the issues with face-to-face teaching / learning, the new learnings among the development stakeholders were: (a) facilitating or implementing the program is just as important as the program itself, (b) managing the program's size and length will help avoid disinterest among the learners, and (c) learning to use the unique contributions of others will lead to the success of a program.

First, the programmer learned that just providing the program is not enough, but instead, a face-to-face teacher must implement or facilitate the program. He said, "This is new, this whole merging of technology and adult education and that you have to have a plan to implement it. ... rather than just handing it over" (programmer, A4). McLagan (1978) may agree with the programmer because she believes that the job of a teacher is to make programs learnable by helping learners: (a) become motivated to change; (b) effectively handle course information and experiences; (c) develop knowledge, skills, values and attitudes; and (d) transfer their learning to the application environment. Knowles' (1980) belief that the role of the adult educator is to manage the educational process also supports the programmer's position on the importance of program implementation. In 1996, Knowles described "a set of procedures for facilitating the acquisition of content by the learners" (pp. 259–261) which signifies that more than just the content (or program) must be considered when facilitating adult learning. Savićević (1999), like Knowles (1980), sees the adult educator as manager of the educational process, who integrates the educational and cultural elements of adult education. To summarize, the programmer learned that face-to-face implementation of the program was the way to manage the Virtual Health Coach program and is supported by McLagan (1978), Knowles (1980, 1996), and Savićević (1999).

Second, the graphic artist learned that managing the program's size and length helps avoid disinterest among the learners. The word "interest" means a *feeling* of curiosity or attentiveness. Taylor (1986) and LeDoux (2002) may agree that adult education must account for and understand the emotional or *feelings* component of learning. Lindeman (1961) said, "emotions and intelligence are continuous" (p. 68). In other words, the graphic artist understood the emotional component of learning. And further, he thought that to improve the learning experience, it was important for him (one of the learning process managers of Virtual Health Coach) to avoid creating in the learner the negative emotion of disinterest (Taylor, 1986; LeDoux, 2002; Lindeman, 1961).

Third, I learned the value of working face-to-face with people that possessed different knowledge and skill from my own. This corresponds with Billington's (2000) research findings, which support the importance of learning environments.

In summary, things learned from this lived experience as it relates to issues with face-to-face teaching / learning were: (a) a face-to-face teacher must manage the implementation of an Internet learning process (McLagan, 1978; Knowles, 1980 & 1996; Savićević, 1999); (b) the face-to-face teacher of an Internet learning process must avoid creating negative emotions in the learner (Taylor, 1986; LeDoux, 2002; Lindeman, 1961); and (c) teachers of the learning process all with different knowledge and skills working together face-to-face is of great value to the creation of an Internet learning process described by Billington (2000) as a learning environment.

Research sub-question #1: What are the issues with face-to-face teaching / learning during the development of the program?

Interview question: A10. Discuss barriers to the project's progress and how you coped with them.

The programmer, graphic artist, and I described the barriers to the project's progress and how we coped with them. The programmer and graphic artist coped with lack of time, money, and staff with face-to-face teamwork. Together they worked extended hours and shifted deadlines and responsibilities. Against all odds, these stakeholders did what they said they would do (Kouzes & Posner, 1993) to demonstrate credibility.

I coped with the military's cultural conservatism by using face-to-face assertive communication skills to negotiate win–win solutions. As manager of the process, Savic´evic´ (1999) might agree that through assertive communication, I creatively integrated the educational and cultural elements of the project.

To summarize the face-to-face issues related to the development stakeholders' barriers to the project's progress and how we coped: the programmer and graphic artist used teamwork to cope with lack of time, money and staff, which helped them do what they said they would do (Kouzes & Posner, 1993) and I used face-to-face assertive communication to creatively integrate the educational and cultural elements (Savićević, 1999) to negotiate win–win solutions with the conservative military.

Research sub-question #1: What are the issues with face-to-face teaching / learning during the development of the program?

Interview question: A13. Describe your relationships with the other stakeholders and how they affected your work?

The development team members all perceived value in their face-to-face relationships with the other stakeholders. First, the programmer valued an open pleasant working relationship with me. It was my job as the programmer's face-to-face teacher to help him know, understand, and value my concept and content in order to electronically transform it into an interactive Internet program. McLagan (1978) may agree that I increased my concept's learnability by: helping the programmer develop knowledge, skills, values and attitudes, and / or creative ideas and by helping him transfer his learning to the application environment. I accomplished this by creating an open, pleasant learning environment.

Second, the graphic artist valued his relationship with all the other stakeholders because those relationships led to mutual planning and involvement by all the stakeholders. The group feedback was helpful to the graphic artist and guided his work. As researcher, I fostered mutual planning and involvement of all stakeholders by scheduling of regular face-to-face meetings with the military and making sure the programmer and graphic artist were always present at the meetings. Knowles (1980) may agree that this type of learning is guided interaction. As the project manager, I gave not only the graphic artist, but also the programmer an advantage that extended beyond the Virtual Health Coach project by helping both of them learn how to learn (Smith, 1982).

And third, as a result of my relationships with all the stakeholders, I respected the unique contribution of each of them. My learner-focused approach took into account the learning differences (Sims & Sims, 1995) among the stakeholders. Spending face-to-face time with all of the stakeholders allowed me to uncover their preferred learning styles, which led to a deeper understanding and appreciation of each one's contribution and to see each stakeholder model through their speech and manner in life what each of them taught the others about their share of the work.

To restate the face-to-face issues related to relationships between the programmer, graphic artist, and myself as well as the other stakeholders and their effects, three statements can be made. First, an open relationship between the programmer and me increased the programmer's learnability (McLagan, 1978). Second, the graphic artist was helped by guided interaction (Knowles, 1980), which helped both him and the programmer learn how to learn (Smith, 1982). And third, as researcher, I developed an understanding and appreciation of each stakeholder's unique contribution by knowing each individual's learning style(s) (Sims & Sims, 1995) and by watching them model what they taught (Henschke, 1998).

Research sub-question #1: What are the issues with face-to-face teaching / learning during the development of the program?

Interview question: A17. Did this project ever seem to drift from a serious vein that should have been more prominent? In other words, were important aspects of this project ever at risk of being lost in the midst of the fun?

None of the three development stakeholders, least of all me, thought that the seriousness of the project was ever jeopardized by fun. Instead, having face-to-face fun was thought, especially by me, to be important to accomplishing the project's goals and according to the programmer, built fun into the program. Helping learners develop creative ideas is the role of a face-to-face teacher (McLagan, 1978), who in this case was me. Having fun with Virtual Health Coach became a "natural part of education and life" (Sims & Sims, 1995, p. 170). As leader of the development team, I fit the profile of the adult educator, which is to facilitate the educational process (Savićević, 1999) and "promote the desired creative integration of the educational and cultural elements of adult education" (p. 133). Fun was part of the learning process and was fostered and encouraged by me.

Research sub-question #1: What are the issues with face-to-face teaching / learning during the development of the program?

Interview question: B2. Discuss the return on your investment of time, money, or intellectual contribution.

The lieutenant colonel and the regional account manager both claimed their return on investment was high, but for different reasons. The lieutenant colonel thought the program was a substantial bang for the buck and it met the goals of the project or, in other words, the project did what it said it would do, "the bottom line of a theory–practice connection" (Kouzes & Posner, 1993, p. 47).

The regional account manager's rating was high because it exceeded his expectations as a new innovative way for his company to build face-to-face relationships with potential customers. Virtual Health Coach allowed the regional account manager to model what he was teaching (Henshcke, 1998). He taught physicians that a pharmaceutical company could build a face-to-face relationship with physicians beyond just for the purpose of selling pharmaceuticals.

To restate the face-to-face issues regarding the project's return on investment, the lieutenant colonel rated the program's return high because it represented a theory–practice connection (Kouzes & Posner, 1993) and the regional account manager rated it high because it allowed him to model what he taught (Henschke, 1998).

Issues without face-to-face teaching / learning

Research sub-question #2: What are the issues without face-to-face teaching / learning during the development of the program?

Conclusions and Recommendations

Interview question: A1. How did the thinking and planning process for this project differ from other Internet-based learning projects you have created?

Regarding issues without a face-to-face teacher related to the thinking and planning process, the programmer, graphic artist and I all found this project different from past work. The programmer was familiar with the thinking and planning process but had never started with a script. In other words, he was forced into group learning. Both his personal traits (programming skill) as well as my traits (the script) influenced his learning (Lewin, 1951). According to Lewin, just by sharing a common objective, they were likely to act together to achieve it.

The thinking and planning process was new to the graphic artist. He became a self-directed learner in what Tough (1979) would call a self-planned learning project. The graphic artist learned how to learn by using intuition and dreams (Smith, 1982) to solve problems. As a self-directed learner, he placed importance on organizational processes in perception, learning, and problem-solving (Ormrod, 1999).

I had no prior experience building an Internet-based learning program, which means I had no memory traces (Ormrod, 1999), from which to build. It could be said that this lack of experience placed me in a state of disequilibrium, which according to Riegel (1973), causes significant changes to take place. This notion is supported by Arlin (1975) and Riegel's (1973) fifth stage of development build on Piaget's stage theory, which represents adulthood and is not a stable plateau equilibrium but instead one where the possibility for change remains (Long, 1983).

Again, the programmer, graphic artist and I all found the project's thinking and planning process different from past work. Working from a script caused the programmer to be involved with group learning (Lewin, 1951). Being involved in the thinking and planning was different for the graphic artist, which caused him to become a self-directed learner (Tough, 1981). And, it could be said that having no related experience put me in a state of disequilibrium, which for me may have been a cause for significant change (Riegel, 1973).

Research sub-question #2: What are the issues without face-to-face teaching / learning during the development of the program?

A5. What one problem was hardest to solve?

_, the graphic artist, and I each expressed our one problem hardest to solve. The biggest problem for the programmer was that computer software technology was not yet sophisticated enough to do what he wanted it to do. He made it work for him by inventing middleware. It could be said that the programmer's actions were characteristic of a learner involved in carrying out a self-directed learning project, as he chose his goal and then decided which activity was appropriate (Tough, 1981) to solve his problem.

The graphic artist struggled with throughput, or how to get people in and out. As a nonhuman planner, Virtual Health Coach had to take the learner from the beginning to the end in a natural way by evaluating responses, and then had to use the learner's response history for choosing particular branches or sequences of material (Tough, 1971 & 1981). The graphic artist's challenge was to create conditions for learners to explore naturally (Papert, 1993) what they wanted to learn, while still moving forward as one would read a book. He solved this problem by adding arrows to subtly move learners in a forward direction. This could be compared to Papert's discussion on how children learn—that is, arranging for children to be in contact with the material, physical or abstract, for Piagetian learning (Papert, 1993).

For me, the biggest problem was giving up some of my content in exchange for process in order to facilitate learning. Gestalt theory emphasizes the importance of organizational processes in perception, learning, and problem-solving (Ormrod, 1999). The project was larger than my content. In keeping with the Gestalt theory of learning, the whole was more than the sum of its parts, and problem solving for me involved restructuring and insight (Ormrod, 1999, pp. 150–153).

To summarize the issues without a face-to-face teacher as they relate to the hardest problem to solve in building Virtual Health Coach, the programmer behaved like a learner involved in a self-directed learning project as he invented middleware to solve his problem (Tough, 1981). The graphic artist solved his problem by creating conditions for the learner to explore naturally what they want to learn (Papert, 1993), while being subtly moved in a forward direction. As researcher, I used restructuring and insight (Ormrod, 1999) to solve my problem of giving up content for the benefit of the process following Gestalt theory that the whole was more than the sum of its parts.

Research sub-question #2: What are the issues without face-to-face teaching / learning during the development of the program?

Interview question: A8. What one piece of the development was most important to get right?

Related to the issues without a face-to-face teacher, the answers to interview question A8 varied. The graphic artist and I both agreed that the look and feel of the program was most important but the programmer thought it was the navigational flow.

The graphic artist understood it was important for learners to be able to relate to the character, the colors to be simple, and the pages to be uncluttered to help the learner relax. Likewise, I wanted the look and feel to make the Internet learner want to stay in the absence of a face-to-face teacher. Getting the climate right for learning follows Gestalt theory that learning involves the perception of the learner, which is often different from reality. Creating a relaxing and inviting look and feel in Virtual Health Coach as a nonhuman planner (Tough, 1981) was, according to Gestalt psychology, important for learning over time to become simpler, more concise and more complete than the actual input (Ormrod, 1999).

The programmer thought navigational flow was most important to get right in the absence of a face-to-face teacher. Smith (1982) may agree that building navigation into an Internet-based program will help those who have not learned how to learn. Those who have learned how to learn almost certainly will enjoy the learning process more than one who goes about it aimlessly (Smith, 1982). Even though flexibility was built in to allow the learner to go back and forth through the process in a more natural way, jumping ahead in Virtual Health Coach was electronically disallowed to avoid learner confusion. Therefore, built-in navigational flow would prevent Virtual Health Coach users from aimlessly going about the process of learning.

To summarize issues without face-to-face teaching / learning during the development of the program, the graphic artist and I thought the most important thing to get right was the look and feel of Virtual Health Coach, which could be compared to Tough's (1981) nonhuman planner. And, the programmer thought navigational flow was most important to help learners, who have not learned how to learn, enjoy the learning process more (Smith, 1982).

Research sub-question #2: What are the issues without face-to-face teaching / learning during the development of the program?

Interview question: A11. If there had been no budget or time restrictions, what would you have done differently?

Regarding what would have been done differently if there had been no budget or time restrictions as it relates to issues without face-to-face teaching / learning, the programmer would have had more of the animated character and the graphic artist would have had more characters. But, I would have done nothing differently. Tough (1981) described teaching *tasks*, which he called major *decisions or actions* that can be performed by either the teacher or the learner. The programmer, the graphic artist, and I demonstrated some of those steps. They were (a) deciding which activities were appropriate, (b) deciding how much money to spend, and (c) having doubts about success (Tough, 1981).

Research sub-question #2: What are the issues without face-to-face teaching / learning during the development of the program?

Interview question: B5. Does the program integrate adult learning principles and Internet technology?

Regarding issues without face-to-face teaching / learning, the lieutenant colonel's and regional account manager's answers to interview question B5 were in agreement. Both agreed that the program integrated adult learning and Internet technology. The lieutenant agreed because he thought Virtual Health Coach followed the principles of adult learning according to Knowles whom he cited in his written response, which is an example of finding and joining one or more fellow experts who can provide companionship—a potential learner problem in adult learning projects (Tough, 1979). The regional account manager agreed because Virtual Health Coach meets the distance learning needs of the deployed military, which is an example of applying the knowledge to real life situations—another potential learner problem in adult learning projects (Tough, 1979). Both the lieutenant colonel and the regional account manager agreed that Virtual Health Coach integrates adult learning principles and computer technology. Tough (1979) might say that it was a result of each one's ability to avoid potential problems in adult learning projects.

Can an Internet program stimulate whole-mind thinking?

Research sub-question: Can an Internet program stimulate whole-mind thinking (cognitive, emotion, motivation)?

Interview question: A3. What did you do differently with this project than with previous projects?

Relating interview question A3 to whole-mind thinking, the programmer, the graphic artist, and I all did something different with this project than with previous projects that can be related to whole mind thinking. The programmer found collaboration to be a new way to work, for he was used to solving problems alone. "Individual development should be considered both a social and a personal phenomenon" (Tennant & Pogson, 1995, p.118).

The graphic artist animated a character to match a voice for the first time. He knew he could animate, he wanted to do animation since he was a child, and just talking about it made him smile and laugh. Taylor (1986) describes experienced-based learning as the "orchestration of emotional states" (p. 69). Learning how to use animation released the emotion of joy in him and the end product gave him a feeling of accomplishment and personal satisfaction. LeDoux (2002) might say that the graphic artist was using his three brain centers for learning animation—cognition, motivation, and emotion.

For me, it was collaborative teamwork that required patience and respect for my team members' contributions that was different. My experience aligns with Mezirow's (1981, 2000) description of the learning process as a whole transforming experience. Some whole-mind elements are shared by both Mezirow's (1981, 2000) findings and my transforming experience: (a) an assessment of role and alienation from traditional social expectations,

(b) exploring options for new ways of acting, (c) building competence and self-confidence in new roles, (d) trying new roles and assessing feedback, (e) reintegrating into the stakeholder team on the basis of conditions dictated by the new perspective, and (f) experiencing the emotional and social aspects of the learning process.

Restating the links between whole-mind thinking and what the development stakeholders did differently with the Virtual Health Coach project: the programmer's problem-solving was both a social and a personal phenomenon (Tennant & Pogson, 1995), the graphic artist's joy and sense of accomplishment regarding animation were elements of emotional and motivational learning (LeDoux, 2002), and my respecting and honoring other stakeholders contributions shared common elements with Mezirow's (1981, 2000) transformational learning.

Research sub-question #3: Can an Internet program stimulate whole-mind thinking (cognitive, emotion, motivation) to learn?

Interview question: A7. Were there any surprises or ah-ha experiences during or after the development?

The surprises or ah-ha experiences of the development stakeholders were all related to fun. And they were all good, not bad. Invention and discovery can be a joyful experience. Lindeman (1961) said, "... from the viewpoint of education, emotions and intelligence are continuous and varying aspects of a single process and the finest emotions are those which shine through intelligence ..." (p. 68). Ormrod (1999) defines learning as "emotional reactions" (p. 3) and therefore it's not surprising that the stakeholders associated ah-ha experiences with the emotion of fun.

Research sub-question #3: Can an Internet program stimulate whole-mind thinking (cognitive, emotion, motivation) to learn?

Interview question: A12. With the same budget and time restrictions, what would you have done differently?

The programmer, graphic artist, and I would not have done anything differently, with the same budget and time restrictions. LeDoux (2002) said learners' emotions such as fears, hopes, and desires influence how they think, perceive, and remember. Perhaps the development team's hope for success of their program influenced how they perceived it.

Research sub-question #3: Can an Internet program stimulate whole-mind thinking (cognitive, emotion, motivation) to learn?

Interview question: A9. Discuss the difference between the process and the content of VHC.

The programmer and I easily distinguished the process from the content. The difference was less clear to the graphic artist, but he finished answering the question saying that the process was not only different from the content but it was more important.

The programmer and I distinguished process from content by describing the process as a constant and the content as something that can change. This distinction perhaps could be applied to the difference between cognition and behaviors. Perhaps it is possible to say that cognition is like a process and that behaviors are like content. Yet, according to Ormrod (1999), learning is a relatively permanent change in behavior (content) due to experience and, learning is a relatively permanent change in mental associations (process) due to experience. So therefore, perhaps it could be said that experience changes content and process forever and, therefore, becomes a unifying factor.

The graphic artist talked himself into the fact that the process, which has a beginning and an end, is more important than the content, but he was clear to say that the content must be right, as well. Ormrod (1999) firmly believed that "both the behaviorist and the cognitive perspectives have something important to say about human learning and that both provide useful suggestions for helping people learn more effectively" (p. 4).

To summarize the perceived differences between process and content as they relate to whole-mind thinking and learning, the programmer and I both thought that process is more important than content but experience may be the factor that unifies the two (Ormrod, 1999). The graphic artist also saw the importance of both process and content, because perhaps both have something important to say about human learning (Ormrod, 1999).

Research sub-question #3: Can an Internet program stimulate whole-mind thinking (cognitive, emotion, motivation) to learn?

Interview question: A18. What other questions do I need to ask that you think would provide important information for this process?

Regarding interview question A18 as it relates to whole-mind thinking, the programmer and graphic artist had nothing more to say. But, I gave a long emotional answer. It is interesting to note that my self-interview came after I interviewed the programmer and the graphic artist but before I interviewed the regional account manager. Clearly my self-interview, after the programmer and graphic artist had nothing more to say on this question, brought forth a summarily spilling of emotions about the project and my life, as if the floodgates opened. It was also interesting that I spoke more and with more enthusiasm and excitement about Virtual Health Coach while interviewing the regional account manager later the same day after my self-interview. The joy and excitement that arose within me during my self-interview spilled over into my interview with the regional account manager. LeDoux (2002) may agree that working on the project engaged my three centers for thinking—cognition, motivation, and emotion. It may be significant that my answer to this open question was one of the longest and most emotional in the interview. My experience seems to align with the elements Mezirow (1981, 2000) identified in perspective transformation. The emotional impact of the experience moved me to want to tell my story of transformation.

How does the design meet the goal of the International Commission on Education for the Twenty-first Century?

Research sub-question: How does the design meet the goal of the International Commission on Education for the Twenty-first Century (UNESCO) for learning throughout life as described by the four pillars of learning: learning to know, learning to do, learning to live together, and learning to be?´

Interview question: A2. Describe in detail your tangible and intangible goals for this project.

Regarding the tangible and intangible goals of this project as they relate to UNESCO's four pillars of learning, the programmer, graphic artist, and I all wanted to make money as a tangible goal, but intangible goals were a larger part of our answers. The programmer's and graphic artist's larger intangible goals were soft measurements of the program's success like appeal and engagement. Skill and knowledge competencies were not sufficient as they learned to program and animate Virtual Health Coach. For the programmer and graphic artist, it could be the case that a new level of *learning to do* to make it appealing and engaging required the additional competencies of attitude, interest, and value (Ormrod, 1999).

An additional tangible goal for me was efficacy. Beyond being appealing and engaging, my goal of efficacy made it "essential to cultivate human qualities" (Delors, 1998, p. 90) into Virtual Health Coach, which amounted to the ability to establish stable, effective relationships between the user and the virtual teacher.

Restating the link between interview question A2 and UNESCO's four pillars of learning: the programmer, graphic artist, and I, in order to reach our tangible and intangible goals, all had to *learn to do* in a untraditional way, which meant going beyond the usual competencies of knowledge and skill to acquire the additional competencies of attitude, interest, and value (Ormrod, 1999) for the purpose of cultivating human qualities (Delors, 1998) into the program.

Research sub-question #4: How does the design meet the goal of the International Commission on Education for the Twenty-first Century (UNESCO) for learning throughout life as described by the four pillars of learning: *learning to know, learning to do, learning to live together, and learning to be?*

Interview question: A6. In your thinking, is this system for Internet-based learning more appropriate for a particular type of learning and why?

The stakeholder answers to interview question A6 can be related to the four pillars of learning. According to Delors' (1998) first pillar of learning called learning to know, adults who did not learn the skills of thought, concentration, and memory in childhood may be at risk for losing them due to information overload. The programmer thought the Virtual Health Coach system for learning helped combat information overload and, therefore, could be used for any kind of Internet-based learning.

The graphic artist thought that this system for Internet-based learning would work for any kind of learning that does not required physical props, such as learning to use a bow and arrow. But, according to Delors (1998), *learning to do*, or applying knowledge, is more complicated than ever before because physical work is being replaced by more mental work. Therefore, furthering the graphic artist's example, people who learn how to use a bow and arrow around other people must also cultivate human qualities (Delors, 1998) to learn bow and arrow safety, bow and arrow etiquette, and the laws governing the sport—qualities that are not necessarily inculcated by traditional bow and arrow training (Delors, 1998, p. 90) and may require the additional competencies of attitude, interest, and value (Ormrod, 1999).

I thought that this system for Internet-based learning was most valuable for intentional *learning to do* that is difficult or has an emotional component. LeDoux, (2002) said that a view of the mind that overlooks the role of emotions "simply won't do" (p. 200).

To restate the relationship between UNESCO's four pillars of learning and types of learning appropriate for this system of Internet-based learning: (a) the programmer thought the Virtual Health Coach system for learning was appropriate for any type of learning because it helped combat information overload thought to happen when adult learners do not *learn to know*, or have never acquired the skills of thought, concentration, and memory (Delors, 1998); (b) the graphic artist thought the learning system was most appropriate for learning that does not require props, but even *learning to do* requires cultivating human qualities (Delors, 1998) and the competencies of attitude, interest, and value (Ormrod, 1999); and (c) I thought this system for Internet-based learning was best for intentional *learning to do* that is difficult or has an emotional component because overlooking the role of emotions in learning "simply won't do" (LeDoux, 2002, p. 200).

Research sub-question #4: How does the design meet the goal of the International Commission on Education for the Twenty-first Century (UNESCO) for learning throughout life as described by the four pillars of learning: learning to know, learning to do, learning to live together, and learning to be?

Interview question: A14. List 3–4 guidelines you could give to future technology companies partnering with an educator of adults to create an Internet-based learning program.

The developer stakeholders' guidelines for future technology companies relate well to how the Commission on Education for the Twenty-first Century's four pillars of learning meets the goals for adult learning in the future. The programmer recommended having one person with both technology skill and creativity or having two people that work as one—each with one of those skills. The Commission recommends a mix of the concrete and the abstract, because "coherent thinking requires a combination of the two" (Ozman & Craver, p. 88). The programmer said the talent of *learning to do* or applying knowledge was not enough and that *learning to be* was also needed for the job or having the freedom of thought, judgment, feeling, and imagination to develop their talents (Delors, 1998). Additionally, if two people work as one, the Commission might argue that *learning to live together* requires that the two discover each other's unique contribution and work together toward common goals (Delors, 1998).

The graphic artist's guidelines were to keep it simple and make sure that it does what it is supposed to do. Keeping it simple could be considered a strategy for avoiding information overload for learners who have not learned the skills of thought, concentration, and memory, which the Commission says are necessary for *learning to know* (Delors, 1998). Making sure the program does what it is supposed to do demonstrates respect for the learner, which can lead to a trusting relationship between the program and the learner—a hallmark of *learning to live together*. Additionally, the program encourages users to seek support during their change effort from someone in their life who will give it to them such as a spouse, a friend, coworker, or child—another must-have for *learning to live together.*

From my own perspective, I recommended that the adult educator *who* partners with a technology company focus on managing the process but not the people for fear of stifling creativity. The Commission is concerned that both imagination and creativity are at risk due to the standardization of individual behavior (Delors, 1998) and, therefore, would likely support my warning not to over manage the people so as to allow the technology company employees to soar and become great contributors. This will only happen, according to the Commission, when education provides the opportunities for discovery and experimentation.

To summarize how the stakeholders' guidelines for future technology companies working with adult educators relate to UNESCO's four pillars of learning, first, the programmer recommended having one person with both technology skill and creativity or having two people that work as one, which relates to *learning to do* (requiring skill and creativity) and *learning to be* (requiring a respectful relationship between two people working toward a common goal) (Delors, 1998). Second, the graphic artist said to keep it simple, a strategy for *learning to know* to avoid information overload, and to make sure it does what it is supposed to do to build a trusting relationship between the program and the learner—a hallmark of *learning to live together*. Additionally, the program encourages users to seek support during their change effort. Finally, as researcher, I suggested the adult educator focuses on managing the process, not the people, thus providing opportunities for discovery and experimentation to allow people to soar and become great contributors (Delors, 1998).

Research sub-question #4: How does the design meet the goal of the International Commission on Education for the Twenty-first Century (UNESCO) for learning throughout life as described by the four pillars of learning: learning to know, learning to do, learning to live together, and learning to be?

Interview question: A15. Was there ever a time during your work on this project that you wanted to quit and walk away from it? If so, why? And, if so, how did you stop yourself from quitting?

Development stakeholder answers to question A15 can be related to UNESCO's four pillars of learning. The programmer, the graphic artist, and I as the researcher all said we never wanted to quit. However, two of us admitted to some negative feelings along the way not because of skill and knowledge, but because of attitude, interest, and value. Work competencies are changing from a focus on knowledge and skill to a focus on attitude, interest, and value (Ormrod, 1999). Regarding *learning to do*, the development team was not expected to only *do* something. We also had to develop effective relationships with the military and the pharmaceutical company, which seemed to be the source of the negative feelings.

The programmer kept an optimistic attitude because he found the work fun, challenging and important. The Commission might agree that the programmer was an example of a learner who *learned to be*, because he seemed to have the freedom of thought, judgment, feeling, and imagination needed in order to develop his talents, and remain as much as possible in control of his life (Delors, 1998, p. 94).

In summary of interview question A15, as it relates to UNESCO's four pillars of learning, there were negative feelings expressed by the graphic artist and me related to the attitude, interest, and value of *learning to do*. And, perhaps, it could be said that the programmer *learned to be*, which might explain his sustained optimism throughout the project.

Research sub-question #4: How does the design meet the goal of the International Commission on Education for the Twenty-first Century (UNESCO) for learning throughout life as described by the four pillars of learning: *learning to know, learning to do, learning to live together, and learning to be?*

Interview question: A16. Compared to other projects you have been involved in, how would you rate your perceived value of this project on a scale of 1–10 with 1 representing least value and 10 most value. Explain your answer.

How the development team valued the project relates to UNESCO's four pillars of learning. All three interviewees rated the project the same. We all said 10. The Commission might say we learned to *live together* on this project, working together toward a common goal, which leads to putting aside differences.

Research sub-question #4: How does the design meet the goal of the International Commission on Education for the Twenty-first Century (UNESCO) for learning throughout life as described by the four pillars of learning:

learning to know, learning to do, learning to live together, and learning to be?

Interview question: B1. Describe your initial interest in participating in the development of this program.

Relating interview question B1 to UNESCO's four pillars of learning, both the lieutenant colonel and the regional account manager were demonstrating *learning to live together* as they expressed interest in how the project would help others. The lieutenant colonel was initially interested in helping military personnel at a low cost and the regional account manager was initially most of all interested in benefiting patients by working with physicians in a new way.

Research sub-question #4: How does the design meet the goal of the International Commission on Education for the Twenty-first Century (UNESCO) for learning throughout life as described by the four pillars of learning: *learning to know, learning to do, learning to live together, and learning to be?*

Interview question: B3. What are your plans and goals for using the product?

UNESCO's four pillars of learning can be related to interview question B3. Both the lieutenant colonel's and the regional account manager's plans and goals for the product went far beyond their initial interest. The lieutenant colonel planned to use Virtual Health Coach at his new job as faculty member of a state university and the regional account manager planned to use Virtual Health Coach as a way to find out more about the needs of his customers. The Virtual Health Coach project fostered *learning to be* by providing the lieutenant colonel and the regional account manager with opportunities to discover and experiment for optimal growth of imagination and creativity (Delors, 1998).

Research sub-question #4: How does the design meet the goal of the International Commission on Education for the Twenty-first Century (UNESCO) for learning throughout life as described by the four pillars of learning: *learning to know, learning to do, learning to live together, and learning to be?*

Interview question: B4. How does the program fill a void, add value, or accomplish a goal for you?

Conclusions and Recommendations 173

Regarding interview question B4 as it relates to UNESCO's four pillars of learning, goals were met for both the lieutenant colonel and for the regional account manager around the *learning to live together* pillar of learning. The lieutenant colonel thought the program added value because work on the project resulted in a rewarding experience for his team members and the regional account manager thought the program helped his company build better relationships with physicians.

Research sub-question #4: How does the design meet the goal of the International Commission on Education for the Twenty-first Century (UNESCO) for learning throughout life as described by the four pillars of learning: *learning to know, learning to do, learning to live together, and learning to be?*

Interview question: B6. Are there other appropriate applications for this learning system? If so, what are they?

The easy-coming and prolific answers given by the lieutenant colonel and the regional account manager to interview question B6 reflect *learning to be*. The lieutenant colonel thought of applications related to the needs of others and the regional account manager thought of applications related to personal needs. The Commission might say that their imagination and creativity bloomed because the project offered them opportunities to discover and experiment (Delors, 1998).

The following section provides a discussion of the findings linking relevant theories with the emerging themes from the interviews.

Emerging theme: Interest

The five stakeholders' interests varied. As researcher, I was interested in creating a program that would do what it was supposed to do (help people make changes to improve their health), yield academic recognition, and make money. The programmer and graphic artist were interested in the project because they saw it as a fun challenge and as profitable work for their company. The programmer and the graphic artist had fun and were paid the amount stated in the Memorandum of Agreement (MOU), but the amount was less than half the amount equal to the hours they worked. I proposed a sum of money to be paid to me for the military's use of my intellectual property, which was rejected. This lack of honoring my unique contribution may have jeopardized the establishment of a learning environment where "life achievements are acknowledged and respected" (Billington, 2000, ¶ 6). Billington believes that adult learning environments best facilitate adult growth and development, a critical element to the stakeholders' ability to be creative and work together in groups.

My interest in creating a program that ended with a practical action (Socrates, 2020 Insite, 2002b) that had a positive conclusion was not realized because the implementation "stopped short at the stage of perplexity" when, in fact, "the constructive process was the proper and necessary sequel" (¶ 10). The program packets were distributed to the Health and Wellness Centers (HAWCs) on military bases across the country but no preparation was offered for implementation, as evidenced by the phone calls received by the programmer and me from confused military staff that continue to be received at the time of this writing. Perhaps managing and evaluating the implementation of Virtual Health Coach could have created the constructive process for the military staff. Failing to facilitate the movement of the HAWC staff past the stage of perplexity resulted in less than positive results (Taylor, 1986).

The military's interest was initially altruistic. The lieutenant colonel saw the value of Virtual Health Coach as "the provision of assistance for individuals interested in reducing their level of risk" (lieutenant colonel, B1). Then, when the military sought funding for the project, their interest changed to a calculated cost savings arguing that the program would extend the reach of their HAWC staff in helping military personnel with bad habits make lifestyle behavior changes to improve their health. But when that argument failed to find military funding, the lieutenant colonel's interest shifted from building a program that would improve the lifestyle habits of military personnel to just building the program as a personal accomplishment. The priority interest became that of the large pharmaceutical company regional account manager who funded the project—to create a program that he would use as a charitable gift to build relationships with prospective buyers of his pharmaceutical products, the military physicians. The Virtual Health Coach project recognition earned promotions for a military physician on the Medical Defense Partnership for Reinvention (MDPR) team and the regional account manager to the position of national account manager. The lieutenant colonel was also promoted to colonel.

The initial altruistic interest in Virtual Health Coach (to improve the lifestyle habits of military personnel) was left to chance—some implementation packets were delivered to military base HAWCs with an enclosed instructional letter, support letters, and a National wellness resource list, but the MDPR was shut down with no transfer of the project to another lead person for implementation and follow up. Simply distributing the implementation packets could be thought of as a general dissemination of knowledge (Verner, 1962), which leaves learning to chance. However, distributing, preparing the HAWC staff on the use of the program, implementing, and evaluating the program could instead be thought of as a systematic diffusion of knowledge (Verner, 1962), which may have improved learning. Preparing the HAWC staff to use the program, involving them in mutual planning for its implementation (Smith, 1982; Knowles, 1995), and then evaluating the program's effect are process elements that may have improved the implementation outcome. Assessing each military base's past experiences (Knowles, 1995; Smith, 1982) with wellness programs and each base's collective readiness to change lifestyle behaviors may have assisted the MDPR in tailoring an implementation planning approach for each base (Prochaska, Norcross, & Diclemente, 1995) to improve the implementation outcome.

The implementation, as it was carried out, lacked a whole-part-whole learning rhythm (Knowles, Holton, & Swanson, 1998). The implementation packet could be thought of as the advance organizer (Ausubel, 1968) (or the first whole) to give the military HAWC staff a framework for using the program (or the part). But, linking these parts together to form the second whole (or the knowledge, skill, and techniques to make it work at each military base—i.e., putting in place mechanisms for getting military staff to use Virtual Health Coach and then providing the resources and support to help staff carry out their behavior change plans) did not happen. Because the second whole is considered the most important of the three components, and according to Gestalt psychology, the whole is greater than the sum of its parts (Ormrod, 1999), the military base HAWC staff never understood how everything linked together to form the "instructional whole" (Elias & Merriam, 1980, p. 191).

My interest in building a program that helped people make behavior changes to improve their health was lost because of the competing and conflicting priority interests of the regional account manager and the lieutenant colonel—personal recognition and promotion. In other words, the focus shifted from the learners (military staff) to the facilitators (lieutenant colonel and regional account manager). And, the lieutenant colonel and regional manager's content-focused approach (delivery of the program) could be described as pedagogical (Knowles, 1980). An andragogical approach would be learner-focused, which implies a concern for facilitating learning (Sims & Sims, 1995; Knowles, 1980) or, in other words, concern for following a process to successfully implement the program.

Emerging theme: Legalities

I was diligent about meeting the military's business and legal requirements. I protected the military's legal interest as well as my own by applying for an intellectual property patent and registering my product concept's trademark—both were tacit requirements for doing new product development for the military. However, the military violated my sole legal right to promote Virtual Health Coach in the public sector per the MOU by allowing Virtual Health Coach to be accessible on open (not password protected) public websites, but desisted after they were confronted with this violation and threatened with possible court action. Regarding this violation of the agreement, the military team's actions were not congruent with the language in the agreement. The military team's credibility was at risk because they did not do what they said they would do—a critical element of leadership credibility (Kouzes & Posner, 1993). Because, theory and practice must be congruent when working in any regard with the development and / or education of adults, there was an andragogical theory / practice disconnection (Henschke, 1998) between the military team's words and actions.

I used a dialogical, criticism-stimulating methodology (Freire, 1973) to ensure legal protection for myself and for my program. First, I protected myself by using challenging dialogue (Freire, 1973) to negotiate an MOU that (a) protected my ownership of the program's source code, (b) gave me sole rights to use Virtual Health Coach in the public sector, and

(c) ensured mutual benefit so that each party would give recognition to the others involved in the development of the program. Since this project was a temporary environment, one of the practical implications was the importance of promoting the military's awareness of "relational contingencies" (Taylor, 1986, p. 70) so that transitions to other settings were understood and effectively managed.

Then, I protected my program by again using challenging dialogue and persuasive cajoling to bring about a change in consciousness (Freire, 1973) that caused the military to refrain from using Virtual Health Coach to collect information that could be perceived as personal health information (PHI), which is legally protected by the new Health Insurance Portability and Accountability Act (HIPAA) Privacy Rule. My use of challenging dialogue created an understanding among the military team that led to actions (Freire, 1973)—actions that legally protected my program and me.

The military required me to register my company with the military's General Services Administration (GSA) before I could receive grant money from the MDPR, and I did. I requested the military to sign a nondisclosure agreement before previewing my intellectual property but the lieutenant colonel refused claiming that the military by nature is trustworthy and therefore does not sign nondisclosure agreements. I complied with the lieutenant colonel's requirement for doing business, but he did not reciprocate by complying with my requirement. The lieutenant colonel's refusal to sign my customary non-disclosure agreement jeopardized the mutual trust and openness—important elements of an adult learning environment (Knowles, 1984, 1995). Though the lived experience of creating Virtual Health Coach could be described as distance learning because the stakeholders mostly worked separately and at a distance, creating a respectful psychological environment is just as important to distance learning as it is to a traditional adult learning environment (Cooper & Henschke, 2003).

Emerging theme: Money

Initially the Internet / CD learning project was proposed as a cost saving disease prevention program to bridge the gap between [health] educational disparities (Stites, Hopey, & Ginsburg, 1998), but that idea was not accepted for military funding. The military team later modified the proposal to more closely meet the MDPR's business focus, which was to support their disease management program. When the MDPR proposed the Virtual Health Coach project as part of their existing disease management program, the regional account manager funded the product development as a charitable gift intended for doctors to whom he was trying to sell pharmaceutical products.

"History is an exercise in personal understanding" (deMarrais, 1998, p. 7). As the story unfolded in the interviews, I developed a sense of where I "might strike gold" (p. 7) and then how I could "extract it in a form that is meaningful" (p. 7). The side story or golden nugget might be that stakeholders work hardest for that which drives them. Though the perception was that the military initially was driven by the potential to save health care dollars, it seems that they were really driven by personal reward and recognition. And, though the perception was that the programmer, graphic artist, and I were driven by personal reward and recognition, it seems as if we were really driven by the creative challenge and the potential to improve health. Gestalt psychology says that perception is often different from reality (Ormrod, 1999).

Many of Tough's (1981) major decisions or actions that can be performed by either teachers or learners in a learning project are similar to the process we stakeholders went through to build Virtual Health Coach such as: choosing the goal, estimating the current level of knowledge and skill, deciding how much money to spend, dealing with lack of desire for achieving the goal, doubting success, and deciding whether to continue. After choosing a goal (to save military health care dollars) and deciding how much money to spend, we dealt with lack of desire for achieving the goal and doubts about success by deciding to continue with a different goal. When the military decided to continue by shifting their goal, they were "able to predict their benefits more accurately than at the beginning of the project" (Tough, 1981, p. 48). And, the military along with the funder (the pharmaceutical company) "experienced some unexpected benefits during the learning project" (p. 48), which increased their motivation for continuing. "The typical adult learner, in fact, has more reasons for continuing ... than for beginning a learning project" (p. 48).

Conclusions and Recommendations 179

Emerging theme: Skill

Building an Internet-based adult learning experience required skill in the following areas: (a) visioning, (b) creativity, (c) animation tailoring, (d) military leadership, (e) andragogical principles, and (f) technology. First, the programmer was skilled in translating my vision into Internet technology and design reality. This requirement perhaps can be best understood if compared to Mezirow's (1981) intricately intertwined three domains of learning—learning for task-related competence, learning for interpersonal understanding, and learning for perspective transformation. Mezirow (1981) extends Habermas' concept of the three domains to say that their inter-relatedness reflects the wholeness of the experience. Perhaps the programmer's use of the terms big visionary, big picture, and the graphic artist's use of the term big grasp reflect the wholeness of the experience of learning how to turn a concept into an Internet learning experience. The programmer could be compared to the adult education philosopher, Lindeman (1961)—a visionary who saw beyond technique to describe the "quintessential format" (Brookfield, 1984, p. 195) of program planning.

Secondly, the systematic process of creativity (Csikszentmihalyi, 1996) was an important skill for both the programmer and graphic artist. Creativity was needed to create a product that could transform the existing domain of online learning into a new domain (Csikszentmihalyi, 1996)—one that integrated andragogy and Internet technology. The long hard work of programming and animation was invisible to the rest of the stakeholders who only saw the fruits of their labor and not the labor itself. Einstein understood that the skill of creativity is making it look easy, when he said, "The secret to creativity is knowing how to hide your sources" (Quotations by Albert Einstein, 2003, ¶ 22). Because the creative process is more important than the created object (Lindeman, 1961), the programmer and the graphic artist worked the amount of time that the creative process required, which was much more than the time for which they were paid. Their imagination and creativity bloomed and they were great contributors because they took the time and the opportunity to discover and experiment (Delors, 1998).

Third, the graphic artist had skill in tailoring the animation to my message. He knew that too much creativity (animation) could have caused my message to be lost. The programmer, graphic artist, and I were not value-free (Mezirow, 1981). We each had an impact on the learner through our "selection of alternative meaning perspectives" (Mezirow, 1981, p. 20) that reflected our own values. The graphic artist had the creative skill to ensure that the animation was learner-centered and not teacher-centered (Knowles, 1981), which means he ensured that the animation was tailored to my message (Smith, 1982) and not just a promotion of his talent.

Fourth, the military demonstrated the following skills: (a) foresight; (b) leadership taskmaster skill; (c) problem-solving; and (d) technical, which were all vital to getting the work done. The lieutenant colonel demonstrated foresight when he recommended that Virtual Health Coach be Internet-based to shift to a learner-based, e-time model that would require ... [military staff] accessibility (Trends, 2003, ¶ 3–10). The lieutenant colonel had a leadership taskmaster skill that kept the project moving forward. He used the MOU to move the project forward like an adult educator would use a learning contract to move learning forward. Much like a learning contract "makes visible the mutual responsibilities of the learner, the teacher, and the institution" (Knowles, 1975, p. 130), the MOU made visible the mutual responsibilities of the programmer, graphic artist, researcher, and the military. Next, the military's skill in problem solving suggested that this new education technology accommodate learning differences (Stites, Hopey, & Ginsburg, 1998) by allowing the user to come and go without losing their place, thus "permitting mastery at one's own pace" (Hornbeck, 1991, pp. 1,2). This problem-solving involved restructuring and the programmer's insight (Ormrod, 1999). Lastly, the military's technological skill and interest made them a good partner for me because they believed that creativity and risk taking provide the innovation to create solutions to long-term problems (Csikszentmihalyi, 1996).

The fifth skill was my knowledge of andragogical principles, which the programmer thought was "crucial every step of the way from beginning to end" (programmer, A13). The lieutenant colonel referred to me as the Big Toe of the development team and was responsible for final approvals of every team member's work. As the adult education practitioner of the stakeholder group, I made "learning how to learn a priority to exploit the learning potential of the new communications technologies to the full" (Tough, 1971, p. 42). Virtual Health Coach as a nonhuman planner was an andragogical model for learning how to learn (Tough, 1971; Smith, 1982) to make behavior changes to improve health without face-to-face teaching / learning.

Emerging theme: Relationships

An open collaborative working relationship between the stakeholders fostered creativity and kept the project moving forward. It could be said that the "challenging and collaborative" relationship was a "transactional process" that transformed stakeholders and "caused them to be changed forever" (Galbraith, 1991, p. 1). The stakeholders were forced to figuratively "live together" (Delors, 1998, p. 22) during this educational project.

The relationships were built in two ways: through discovering the unique contributions of each other which led to respect, and through working together toward common goals which led to putting aside differences (Delors, 1998). The programmer, graphic artist and I were forced to quickly be a team that spoke with one voice at the military meetings to show solidarity. Sometimes we even worked as one to compliment one another's skills. The programmer, graphic artist, and I found power in working and speaking as one. Pfeffer (cited in Kouzes & Posner, 2003) gives a "persuasive business argument for speaking with one voice: power!" (p. 123). Further, Pfeffer's investigations reveal that organizational groups or departments with the greatest unity get more resources. Pfeffer uses the word unity for agreement on shared values. "Because of their unity, these groups also have more efficient internal and external communication" (Kouzes & Posner, 2003, p. 123). As a result of unity, the programmer, graphic artist, and I found joint action was easier to achieve.

The term group learning could be used to describe the stakeholders working toward a common objective. According to Lewin (1951), though people come to a group with very different dispositions, if they share a common objective, they are likely to act together to achieve it. For the lieutenant colonel and the regional account manager, the objective changed from saving money for the military by extending the reach of their HAWC staff to personal recognition and promotion. Although the programmer, the graphic artist, and I did not know it at the time, the objective of the project was no longer common to all the stakeholders. In light of this, it is not surprising that the outcome was less than optimal.

Emerging theme: Doubt

Doubt among stakeholders about working with fellow stakeholders and about stakeholder talent had to be resolved before the project could go forward. Because an andragogy theory / practice connection can be made through modeling (Henschke, 1998), there was incongruence between what was expected and what really happened in regards to stakeholder behavior and talent.

Tough (1981) described some of the natural learning process elements as follows: (a) estimating the current level of knowledge and skill, (b) having doubts about success, and (c) deciding whether to continue. Though the programmer's doubt about the technical skill of his business partner was an issue early in the project, the development of Virtual Health Coach made it "essential to cultivate human qualities that were not necessarily inculcated by traditional training" (Delors, 1998, p. 90), which amounted to the ability to establish stable, effective relationships between the stakeholders. It could be, then, that work competencies changed from a focus on the knowledge and skill to do something, to a new focus on attitude, interest, and value (Ormrod, 1999).

Emerging theme: Trust

Establishing a climate of trust was an important element for both the project and the product. A climate of trust was essential in creating the project's climate for learning between the programmer, the graphic artist, and me. The climate could be described as one that demonstrated mutual respect, collaboration, mutual trust, openness, fun, support, and humanness (Knowles, 1984).

There was trust among the developers of the program (programmer, graphic artist, and me) as well as trust for the users of the program. Early in the process, the military earned my trust through words and later lost my trust through actions. "Do[ing] what you say you will do

(DWYSYWD) is the critical difference of what leadership credibility is all about ..." (Kouzes & Posner, 1993, p. 47), and describes the cause and effect relationship between words and actions. The military said they would not promote Virtual Health Coach in the public sector but they did.

Likewise, a pleasing physical climate was created in the program to convey trust by using "colors ... toward the bright side rather than the dull side of the rainbow" (Knowles, 1980, p. 223) and by using traditional learning symbols that the learner would remember from previous learning such as a blackboard and chalk to foster a trust in this new process for learning. The programmer said, "... we had to flash things in front of them things that they remember as part of the learning climate." (A8).

Emerging theme: Fun

Maybe the project was fun because "the process of discovery involved in creating something new appears to be one of the most enjoyable activities any human can be involved in" (Csikszentmihalyi, 1996, p. 113). Or, perhaps the programmer, graphic artist, and I had fun because of our creative personalities. According to Csikszentmihalyi, "creative individuals are remarkable for their ability to adapt to almost any situation and to make do with whatever is at hand to reach their goals" (p. 51). Another "fun" trait of creative people is their "playfully light attitude" (Csikszentmihalyi, 1996, p. 61), "passion for their work", and their "positive impulses that produce happy creations" (p. 72). Recall the graphic artist discussing his "happy accidents" (graphic artist, A5). And, "creative people love what they do" (Csikszentmihalyi, 1996, p. 107). The programmer said, "I couldn't wait to do the next thing. ... it was real exciting" (A15). In fact, "creative people do what they do primarily because it's fun" (Csikszentmihalyi, 1996, p. 107). Recall my comment, "There's never too much fun ... at all, especially with a project like this" (author / researcher, A17). And so, it may have been that the programmer, the graphic artist, and I naturally had fun because of our creative personalities.

Creating Virtual Health Coach required an andragogical learning climate (Knowles, 1984) that included fun. Benjamin Franklin understood the importance of having fun when he consented to Junto members "downing a glass of wine before moving from one discussion topic to another" (Smith, 1982, pp. 48-49). "Learning should be one of the most pleasant and gratifying experiences in life; it is, after all, the way people can achieve their full potential" (Cooper, Henschke, & Isaac, 2003, p. 3). I knew that without fun, there would be a "loss of energy and the creativity" (author / researcher, A17). The programmer and graphic artist created their own physical and psychological climate conducive to learning (Galbraith, 1991; Knowles, 1984, 1995; Verner, 1962; Mezirow, 1981). The office where they worked was open without walls separating workstations, it was well lighted and the walls were decorated with brightly colored original artwork painted by the graphic artist. There was a climate of mutual respect, collaboration, fun, support, and humanness (Knowles, 1984).

The programmer and graphic artist worked to create the same learning climate for Virtual Health Coach users. They built fun into the program through cartooning and bright colors to relax the learner (graphic artist A17). "There are a lot of emotions with color" (author / researcher in graphic artist, A8). The animated cartoon character brought fun to the program as a nonhuman resource for planning (Tough, 1971). The cartoon coach brought to the learner my expertise, personality, and teaching style in a fun nonhuman characterization (Tough, 1971). The intention of the programmer and graphic artist was to provide fun for the learner to create a happy emotional response. Because learning could be described as the "orchestration of emotional states" (Taylor, 1986, p. 69) where "emotions and intelligence are continuous" (Lindeman, 1961, p. 68), creators of a program for learning and changing must "account for and understand these complex processes" (LeDoux, 2002, p. 24).

Emerging theme: Leadership

I was the leader of the production effort and the lieutenant colonel was the leader of the funding effort. In the universal role of adult educator, I may have benefited by managing the educational process: counseling, directing, and evaluating the educational process to preserve the initial intended outcome. Further, if I had assumed this broader role of adult educator as manager of the educational process

(Knowles, 1980), I could have more easily promoted the "desired creative integration of the educational and cultural elements" (Savićević, 1999, p. 133). As it happened, the lieutenant colonel (leader of the funding effort) did what he said he would do (Kouzes & Posner, 1993), which was to acquire funding and provide development support. However, I (leader of the production effort and manager of the educational process) did not do what a manager of the educational process should do, which would be to ensure that the project would be process-oriented and learner-centered and that all elements of the learning process were addressed (Knowles, 1984).

The program by itself could be thought of as a content model. The program along with its implementation could be thought of as a process model. Andragogical models have been referred to as process models, in contrast to the content models employed by most traditional educators (Knowles, 1973). Perhaps if I, as manager of an andragogical education process, had viewed the implementation process "as a value chain, with each step adding value to the preceding steps" (Knowles, Holton, & Swanson, 1998, p. 257), I may have used my leadership skill to preserve the initial intended outcome of the project, which was to decrease military health care costs and improve lifestyle habits.

Emerging theme: Getting it right

Getting it right was important: the right technology company, the right learning climate, the right character, the right flow, making sure it did what it was suppose to do, and deciding not to collect personal health information.

First, it was important to choose the right technology company. The winning company was chosen for its perceived humanness (Savićević, 1991) and ability to create a "whole transforming experience" (Mezirow, 1981, p. 7), one that was the result of a new or "alternative meaning perspective from old habits of seeing, thinking or acting" (p. 7). The selected company knew "the importance of organizing learning experiences around life situations, rather than according to subject-matter ..." (Cooper, Henschke, & Isaac, 2003, p. 1) as evidenced by their tag line touting their ability to integrate technology and human touch, which immediately oriented me to the company and made me take notice.

Next, the learning climate was important to get right. The graphic artist thought the one problem hardest to solve was "probably setting the stage" (graphic artist, A14) or climate setting. A learning climate of mutual trust is conducive to adult learning (Knowles, 1984, 1995; Cooper, Henschke, & Isaac, 2003). If the graphic artist set the stage in a way that made the learners "feel that they are being talked down to, ignored, or regarded as incapable ... then their energy is spent dealing with these feelings at the expense of learning" (Cooper, Henschke, & Isaac, 2003, p. 3). Or, in the case of Internet learning, these feelings could cause the learner to leave the virtual classroom.

Regarding the virtual classroom, the graphic artist also did not want to "clutter it up with too much craziness that would take away from the content" (graphic artist, A8). He sought to create a learning climate that was "neither too crowded nor too spacious" (Knowles, 1980, p. 223). "I think ... that solid blue ... is calming. It kind of helps you" (graphic artist, A8). Blue is a cool color. "Cool colors are calming" (Bear, 2004, ¶ 2). Knowles (1980) said, the "physical environment should be one in which adults feel at ease" (p. 46). And, about blue, the graphic artist said, "If it were warm colors, I think it would have been too much for the eye and it would have taken away" (graphic artist, A8). "In nature, blue is water and green is plant life—a natural life sustaining duo ... comforting and nurturing" (Bear, 2004, ¶ 2). "The colors that were used are simple ... it frees your mind and lets you focus on ... the content" (graphic artist, A8). Perhaps blue frees the mind because "cool colors appear smaller than warm colors and they visually recede in the page" (Bear, 2004, ¶ 3).

To foster a learning climate, the programmer chose to use old traditional learning symbols like "clipboards, and chalkboards ... The goal was to create a new climate for learning with some traditional aspects ... almost a link to past experiences ... and the reason is that we wanted them to realize that it is a learning climate" (programmer, A8). But, "a few adults report that chalkboards are a symbol of childishness to them, which may help to explain the growing popularity in adult education of newsprint-pads on easels" (Knowles, 1980, p. 47). Therefore, traditional classroom symbols may not have been a good choice for establishing a climate conducive to learning for adults.

Next, the animated character and his voice were important to get just right. The programmer and the graphic artist "realized that people ask their best friends ..." (programmer, A2). Regarding asking best friends for help in making an intentional change, "non-professional helpers contribute far more than the combined total for professionals and nonhuman resources" (Tough, 1982, p. 65). So, the programmer thought the character "had to sound like [he'd] lived it before ... lived this whole experience, not preaching at us, just teaching us from experience" (A2). "... People often gain from someone similar to themselves, rather than from a professional change agent ..." (Tough, 1982, p. 67).

Then, the program's flow was important to get right. About the flow of the program, the programmer said, "if you strip out the content, the basic structure and flow is perfect" (programmer, A8). From the programmer's description of the relationship between flow and structure, perhaps one could say that learning is about how structures grow out of one another to create a logical and emotional form (Papert, 1993). Papert (1993) saw the tremendous potential of the computer as a tool to facilitate the learning process. Perhaps it was the structure of Virtual Health Coach that gave Internet learning logical and emotional form. Bruner (1990) discussed the connection between human learning and artificial intelligence (the use of computers to model the behavioral aspects of human reasoning and learning). Bruner said, "human beings do not terminate at their own skins; they are expressions of a culture. To treat the world as an indifferent flow of information to be processed by individuals each on his or her own terms is to lose sight of how individuals are formed and how they function" (p. 12). Verner (1962) described flow of a systematic diffusion of knowledge as that which results from rational thought. Taylor (1986) supports the idea that flow in the learning process describes an ordered approach. She said there is "an inherent order in what the learner is experiencing" and that learning is a "connected flow of events over time with a specific chronological pattern" (p. 68). And perhaps this process for learning is what needs to be done to address the adult education practitioner concern that the practice of Internet learning is ahead of the practice of adult learning (Isenberg & Titus, 1999, Figure 1). It may be the case that the back-and-forth relationship between practice (of Internet learning) and research (on adult learning) (Isenberg & Titus, 1999) is what the programmer is calling flow.

But, the graphic artist warns that all of the important aspects mentioned above are useless if the program does not do what it is suppose to do. His warning was, "Really understand it from all sides and really take your time with that because if you don't, it doesn't matter how you animate it, how it looks, if the function's not right and it's not doing what it really needs to do, then it's useless"(graphic artist, A14). About facilitating change, Tough (1982) supports the graphic artist when he said, "If we thoroughly and accurately understand the natural phenomenon before we try to be helpful ... and if we try to fit into the person's natural process instead of making the person fit into ours, I believe we can be of great benefit" (p. 76). And, if doing what you say you will do earns and strengthens leadership credibility (Kouzes & Posner, 2003, p. 47), then a program that does what it's suppose to do would also earn credibility.

Last of the important things to get right was the decision not to collect personal information. The International Commission on Education for the Twenty-first Century (Delors, 1998) would support our collective right decision to not collect demographic information from the users of Virtual Health Coach. The programmer called it a very critical decision. It is the Commission's wish that adult education practitioners "devise a form of education which might make it possible to avoid conflicts or resolve them peacefully by developing respect for other people, their customs, and their spiritual values" (Delors, 1998, p. 92). It is my opinion that personal health information could be included on a list of human things and for which a law was created to ensure its respect and protection. Thomas Jefferson in the Declaration of Independence respected life, liberty and the pursuit of happiness for citizenry. Laws that protect personal health information help position members of a society to be in control of their destinies.

Emerging theme: Educational constraints

The three educational constraints were creativity, intellectual, and evaluation. The first educational constraint was creativity. The military gave the appearance of being closed to creative education: the controversial Fluffy Floaters, and Slimy Sinkers weight management lesson; the olfactory learning style; and the animated character's voice. In reality, the military was using creativity's "systems model" (Csikszentmihalyi, 1996, p. 27–31) to make decisions about the program in the military environment. The creativity systems model says that "to have any effect, the idea must be couched in terms that are understandable to others, it must pass muster with the experts in the field, and finally it must be included in the cultural domain to which it belongs" (p. 27). The MDPR team was a group of experts in their field and they used their intuition to make decisions about the program for their military environment. Members of the team intuited that the weight management lesson, the olfactory learning style, and the animated character's voice did not fit in their cultural domain. Though the weight management program was taken out, the olfactory learning style and the voice were allowed to stay. At first, the olfactory learning style did not pass muster until the idea was couched in terms that were understandable. It was only after I created for the lieutenant colonel a sense of ownership by naming the animated character after him, that he supported the idea. This act of naming the animated character after the lieutenant colonel improved the climate and the project's effectiveness by demonstrating respect for the lieutenant colonel's abilities and life achievements and honoring his contribution (Billington, 2000; Knowles, 1984, 1995).

The second educational constraint was intellectual. The programmer said, "They had us dumb it down" (programmer, A10). But, it could be that the changes requested by the military improved the program. In other words, adding to or changing words to increase understanding seemed like a constraint, but in fact, may have improved the learning. Tailoring the language in Virtual Health Coach was intended to accommodate learning differences (Stites, Hopey, & Ginsburg, 1998; Billington, 2000; Knowles, 1984; Brookfield, 1986; Smith, 1982). Placing the simpler words in parentheses next to the academic titles of the learning styles allowed the learner to associate hard words with simpler ones, thus fostering learning how to learn. There is support for using computers to help people learn how to learn (Smith, 1982; Field, 1997). The International Commission on Education for the Twenty-first Century challenges education practitioners to foster the learner's thought, concentration, and memory skills (Delores, 1998)—all required elements for learning how to learn. Regarding the potential learner confusion due to inconsistencies in the stages-of-change language, I should have ensured that the stages-of-change titles were consistent throughout the program. Allowing the stages-of-change language to be changed in one section and then not changing the other sections where the words appear was a development blunder and was no fault of the military.

The third educational constraint was evaluation. Both leaders that emerged during the project, the lieutenant colonel and I allowed biased evaluations of the project and then used the results to promote our differing opinions. An adult educator is not value-free (Mezirow, 1981). "His [the adult educator's] selection of alternative meaning perspectives will reflect his own cultural values ..." (p. 20). It was not surprising that the programmer and graphic artist received good feedback about the program from their satisfied customers because the programmer and graphic artist were looking for good feedback. And it was not surprising that the military received bad feedback from their staff because the lieutenant colonel was looking for bad feedback to support his opinion of the character and voice. Both were guilty of sampling bias, which does not result from random, chance differences between samples and populations. "Sampling bias is systematic and generally the fault of the researcher" (Gay, 1996, p. 126). Full awareness of the existing bias should be and is reported in this section.

Unbiased evaluation of the program was not due to lack of money and lack of interest. The MOU was the plan for how the military, the programmer, the graphic artist, and I would carry out the project. It could be compared to a learning contract for the project. According to Knowles (1975), a learning contract specifies what the evidence will be to show accomplishment, and lastly, states how the evidence will be validated. One of Galbraith's (1991) six guiding principles for creating a transactional process is to "foster critical reflection" (p. 16). The MOU did not include evaluation not only because of lack of time and lack of money but also because of lack of a plan to do it.

Emerging theme: Situational constraints

The situational constraints were in the areas of development, power, information, and implementation. The first situational constraint was development. Regarding the development constraints related to time and money, the programmer and the graphic artist were remarkable in their ability to adapt and "make do with whatever is at hand to reach their goals" (Csikszentmihalyi, 1996, p. 51). Perhaps most of the work was done after hours to avoid distractions. "It was not done during normal working hours. It was done with a lot of 12-hour, 16-hour days including weekends" (programmer, A10). And forgetting self, time, and surroundings is common to creative people according to Csikszentmihalyi (1996). The author quotes the poet Mark Strand about being creative, "You lose your sense of time, you're completely enraptured, you're completely caught up in what you're doing" (cited in Csikszentmihalyi, 1996, p. 121).

Though the programmer was forced to do the job of two people, he got the job done. And, as it turned out, the programmer disapproved of his previous partner's approach. Therefore, losing the partner may have been an opportunity instead of a constraint. About the first draft of Virtual Health Coach, the programmer said,

> The way [the previous partner] structured it originally was as a big giant database program, where you go in and create the questions, and it would display each question on each page. But it would be no unique experience. Everything's exactly the same. That was the opposite of what we needed to create here (programmer, A14).

And, perhaps there was less animation and voice than what was originally proposed and the program was undervalued compared to the hours worked.

> But what makes science intrinsically rewarding is the everyday practice, not the rare success. ... [and] what is rewarding is not a mysterious and ineffable external goal but the activity of science itself. It is the pursuit that counts, not the attainment (Csikszentmihalyi, 1996, p. 122).

The second situational constraint was power due to being female amid male-dominated industries—the military and computer technology. First, I gained power over my intellectual property rights with the help of lawyers who offered expertise beyond my own regarding the MOU, the product copyright, and the product patent. Adults are the richest learning resource for one another for many kinds of learning (Cooper, Henschke, & Isaac, 2003).

I had power-with the military and the technology company, not power-over them.

> Too often, power has been viewed in a hierarchical way of power-over others, rather than power-with others. The dominant controlling version of power is power-over. This is the negative end of the continuum. The positive end of the continuum is power-with. Power-with promotes the well-being of self and others, and is inspirational and considerate of others (Marotta, 1999, ¶ 5).

Power-over could be compared to pedagogy and power-with could be compared to andragogy. My power-with behaviors were (a) learning military and computer technology jargon, (b) being prepared, (c) being on time, and (d) dressing well. I also achieved power-with both the military and the technology company by demonstrating some of the personal characteristics of a facilitator of learning (Ross, n.d, p. 30): (a) diligent in keeping oneself current and increasing one's mastery with respect to the knowledge and skill (learning the industry jargons), (b) conscientiousness and proficiency in planning and preparation (being prepared), (c) dependability (being on time), and (d) awareness of societal expectations (dressing well). I succeeded most in creating a climate of mutual respect (Knowles, 1984, 1995) when I met with the military and the technology company face-to-face. Disrespectful behaviors by the military seemed to be limited to distance learning situations (i.e., phone calls, electronic mail, documents, etc.). This may be explained by Bullen (n.d.) who said that practitioners are not able to literally apply the principles of andragogy to distance learning.

The programmer, graphic artist, and I gained power by "speaking with one voice" (Kouzes & Posner, 2003, p. 123). Pfeffer (in Kouzes & Posner, 2003) said, "… those organizational groups or departments with the greatest unity get more resources" (p. 123). Pfeffer uses the word unity,

> for agreement and consensus around paradigms—essentially what we have been referring to as shared values.

Because of their unity, these groups also have more efficient internal and external communication. As a result, their coordination costs are reduced, and joint action is easier to achieve (cited in Kouzes & Posner, 2003, p. 123).

The third situational constraint was information constraint due to withholding of information and competing stakeholder agendas. I had a need to know about things that affected me such as the decision not to distribute the military physician implementation packets and the lack of implementation package management, which led to the MOU violation of the Virtual Health Coach access on public websites. Knowles' (1975) comparison of pedagogy and andragogy (Figure 1. p. 20) depicts the difference between the pegagogy and adragogy design elements. By this time, the project had taken on two pedagogical traits. The climate had become competitive rather than collaborative and the formulation of new objectives was done by the teacher (military) rather than through mutual negotiation with all five stakeholders.

The fourth situational constraint was an implementation constraint. Instead of implementing the program to create a change in lifestyle habits of military personnel, implementation packets were simply distributed. The work of the project was limited to product development and did not involve military staff change management. Regarding change management, Tough (1982) suggested that people participating in a change initiative might become more competent in "actually implementing the change" ... and it may require "developing a repertoire of other techniques" (p. 80), which the military did not incorporate.

Emerging theme: Evaluation

There were intended and unintended outcomes. An intended outcome was that the program was completed and implementation packets were distributed to military HAWCs. Unintended outcomes were the promotions of the military physician, the regional account manager, and the lieutenant colonel.

When the project was finished, all stakeholders seemed pleased that they did what they said they would do and had no regrets. Though they said they had no regrets, the programmer and I later learned that an implementation plan that included training of program facilitators was an important missing piece.

At the end, all interviewees looked ahead to the future and looked back on the experience. Each stakeholder thought of other applications for the Virtual Health Coach's system for Internet learning suggesting that the Internet learning process is more important than the Virtual Health Coach content and all stakeholders expressed good feelings about having participated in a project that required them to learn about online learning. "Because if lifelong learning is absolutely essential and learning how to learn is feasible, then learning about learning takes on real importance. Time and energy given over to it stand to yield rich returns" (Smith, 1982, p. 15).

PROTOCOL

This section will attempt to articulate a process that I used to create Virtual Health Coach. There are suggested protocol elements that relate both the literature to the product and the literature to the lived experience. Some process elements coincided with what the literature said and some did not happen that way. Those interested in doing this may want to consider elements of the protocol that eventually brought this program to fruition.

The following is a listing of literature protocol elements from Chapter Two. These sentence fragments may have in some cases been changed slightly without changing the meaning to give a standard appearance and to give them more of a protocol appearance. These fragments could serve as literature protocol elements for practitioners who are attempting to transition traditional classroom learning experiences into Internet-based learning experiences. The page numbers where the protocol elements can be found in the text are in parentheses at the end of each element.

1. Ensure the program serves not only as a learning process guide but also as a librarian directing users to appropriate resources in a climate of respect (p. 15).
2. Create a way of changing general dissemination of knowledge into a systematic diffusion of knowledge. Thus, facilitation of learning on the Internet would be enhanced and not just left to chance (p. 17).

Conclusions and Recommendations 195

3. Create a challenging dialogue methodology (p. 17).
4. Include (a) preparing the learners for the program / course, (b) establishing a climate conducive to learning, (c) creating a mechanism for mutual planning, (d) diagnosing the needs for learning, (e) formulating program objectives (which is content) that will satisfy these needs, (f) designing a pattern of learning experiences, (g) conducting these learning experiences with suitable techniques and materials, and (h) evaluating the learning outcomes and rediagnosing learning needs (pp. 17 & 19).
5. Allow a facilitator to tailor an Internet learning experience to unique characteristics of the learner (p. 19).
6. Follow the learner's own natural process for intentional learning and changing and, at the same time, make the learner aware of the benefit of doing so (p. 19).
7. Ensure controlled decision-making, not … unlimited choices. (p. 20)
8. Ensure that it happens as a result of a systematic process, one that involves the learner through challenging dialogue, is respectful of past experiences, is modeled after a normal natural process, allows controlled decision-making, is tailored to the learner's unique needs, and creates a climate that makes the learner feel welcome and safe to experiment (p. 20).
9. Lead the learner through a systematic diffusion of knowledge by promoting rational thought through a continuous exchange between the *virtual* teacher and the learner (p. 21).
10. Ensure that the Internet learner is allowed to practice all skills in one continuous procedure in the second whole. Perhaps this could be accomplished through the online creation of an action oriented learning contract (p. 21).
11. Address the eight elements of an andragogical process design in a systematic and sequential way that seems natural to the learner: (a) preparing the learner; (b) establishing a climate conducive to learning, both the physical and the psychological atmosphere; (c) having a mechanism for mutual planning; (d) involving the learners in diagnosing their own learning needs; (e) formulating their own program objectives; (f) designing their own learning plans; (g) helping the learners

carry out their own learning plans; and (h) involving the learners in evaluating their learning (p. 22).
12. Use carefully crafted preprogrammed questions and answers, which could result in the creation of a learning contract that could be printed for portable use, revisited and changed at any time (p. 23).
13. Transform users and cause them to be changed forever (p. 23).
14. Include an adult education philosophy statement and description (p. 23).
15. Tailor answers to the learner's stage of change (p. 24).
16. Include special social and psychological understanding and expertise (p. 25).
17. Create critical points in the movement toward self-direction regarding the learner's relationship with the program's events and the learner's perceptions and emotions (p. 25).
18. Create learning environments where individual needs and uniqueness are honored, and where life achievements are acknowledged and respected. Allow online learners to tailor their learning experience to meet unique needs that can be accomplished through the use of a text box answer option to most multiple-choice questions (p. 25).
19. Ensure moderation when applying the principles of andragogy to Internet learning and validate adult learner assumptions in the context of the Internet classroom (pp. 26 & 27).
20. Follow a process to deliver content and, at the same time, assist students in following their preferred learning style (p. 27).
21. Creatively integrate educational and cultural elements (p. 28).
22. Realize group membership advantage through a chat room function where individuals working toward a common goal could support one another (p. 29).
23. Model the natural and human behaviors of learners who are involved in self-directed learning projects: (a) choosing the goal, (b) deciding which activities are appropriate, (c) obtaining the printed materials and other resources, (d) estimating the current level of knowledge and skill, (e) dealing with difficulty in grasping parts, (f) deciding when and where to learn, (g) deciding how much money to spend, (h) dealing with lack of desire for achieving the goal,

Conclusions and Recommendations

(i) disliking the activities necessary for learning and having doubts about success, and (j) deciding whether to continue (p. 29).

24. Build in flexibility to allow the learner to go back and forth through the process in a more natural way but electronically disallow the behavior of jumping ahead only when it would create confusion or be illogical (p. 29).
25. Address intangible barriers such as lack of motivation and confidence as well as those that are tangible such as lack of knowledge and lack of money, which may give an Internet learning program more humanness (pp. 29 & 30).
26. Account for and understand these complex processes of learning—cognition, motivation, and emotion (p. 32).
27. Include a social and historical critique (p. 33).
28. Provide a process oriented experience and include elements that will provide a whole-mind experience (p. 34).
29. Include an advance organizer that links new learning to a person's cognitive structure (p. 45).
30. Install elements of a culture (the sum total of the attainments and learned behavior patterns) into artificial intelligence (Internet learning) by extracting it from the learner through questions and answers (p. 45).
31. Equally engage all learners (teachers and students) (p. 45).
32. Surprise the computer learner with an andragogical experience on the Internet to create a new schema for the learner (p. 46).

Merging the conceptualization of how the building of an Internet learning program could be done according to the literature review in Chapter Two with the reality of how it was done: Sections of Virtual Health Coach with coinciding protocol elements from the literature review in Chapter Two (1–32).

Front Page and Front Page Links—Coinciding protocol elements: 4, 6, 14, 24, 28, and 29.

Section 1—"*Build confidence by thinking about other times in your life when you've been successful in other ways*"—Coinciding protocol elements: 3, 5, 7, 8, 9, 16, 17, 18, 21, 24, 26, 27, 28, 30, and 32.

Section 2—Think about past barriers to change and coping strategies to get around those barriers this time—Coinciding protocol elements: 2, 3, 5, 7, 8, 9, 17, 25, 26, 27, 28, 24, 29, 30, and 32.

Section 3 – Reveal your favorite way(s) to learn and how to follow your favorite learning style(s)—Coinciding protocol elements: 5, 6, 7, 8, 9, 13, 17, 19, 20, 21, 24, 29, 30, and 32.

Section 4—Discover why you want to change and the reasons why you haven't up until now—Coinciding protocol elements: 3, 5, 6, 7, 8, 9, 13, 16, 17, 18, 21, 24, 25, 26, 27, 28, 29, 30, and 32.

Section 5—Find out what habit you're most ready and willing to change. Many people have more than one bad habit and don't know where to start — Coinciding protocol elements: 6, 7, 15, 16, 17, and 29.

Section 6—Create your very own behavior change plan that answers the questions:

1. What will you do?
2. How will you do it?
3. How will you know you did it?
4. How will you cope with anticipated barriers?
5. How will you pay attention to your preferred learning style to learn something new?
6. Who will support you?
7. How will you reward yourself?

Coinciding protocol elements: 2, 3, 4, 5, 6, 7, 8, 9, 10, 11, 12, 13, 15, 16, 17, 18, 19, 20, 21, 23, 24, 25, 26, 27, 28, 29, 30, 31, and 32.

Resource Page—Automatically created for the learner, which offers resources that are tailored to their plan including what they plan to do, how they will do it, and preferred learning style—Coinciding protocol elements: 1, 2, 7, 8, 9, 10, 11, 15, 16, 17, 19, 20, 22, 25, 26, 28, 29, 30, 31, and 32.

Chat Room—Coinciding protocol elements: 16, 17, 19, 20, 21, 22, 25, 29, 30, and 31.

Protocol elements resulting from the lived experience

The following protocol elements (1-20) are the result of my lived experience creating Virtual Health Coach with four other stakeholders. These protocol elements are not found in the literature but were discovered as the study data were analyzed. Part is capsuled in the emerging themes section of this book and part is capsuled in the section where the research sub-questions are linked with the interview questions.

As the manager of the adult learning process for building a program that integrates andragogy and Internet technology, there is a need to:

1. Facilitate the implementation of the program. The adult educator must plan, implement, and manage the Internet-based program and not leave it to chance.
2. Involve all the stakeholders in the planning, the implementation and the evaluation process.
3. Manage the stakeholder relationships with open and assertive communication.
4. Share and manage the expectations of all the stakeholders.
5. Focus on managing the adult learning process and not the stakeholders. Let them do what they do best.
6. Foster a fun, creative work environment.
7. Celebrate and honor all the stakeholders' unique contributions.
8. Find the right technology company to partner with that has both technological skill and creative talent.
9. Listen to the stakeholders and offer compromising solutions.
10. Create stakeholder solutions that fall within the project's budget.
11. Be open to new ideas. Adult educators are only process experts, in contrast to content experts.
12. Demonstrate that the process is more important than the content.
13. Keep the Internet-based program simple and make sure it does what it is suppose to do.
14. Do what you say you will do to build trust and credibility among stakeholders.
15. Work as a team. The team is smarter than any of the individual members. Cover for one another and make each other look good. Provide for many face-to-face meetings and other opportunities to be face-to-face.
16. Be prepared for stakeholder meetings.

17. Never lose sight of the program's philosophy.
18. Practice self-management (get enough sleep, model what you teach, never let the team see you worry or sweat, keep balance in your life).
19. Be legally and financially responsible and seek counsel in both areas. Make no assumptions about roles and commitments. Ensure the pay equals the work and that outcome data are available to all stakeholders.
20. Be the leader of the adult learning process. The experience of building an Internet-based adult learning program is itself an adult learning process and must be managed by the adult educator.

Integrated protocol

The result of this research is an integrated protocol combining the protocol elements from the conceptualization of how to build an Internet adult learning program based on a review of the literature (1–32) with the protocol elements from the lessons learned based on the lived experience (1–20). These elements are then linked to Tough's (1981) teaching tasks, which he called major decisions or actions that can be performed by either the teacher or the learner in the learning process. The linkage was made for the purpose of giving the new integrated protocol order and flow and to show the naturalness of the process. I integrated the two protocols as they related to my research and lived experience knowing that other adult education practitioners' experiences will be very different and will bring forth new protocol elements not expressed in this book. Table 7 depicts the combining of the protocols and Tough's (1981) teacher / learner tasks to create the integrated protocol.

Answering the Research Questions

The main research question was: Is it possible to support the principles and technology of adult learning, while creating an Internet learning experience? Yes, the program's elements are evidence that the principles and technology of adult learning were supported in the program. A proof-of-concept called Virtual Health Coach was created for the purpose of helping users make lifestyle behavior changes to improve their health in the areas of

TABLE 7. Combining of the Protocols and Tough's (1981) Teacher / Learner Tasks to Create the Integrated Protocol

Tough's (1981) Learning Tasks in Sequential Order (p. 29 in Text)	Integrated Protocol	Literature Protocol (1–32) (pp. 194–197)	Lived Experience Protocol (1–20) (pp. 199–200)
Choosing the goal	Include an adult education philosophy statement and description	14	
	Never lose sight of the program's philosophy		17
	Ensure the program serves not only as a learning process guide but also as a librarian directing users to appropriate resources midst a climate of respect	1	
	Transform users and cause them to be changed forever	13	
	Provide a process oriented experience and include elements that will provide a whole-mind experience	28	
	Equally engage all learners (teachers and students)	31	
	Surprise the computer learner with an andragogical experience on the Internet to create a new schema for the learner	32	
Deciding which activities are appropriate	Create a way of changing general dissemination of knowledge into a systematic diffusion of knowledge. Thus, facilitation of learning on the Internet would be enhanced and not just left to chance	2	
	Create a challenging dialogue methodology	3	
	Include (a) preparing the learners for the program / course, (b) establishing a climate conducive to learning, (c) creating a mechanism for mutual planning, (d) diagnosing the needs for learning, (e) formulating program objectives (which is content) that will satisfy these needs, (f) designing a pattern of learning experiences, (g) conducting these learning experiences with suitable techniques and materials, and (h) evaluating the learning outcomes and rediagnosing learning needs	4	

(Continued)

TABLE 7. (*Continued*)

Tough's (1981) Learning Tasks in Sequential Order (p. 29 in Text)	Integrated Protocol	Literature Protocol (1–32) (pp. 194–197)	Lived Experience Protocol (1–20) (pp. 199–200)
	Allow a facilitator to tailor an Internet learning experience to unique characteristics of the learner	5	
	Follow the learner's own natural process for intentional learning and changing and, at the same time, make the learner aware of the benefit of doing so	6	
	Ensure controlled decision-making, not … unlimited choices	7	
	Ensure that it happens as a result of a systematic process—one that involves the learner through challenging dialogue, is respectful of past experiences, is modeled after a normal natural process, allows controlled decision-making, is tailored to learner's unique needs, and creates a climate that makes the learner feel welcome and safe to experiment	8	
	Lead the learner through a systematic diffusion of knowledge by promoting rational thought through a continuous exchange between the virtual teacher and the learner	9	
	Ensure that the Internet learner is allowed to practice all skills in one continuous procedure in the second whole. Perhaps this could be accomplished through the online creation of an action oriented learning contract	10	
	Address the eight elements of an andragogical process design in a systematic and sequential way that seems natural to the learner: (a) preparing the learner; (b) establishing a climate conducive to learning, both the physical and the psychological atmosphere; (c) having a mechanism for mutual planning;		

(d) involving the learners in diagnosing their own learning needs; (e) formulating their own program objectives; (f) designing their own learning plans; (g) helping the learners carry out their own learning plans; and (h) involving the learners in evaluating their learning	11
Use carefully crafted pre-programmed questions and answers, which could result in the creation of a learning contract that could be printed for portable use, revisited and changed at any time	12
Tailor answers to the learner's stage of change	15
Include special social and psychological understanding and expertise	16
Create critical points in the movement toward self-direction regarding the learner's relationship with the program's events and the learner's perceptions and emotions.	17
Create learning environments where individual needs and uniqueness are honored, where life achievements are acknowledged and respected. Allow online learners to tailor their learning experience to meet unique needs that can be accomplished through the use of a text box answer option to most multiple-choice questions	18
Follow a process to deliver content and, at the same time, assist students to follow their preferred learning style.	20
Creatively integrate educational and cultural elements	21
Realize group membership advantage through a chat room function where individuals working toward a common goal could support one another	22

(Continued)

TABLE 7. (*Continued*)

Tough's (1981) Learning Tasks in Sequential Order (p. 29 in Text)	Integrated Protocol	Literature Protocol (1–32) (pp. 194–197)	Lived Experience Protocol (1–20) (pp. 199–200)
	Model the natural and human behaviors of learners who are involved in self-directed learning projects: (a) choosing the goal, (b) deciding which activities are appropriate, (c) obtaining the printed materials and other resources, (d) estimating the current level of knowledge and skill, (e) dealing with difficulty in grasping parts, (f) deciding when and where to learn, (g) deciding how much money to spend, (h) dealing with lack of desire for achieving the goal, (i) disliking the activities necessary for learning and having doubts about success, and (j) deciding whether to continue	23	
	Include a social and historical critique	27	
	Include an advance organizer that links new learning to a person's cognitive structure	29	
	Install elements of a culture (the sum total of the attainments and learned behavior patterns) into artificial intelligence (Internet learning) by extracting it from the learner through questions and answers	30	
Obtaining the printed materials and other resources	Find the right technology company to partner with that has both technological skill and creative talent		8
	Be prepared for stakeholder meetings		16
	Involve all the stakeholders in the planning, the implementation and the evaluation process		2

Estimating the current level of knowledge and skill	Ensure moderation when applying the principles of andragogy to Internet learning and validate learning assumptions in the context of the Internet classroom	19
	Be open to new ideas. Adult educators are only process experts, in contrast to content experts	11
	Celebrate and honor all the stakeholders' unique contributions	7
	Do what you say you will do to build trust and credibility among stakeholders	14
Dealing with difficulty in grasping parts	Practice self-management (get enough sleep, model what you teach, never let the team see you worry or sweat, keep balance in your life)	18
	Demonstrate that the process is more important than the content	26
	Account for and understand these complex processes of learning—cognition, motivation, and emotion	12
	Address intangible barriers such as lack of motivation and confidence as well as those that are tangible such as lack of knowledge and lack of money, which may give an Internet learning program more humanness	25
Deciding when and where to learn	Share and manage the expectations of all the stakeholders	4
	Build in flexibility to allow the learner to go back and forth through the process in a more natural way but electronically disallow this behavior of jumping ahead only when it would create confusion or be illogical	24
Deciding how much money to spend	Be legally and financially responsible and seek counsel in both areas. Make no assumptions about roles and commitments. Ensure the pay equals the work and that outcome data is available to all stakeholders	19

(Continued)

TABLE 7. (*Continued*)

Tough's (1981) Learning Tasks in Sequential Order (p. 29 in Text)	Integrated Protocol	Literature Protocol (1–32) (pp. 194–197)	Lived Experience Protocol (1–20) (pp. 199–200)
Dealing with lack of desire for achieving the goal	Create stakeholder solutions that fall within the project's budget		10
	Focus on managing the adult learning process and not the stakeholders. Let them do what they do best		5
	Be the leader of the adult learning process. The experience of building an Internet-based adult learning program is itself an adult learning process and must be managed by the adult educator		20
Disliking the activities necessary for learning and having doubts about success	Foster a fun, creative work environment		6
	Keep the Internet-based program simple and make sure it does what it's suppose to do		13
	Work as a team. The team is smarter than any of the individual members. Cover for one another and make each other look good. Provide for many face-to-face meetings and other opportunities to be face-to-face		15
Deciding whether to continue	Listen to the stakeholders and offer compromising solutions		7
	Manage the stakeholder relationships with open and assertive communication		3
	Facilitate the implementation of the program. The adult educator must plan, implement, and manage the Internet-based program and not leave it to chance		1

smoking, weight management, stress, alcohol use, substance use, exercise, and personal safety. The program has andragogical elements throughout. The program can be found on the Virtual Health Coach Website at www.virtualhealthcoach.com.

Evidence of the process used to create an Internet-based program by a group of five stakeholders over a two-year period of time supported the principles and technology of adult learning in most cases except that I, as the adult education manager, did not manage the program's implementation and therefore, the intended outcomes of the project were never realized. The assumption is that if the adult education manager had managed the project, including the program's implementation and evaluation, the project would have succeeded in reaching its intended outcome, high participation rates and healthier lifestyles among military staff.

There were four research sub-questions. The first sub-question was, What are the issues with face-to-face teaching / learning during the development of the program? This study revealed that the adult educator attempting to build an Internet program must manage face-to-face the education process required to build an Internet program. And the adult educator must face-to-face facilitate the implementation and evaluation of the Internet program. Face-to-face open relationships, teamwork, and assertive communication between stakeholders are valuable in getting the work done. Mutual planning and face-to-face involvement of all the stakeholders are beneficial to every member of the group.

The second research sub-question was: What are the issues without face-to-face teaching / learning during the development of the program? This study revealed that just sharing a common objective makes a group likely to achieve its goal even without face-to-face teaching / learning. This principle of group learning can describe the stakeholders' educational process for achieving the goal of building the Internet program. Likewise, Virtual Health Coach users are also engaged with group learning when they find other users planning to achieve the same goal in the virtual chat room. The look and feel was important to get right without face-to-face teaching / learning because in one click, users are gone if they don't like what they see. Also, navigational flow of this nonhuman planner was most important for users who had not learned to learn.

The third sub-question was: Can an Internet program stimulate whole-mind thinking (cognition, emotion, and motivation) to learn? Yes. Virtual Health Coach users are surprised with an andragogical experience on the Internet. The stakeholders had fun building the program and therefore built fun into it with bright colors, nonhuman character animation, and voice. The program is process oriented and includes elements that will provide a whole-mind experience by fostering thinking, motivation, and emotions. Virtual Health Coach creates critical points in the movement toward self-direction regarding the learner's relationship with the program's events and the learner's perceptions and emotions.

Finally, the last research sub-question was, How does the design meet the goal of the International Commission on Education for the Twenty-first Century (UNESCO) for learning throughout life as described by the four pillars of learning: *learning to know, learning to do, learning to live together, and learning to be*? First, regarding *learning to know*, the design meets the UNESCO's goal for learning by helping combat information overload thought to happen when adult learners have never learned how to learn. This is accomplished by navigational flow, by limiting choices, and through the use of a learning contract called a behavior change plan.

Regarding *learning to do*, the design is appropriate for knowledge, understanding, attitude, value, and interest, but not for skill alone. Skill requires practice with props, though rarely does it happen that one is required only *to do*, but instead must usually *do* something in a relationship with others.

Regarding *learning to live together*, the design of the program demonstrates respect for the learner, which can lead to a trusting relationship between the program and the learner, a hallmark of *learning to live together*. Also, the behavior change plan includes identifying who will support the user in their change effort, another must-have for *learning to live together*.

Regarding *learning to be*, the design provides opportunities for discovery and experimentation to allow people to become great contributors to their own problem solving efforts. Virtual Health Coach has strategies to address learning barriers that involve discovery and experimentation. For example, a suggested coping strategy to understand the dangers of alcohol abuse is to compare the weight of a two-pound versus a five-pound bag of sugar for the purpose of understanding the difference between a normal healthy two-pound liver and an unhealthy alcohol abused five-pound fatty liver. This experiment may help an alcohol abuser learn to be healthier.

To summarize the answers to the research question and sub-questions, the answers to the main research question and the four sub-questions are all affirmative. However, the study found that the adult educator must manage the planning, implementation and the evaluation of an Internet program that integrates the principles of andragogy in order for it to succeed in meeting the learning needs of the adult learner.

Current Status of Virtual Health Coach

At the completion of this study, Virtual Health Coach was patent pending and licensed for use by an Internet-based wellness solutions company and by a large health care system in the Midwest. Also, all five branches of military service—Army, Air Force, Marines, Navy, and Coast Guard—has access to Virtual Health Coach as a result of my MOU with the military. It should be noted that I was not involved (as this study revealed) in the implementation or outcome measuring of Virtual Health Coach in the military population, nor was I involved with the implementation or outcome measuring in the Internet-based wellness company. In both instances, efficacy and level of satisfaction with the program is not known. However, I was involved in the planning and implementation of the health care system's Virtual Health Coach and had real-time continuous access to the data collected by the program.

A public Virtual Health Coach Website at www.virtualhealthcoach.com was launched in the fall of 2004 with a national press release that offered membership subscriptions to individuals and corporations. The public Website is the result of a new company called Virtual Coach, Inc. New features added to Virtual Health Coach were: (a) an automated electronic mail function sends pre-programmed tailored messages out to users at timed intervals that allows the program provider to track and measure the program's efficacy and popularity, (b) a tools section that offers an online journal and calendar for users to track and measure progress toward goals, and (c) a portability function that allows users to access Virtual Health Coach from their cell phone or personal assistance device such as a Palm Pilot or Blackberry.

Outcome data was promising. In the first year of offering Virtual Health Coach to its employees as one of four possible smoking cessation interventions, more than 1,500 Midwest healthcare system employees used Virtual Health Coach. One year post-intervention survey data showed a 35% quit rate among the 40% of the more than 1,500 users who responded to the pre-programmed electronic survey. For the purpose of comparison, the American Lung Association's group class held over several weeks (called Freedom From Smoking) was referred to as the gold standard of smoking cessation programs (Coruthers, 2005, ¶ 4). On a telephone call with me, also at the completion of this study, the American Lung Association's Manager of Tobacco Control Programs in Washington D.C., reported "two good examples" of one year post-Freedom From Smoking class quit rates—"27.1% and 28.6%"—approximately seven points below Virtual Health Coach's one year post-intervention quit rate. Unfortunately, outcome data was not available to me for the Virtual Health Coach program used by the Internet-based wellness solutions company nor was outcome data available from the military. At the publication of this book, Virtual Health Coach is marketed to employee assistance programs that promote it as a tool for helping corporations manage the high cost of employee healthcare.

Recommendations for Future Research

Adult education practitioners may benefit from future research that scientifically compares the outcomes of this learning system implemented and managed by an adult educator with outcomes of this learning system *not* implemented and managed by an adult educator. Quantitative and qualitative research methodologies could measure differences in not only learning outcomes but also learner satisfaction with Virtual Health Coach managed and not managed by an adult educator. In other words, compare the satisfaction level and number of Virtual Health Coach users that make lifestyle changes to improve their health when the program is implemented and managed by an adult educator with the satisfaction level and number of Virtual Health Coach users that make lifestyle changes to improve their health when the program is *not* implemented and managed by an adult educator. Based on the results of this completed study, it might be possible

Conclusions and Recommendations

that the success rate may be influenced by a program managed by an adult educator as compared with a program managed by someone who is an educator other than an adult educator. Furthermore, the satisfaction level among users of a program managed by someone who is an educator other than an adult educator may be influenced as compared with a program managed by an adult educator. The term adult educator is key. For these future studies, the term adult educator would mean one who has received education and training in, and practices andragogical principles and techniques.

Adult education practitioners may also benefit from a future research study that scientifically compares the learning outcomes and satisfaction of Virtual Health Coach users with the learning outcomes and satisfaction of a same-content, same-process, face-to-face class that is implemented and managed by an adult educator. In other words, with everything else being equal, how do the results and satisfaction of andragogical online teaching / learning compare to the results and satisfaction of andragogical face-to-face teaching / learning.

APPENDIX A

Interview Questions for the Author / Researcher, the Programmer, and the Graphic Artist

1. How did the thinking and planning process for this project differ from other Internet-based learning projects you have created?
2. Describe in detail your tangible and intangible goals for this project.
3. What did you do differently with this project than with previous projects?
4. What new learning did you come away with from the experience?
5. What one problem was hardest to solve?
6. In your thinking, is this "system" for Internet-based learning more appropriate for a particular type of learning and why?
7. Were there any surprises or ah-ha experiences during or after the development?
8. What one piece of the development was most important to get right?
9. Discuss the difference between the process and the content of Virtual Health Coach.
10. Discuss barriers to the project's progress and how you coped with them.
11. If there had been no budget or time restrictions, what would you have done differently?
12. With the *same* budget and time restrictions, what would you have done differently?
13. Describe your relationships with the other stakeholders and how they affected your work (author / researcher, Air Force lieutenant colonel, pharmaceutical company regional account manager).

14. List 3–4 guidelines you could give to future technology companies partnering with an educator of adults to create an Internet-based learning program.
15. Was there ever a time during your work on this project that you wanted to quit and walk away from it? If so, why? And, if so, how did you stop yourself from quitting?
16. Compared to other projects you have been involved in, how would you rate your perceived value of this project on a scale of 1–10 with 1 representing least value and 10 most value. Explain your answer.
17. Did this project ever seem to drift from a serious vein that should have been more prominent? In other words, were important aspects of this project ever at risk of being lost in the midst of the fun?
18. What other questions do I need to ask that you think would provide important information for this process?

APPENDIX B

INTERVIEW QUESTIONS FOR THE AIR FORCE LIEUTENANT COLONEL AND PHARMACEUTICAL COMPANY REGIONAL ACCOUNT MANAGER

1. Describe your initial interest in participating in the development of this program.
2. Discuss the return on your investment of time, money, or intellectual contribution.
3. What are your plans and goals for using the product?
4. How does the program fill a void, add value, or accomplish a goal for you?
5. Does the program integrate adult learning principles and computer technology?
6. Are there other appropriate applications for this learning system? If so, what are they?

APPENDIX C

CONSENT

Office of Research Administration

University of Missouri St. Louis

8001 Natural Bridge Road
St. Louis, Missouri 63121-4499
Telephone: 314-516-5900
Fax: 314-516-6759
E-mail:ora@umsl.edu

Informed Consent for Participation in Research Activities

THE EXPERIENCE OF APPLYING ANDRAGOGICAL PRINCIPLES TO INTERNET COMPUTER TECHNOLOGY

Participant _____ HSC Approval Number: 030108I
Principal Investigator: Susan Isenberg   PI's Phone Number: (314) 831-4668

You are invited to participate in a research study exploring the experience of applying adult learning principles to Internet computer technology conducted by Susan Isenberg, a doctoral student in the College of Education—Adult Education Division of Educational Leadership & Policy Studies at the University of Missouri–St. Louis. You have been asked to participate in this research because you were involved in the creation of the Virtual Health Coach program. We ask that you read this form and ask any questions you may have before agreeing to be in the research. Your participation in this research is voluntary. Your decision whether to participate will not affect your current or future relations with the University. If you decide

Appendix C

to participate, you are free to withdraw at any time without affecting that relationship.

The purpose of the research is to answer the following questions: Is it possible to address the adult's learning needs while creating an Internet-based learning experience? I will be taking an historical look at the process through which Virtual Health Coach was created. I anticipate that new learning will emerge as a result of integrating present knowledge of adult learning and present knowledge of computer technology. Further, it is my hope that findings will lead to a protocol for how to integrate the two.

If you agree to participate in this research, you can expect:

- I will use interview as one of the methods to obtain information needed to answer the study questions. I would like to interview you because of the role that you played in the program's creation. This is not a program evaluation study but rather an intellectual audit review of the experience of applying the science of adult learning to the science of Internet technology.
- The interview will require only one session no longer than two hours at a location that is convenient for you, confidential, and quiet. I will send you the interview questions before we meet so that you will have time to prepare, if needed. I will audiotape the interviews with your consent only.

Approximately five people may be involved in this research at the University of Missouri–St. Louis.

Your participation in this study is voluntary and there are no risks and discomforts that may be associated with this research.

There is no cost to you, nor any remuneration given to you.

The potential benefit to you is that you may gain insight into efficient and effective ways of applying adult learning principles to other areas of learning. Also, you may learn from the collaboration process that could benefit your next one.

During the course of the study, you will be informed of any significant new findings (either good or bad), such as changes in the risks or benefits resulting from participation in the research, or new alternatives to participation, that might cause you to change your mind about continuing in the study. If new information is provided to you, your consent to continue to participate in this study will be re-obtained.

The only people who will know that you are a research subject are members of the research team. No information about you, or provided by you during the research, will be disclosed to others without your written permission, except:

- if necessary to protect your rights or welfare (for example, if you are injured and need emergency care or when the University of Missouri—St Louis Institutional Review Board monitors the research or consent process); or
- if required by law.

Your answers will be treated confidentially.

When the results of the research are published or discussed in conferences, no information will be included that would reveal your identity. If photographs, videos or audiotape recordings of you will be used for educational purposes, your identity will be protected or disguised. Any information that is obtained in connection with this study, and that can be identified with you, will remain confidential and will be disclosed only with your permission or as required by law.

When you are audio taped, you have the right to review / edit the tapes, state who will have access if the tapes will be used for educational purpose, and when the tapes will be erased.

The research team will use and share your information until the completion of the research. At that point, the investigator will remove the identifiers from your information, making it impossible to link you to the study.

The researcher conducting this study is Susan Isenberg. You may ask any questions that you may have now. If you have questions later, you may contact her at (314) 831-4668 or s_isenberg@yahoo.com

Appendix C

Do you already have contact restrictions in place with UM-SL?   [ ] Yes   [X] No

(Example: no calls at home, no messages left for you, etc.)

Please specify any contact restrictions you want to request for this study only.

When the results of the research are published or discussed in conferences, no information will be included that would reveal your identity. Any information that is obtained in connection with this study, and that can be identified with you, will remain confidential and will be disclosed only with your permission or as required by law. All data will be secured and protected by being stored in the researcher's locked office file cabinet.

If you suffer an injury in the presence of the investigator, the investigator will assist you in seeking emergency services. If you suffer an injury in the absence of the investigator, you are responsible for seeking emergency services. You or your third party payer, if any, will be responsible for payment of treatment.

You can choose whether to be in this study. If you volunteer to be in this study, you may withdraw at any time without consequences of any kind. You also may refuse to answer any questions you do not want to answer and still remain in the study. If you decide to end your participation in the study, please complete the withdrawal letter found at http://www.umsl.edu/services/ora/IRB.html, or you may request that the Investigator send you a copy of the letter.

If you have any questions about your rights as a research subject, you may call the Chairperson of the Institutional Review Board at (314) 516-5897.

If you are an UM-SL employee, your participation in this research is, in no way, part of your university duties, and your refusal to participate will not in any way affect your employment with the university or the benefits, privileges, or opportunities associated with your employment at UM-SL. You will not be offered or receive any special consideration if you participate in this research.

Remember: Your participation in this research is voluntary. Your decision whether to participate will not affect your current or future relations with the University. If you decide to participate, you are free to withdraw at any time without affecting that relationship.

You will be given a copy of this form for your information and to keep for your records.

I have read the above statement and have been able to express my concerns, to which the investigator has responded satisfactorily. I believe I understand the purpose of the study, as well as the potential benefits and risks that are involved.

All signatures must match.

_____   _____   _____
Participant's Signature   Date   Participant's Printed Name

_____   _____   _____
Parent or Guardian's Signature   Date   Parent or Guardian's
                                             Printed Name

_____   _____   _____
Witness' Signature   Date   Witness' Printed Name

_____   _____
Researcher's Signature   Date

APPENDIX D

Verbatim Transcripts (in sequential order)

Programmer Interview

The interview questions and the interviewer questions and comments are in bold.

1. How did the thinking and planning process for this project differ from other Internet-based learning projects you have created? Therein lies the problem. There were no other projects. This was like our first web-based learning project. We've never had a learning project per se. The planning process is not real different from others. We plan, structure, organize, outline, and then scope out the project following your diagram of the project. So, that's all basically the same. The difference here is the fact that we started from the script. And, the whole process was to see how much we could do with what little money we had to work with. We asked, how far can we go with what money we had. Then we had to restructure. There's usually an approved budget before we start. This project was a little different. **The budget was approved, wasn't it?** Yeah, but, in reality it was fudge. Our initial budget was almost triple what we ended up getting. **Oh, that's right.** We ended up saying; we'll do it for whatever money you can get us. Then, they gave us a third of what we asked for and we tried our best to make a realistic working project, which I think we succeeded in doing. It wasn't what we originally thought. **Which was animation all the way through?** Which was a lot more animation, a lot more interactivity. There were whole pieces we took out—the email portion, the pull up, the stuff we just removed altogether to try to fit within the budget. But, that's a whole other question.

2. Describe in detail your tangible and intangible goals for this project. Hmmm. **Black and white goals were that we had deadlines.** Right. Well, and there was money. That was always a big, you know (trailed off). **There**

were timelines. And there were money limits. Right. As far as, I mean, intangible goals, what do you mean by that? Does that mean it sounds or seems like unreachable? You can't get. **Well, tangible just means that you can describe it and that it's very black and white like ... Tangible things are like time and money. Intangibles are like, you know, the emotions of it, the feel, the tone, or anything that you were hoping to achieve besides being functional, besides being on time and what we wanted, what we needed to please the Air Force.** Oh yeah, as far as the work, yeah those were all tangible goals. That's correct. You put words in my mouth (little laugh). You are correct. Intangibles I guess were the right, I guess, personality for the health coach. Create a personality that didn't exist. Trying to get it even down to the voice I think was, I mean, it was intangible. Nothing you could taste or feel. It was ... it had to have ... it had to be fun, it had to appeal to a certain audience. And we had to try to determine what that personality would be and create that. And I thought that was a really unique goal that we set out to do and that we surpassed, that we definitely succeeded on. **Because I walked in with 66 pages of content and that's all I had, that's all I knew. I didn't know what the voice would be like or the character.** Right. **You all just came up with that.** Right. Well, I think we did. **You came up with several iterations. Trial animations. Trial voices.** Right. And there was science behind it. I pulled up some studies and some research on the type of people that would use this product and tried to get an age range, gender, and everything, and tried to figure out who'd be the most likely people to use it and what would appeal to them the most. So, we read what was there, we tried a voice that sounded like an authority figure but wouldn't sound like you were being preached at. We realized that most people don't listen to their doctors, why would they listen to this. We realized that people ask their best friends. People who try to lose weight, they turn to Richard Simmons, or people try to get motivated to reduce their stress they turn to Tony Robbins. So, we thought, well let's ... someone has to be ... sounds like they've lived it before ... they've lived this whole experience. They're not preaching at us, they're just teaching us from experience. And, so, with several different versions of a voice we ended up with kind of a Bronx New York accent that sounds like this person lived a hard life and learned by making every mistake there was. And, was a better authority than the people who read it from books or try to teach you how to be better ... if that makes sense. And to realize that at that point the voice was a little too harsh and was almost too comical. So we softened it by making it a little bit more feminine. By making it more feminine, it had just the right appeal. It had just the right appeal across the board. It didn't offend anybody but one person in the military (little laugh). **And I think he was afraid of it being offensive.** Right. **I don't think it really offended him but he was afraid to put it forward.** But we had put it in front of a lot of people and it was unanimous. That was the right one. That was the right character. And, all of the sudden, it had its own personality. All of the sudden, its personality was born. It was fun, entertaining, motivating, all those goals that we wanted, all the intangibles were starting to take shape and once it was all said and done, it worked except for the fact that we want more. You're left wanting more [animated character]. We'll get into the budget topic later (little laugh). **He came and then he goes away in the middle and he comes back.** He can certainly be involved in more. That was one goal that we didn't reach.

3. What did you do differently with this project than with previous projects? I think what was different for me was, when we put this thing together, it was a collaboration rather than me just telling you how it was going to be. Rather than me dictating. Because, typically with a project, I get a bunch of information and then I usually organize it in such a way, and people say, you're the professional. That wasn't the case here. You and I went back and forth with this idea until we slowly started to put it together. I think that was different ... is to have someone to collaborate in the structure and assembly, which is usually not the case. I mean, with all the employees here, I have to put all the stuff together. I guess that was different for me. **Plus, we had a third factor, who was raising their hand and saying, "What about this?" and "What about that?" and that was the military. They thought that they were a big part of building of it. But, in fact, they were just kind of over-seers and would say Yeah or Nay.** Right. And there were some things we did just to please them. But, that's all right because they were the customers at this point. **Right.** We changed a section that we later determined that we have to change back (little laugh). **The Wish List. It turned into a wish list versus the stages of change, which we now have to turn back to the way it was.** Right. We have to. Because now it really doesn't make sense. It says, ok, pick three things but they don't know why they're picking those three things. The way it was written originally was correct because it *did* walk you through the stages of change so you understood why you were making that decision. So, that was a compromise that we had to make. We didn't have a choice. They didn't understand it. I don't know if we didn't explain it to them well enough or we didn't make a convincing argument. But, I think they were looking at it from a user's perspective but without having the knowledge of stages of change beforehand. I think that was the problem that they were looking at it from their own perspective, which is a health care professional, who already understands the theory behind it and stages of change and that's not what this is designed for. It's to help those who don't understand it. So, I think that they had the checkbook and they had the power so therefore, we made the compromise. And I think we've already agreed that we wouldn't do that again. But, it's ok because that was their version and they're responsible for it. But, our version is going to be different. It's going to be like it should be. **The idea behind that was that first you teach someone something and then you allow a person to apply it. And, as you said, they learned about it but then, they really weren't applying it. They went back to "What would you like to do most?" and not using the same language that was used in the explanation.**

4. What new learning did you come away with from the experience?
I think that [what was just said] covers the learning coming away from the experience, which is that we didn't compromise the integrity of the project by changing it to please them. It still was effective. It still does what it's supposed to do. It makes no difference now because we found out that they really didn't have that much interest in the project. That it was a stepping stone for certain individuals to move on in their lives and they had no intention of using it, we found out much later. Although, there's more activity now ... now that there's nobody in charge of it. It's being installed at several places right now. **Are you seeing evidence of that?** I'm getting phone calls and people are sending me emails to help them install it. I've had two in the last

month and a half. **People are rediscovering it.** But, I don't know who's in charge of it. **That's what happens when you have a project that lacks leadership. They are never able to implement in a satisfactory way.** And we never got to that part. Because at our last meeting was, "Well, [lieutenant colonel] is retiring, the place is disbanding, and there's no money left in the military for that particular office". There was nobody to head it up, nobody to implement it. So, it's just out there. **I *did* follow up with the Surgeon General's office, who said they weren't interested in it right now. It's going to take a little time and we'll have to go back to someone else.** Maybe that's something that we learned when we walked away. This is new, this whole merging of technology and adult education and that you have to have a plan to implement it. We actually have to do that. I think this is something that you and I are just going to have to learn. Ok, we just can't hand it over and have some instructions on the back of the CD. It's bigger than that and there has to be some promotion or instruction instead of just handing it to them. There has to be a method for how we get people involved in using this technology. I think that's something we discovered after the fact. In fact, we've been building those pieces. I think we have a clear plan today, a year later, of how to get it in the door, implement this thing and get people started that I don't think we had at the beginning of the project. It's something that we kind of fell in to. No one else was doing it. **I think part of that (what learning we did come away with) is part of the implementation. It was so new, the innovation as it was, from anything anyone has ever seen before. But, one of the problems with the military is that we satisfied the terms of the contract and then we had no more say in it. The terms of the contract according to the military were, "We'll help you get it built and then it's ours and it's also yours in the public". And so there really was a stopping point and they would have had to pay for me, for you, to help them implement.** And, that's exactly what happened. **It was a lack of commitment to take that project all the way through to the end, because that would have taken more money. Clearly, they didn't have enough money. They didn't have the foresight to really create a plan from beginning to end. Their goal was completion of the program and to get it out to physicians and that was it.** They had no plans to go further than that, which we didn't realize until we met with them. **It's like giving someone a textbook.** Without giving instructions on how to use it. You open a textbook and read from left to right. But, we did make an effort. **But, it was timing too. And who is to say we can't go back and pick back up as long as we have new people.** With someone actually in charge. This is something that we know when we go take it somewhere else. We already know up front. We'll tell them up front. And part of getting this package is that you get this front end consulting and all the materials you need to implement it rather than just handing it over. That's such a crucial part to get people into this. Because it's new and different. **The advertising department and the understanding of what it is and how to use it. Also, how to use the data. They won't see the value of it unless they are able to use the data.**

5. What one problem was hardest to solve? I remember you telling me stories about wearing out your carpet. Pacing. There wasn't one, there were a ton of them to solve. **How would you categorize the problems you were having a hard time solving? Related to programming, the technical part of it?** There weren't too many problems with that. **I think part of it was flow, how to get from one point to the next. The whole thing about there being two sections. There's the advising, thinking, decision-making, and then there's creating the plan. You change colors so people could see the difference between the two sections. To me, it was how to make this a systematic forward movement so you end up in a different place than where you started. And I think, too, part of it for me was how do you keep them moving forward without continuously going backwards.** I didn't necessarily see that as a problem. To me, that's a barrier. I saw that as part of the development process, to try to figure out the best way to structure it. But, that was something we spent a lot of time on. We worked on a lot of different ideas. We had navigation on the left side and across the top, we had drop-down menus, we had check boxes for each section. These are things we slowly developed as we went along. One thing that the military *did* contribute during that process was that we were under the assumption that people would sit down and spend a half hour or forty-five minutes and go through the whole program or maybe not. That was the way it was set up. When we went to present it, they said, "What if we leave, what if we stop and come back to it later?" We said, "Uh, well, you'll have to find your place". So, that was one big thing that they brought to the project that we built into the program the ability to remember where you left off. So that makes it easier to complete at your leisure. **This addresses one of the characteristics of adult learners. They're busy people and they come and go.** There were programming issues. There were printing issues. That was probably the biggest problem that we ran into. We assumed that the Flash technology was capable of doing all the printing that we needed it to do. And, when you printed the plan, it would not consistently print from one computer to another, one platform to another. That was a problem, a huge problem. And, that got resolved but it caused us to take a slight detour to put in a completely different technology with the Flash technology to fix it. **What technology was it that you integrated with Flash?** We ended up writing a program using Delphi, which is a Windows programming platform. **That's the thing we talk about on the front of the program?** That's Flash, that's Micro Media. They don't care if you use their player. That's how it runs, with its own player. It's like one giant movie, an interactive movie. In order to distribute the player, you paste on the front somewhere that it's made with a Micro Media product and then they don't care if you distribute it for free. But, we built with Delphi and used a Windows based programming environment to create this external program. Then, we had to figure out a way for Flash to talk to it. And then, back and forth (little laugh). **Have you used that since then?** No. **That the only application of it?** Right. It was just because Flash technology wasn't up-to-date yet. The new versions now, of course, it's almost been two years since we started with this, if you go down the bug list, of things that they've fixed, there are about fifty items related to printing that were the problems we ran into. But, we had a time constraint. We couldn't wait for the corporation of Macro Media to fix the problems. We had to work around them in order to meet our deadline. So, we had to come up with something different. That was probably the biggest problem of all. **I remember when I first came to you about the questions and answers, the only thing that I had seen was the technology used for health risk assessment, where you have to answer a whole bank of questions first before you see the answer. Wasn't that different for**

you, giving feedback immediately to each question? Yes, it was. **So it gave the feeling of a live conversation**. That was definitely different but actually, it wasn't a problem because of the technology we were using. We're kind of fortunate that the technology, Flash, existed at that period of time because Flash stores everything anyway. So, if we would have made this strictly Web-based or what's called a client server application, which means there's a client application and server application. The client just sends information back and forth. You can't always go back and review it as easily or display those answers as easily as we were able to do. So, I think that we were fortunate to have that technology at that time. **It seems to me that you said you took Flash to the maximum of its potential at that time.** Yes. **Weren't you even going to submit it [VHC] for an award?** We were going to submit it to Flash or to Macro Media because they want to see what everyone is doing with their technology. We never did it. I think they would have been impressed. I wish we would have. They have a brand new version of Flash out. It's called Flash Professional. They've added in all those tools and things that we had to create on our own now. I'm reading the blurb on it and they were so amazed over what people were able to do with it and that they never really intended Flash to be as powerful as it has become and just because of everyone making it do things they didn't know it could do. They were amazed that people were integrating things with it … data based technology and everything else. So, they've applied all those tools now. So now, they brag about how with Flash Professional you can build an application for the Web and for the desktop. And that's exactly what we did! We made it a desktop application that we imported over to the Web, which is what it was never intended to do. We had an issue of trying to read from flat files. When it's a desktop, you're not writing back and forth to a server. You're writing to someone's hard drive on the computer. So, we had to make our own technologies. There again, we had to build an external program that was kind of middleware to communicate with the computer and with Flash. Because Flash would send data a certain way, we had to reconstruct it in order to save it to that person's personal computer in a format that *it* understood and then read it back and forth and translate it. Well, now they *have* that. It's built in. If we built it today, it would be a lot easier. **You probably could do the whole thing for that amount**

of money now. Possibly. **You would have to do a lot less programming. Less fixing things, creating and inventing things to fix things that don't work.**

6. In your thinking, is this "system" for Internet-based learning more appropriate for a particular type of learning and why? Is it style of learning you're referring to? **Well, this is learning to make behavior changes. There are other kinds of things that you could teach, like how to play baseball. There are all kinds of things you could learn on the Internet. Is this more appropriate for something like what we did which was intentional learning, kind of high-stakes learning where it's very difficult? I could use the GED exam as an example of high stakes learning. Where you're really out to achieve a goal versus fun learning or just because you're interested. And not because you're really trying to accomplish something.** No. I think it can be applied to just about anything. The question should probably be different. I've had so much exposure to the Health Coach that what I keep thinking about is type of learning or style of learning. You know, is this more appropriate to print learners? How else could you phrase it? **Well, do you think it would be appropriate for any kind of Internet learning?** Yes. **You set out to learn something on the Internet. Would it be appropriate? My intention is to create a protocol to take any content and apply it to this protocol for Internet learning to ensure that learners, adults in particular, meet their learning goals on the Internet. Because the feeling of some adult practitioners is that learners aren't getting their goals met on the Internet because they go back and forth, they don't remember where they went, and they are like in a library without a librarian.** And, they have to create their own course outline. **There's no process, no systematic approach and they're all over the place. Just like if you have to learn Math 101.** Yeah, where do you start? You get bits and pieces from all over the place and you don't know if any of that information is correct. Yeah, I think you could use it for anything. Especially when you're trying to achieve a goal. It creates a plan. I don't know if it helps you establish your goal because it doesn't do that. It provides you help in developing a plan to reach your goals. It doesn't really help you create the goals. You have to come into it with that. **In VHC,**

it has already been applied. In other words, we've already taken a content and applied it to this protocol. So, there could be a part that asks; What would you like to learn? It could quiz you. So, instead of talking about stages of change, like for running a business, being an entrepreneur, there aren't stages of change that you're concerned with, they are the stages of readiness to building your business. Setting goals and creating your plan and things like that. So, it could be applied to personal finance. To set goals and build a plan. It won't necessarily do the investments for you. But, it will help you plan for how you're going to deal with getting to that point. I want a will, and I want to have retirement down the road. Now, I could go talk to a financial planner but to me, that is a step in my overall plan and so, I can see it being applied there. So, my overall plan is not to just go to an advisor and "Here we go". Maybe there are other people I need to contact for insurance purposes. You're supposed to start a savings account. **It's about making decisions about what's important to you.** Right. And set that goal and come up with a plan. I can see it being applied to anything. It's a great format, structure to apply to just about anything. **And that process that I've used has been identified in the adult education literature. Starting way back in the 60's they talked about a learning process that takes the learner through all of those steps. And it's as if practice has leaped ahead of theory in the way of Internet learning. Because the Internet came along and people have been using that and it has advanced a lot faster than adult learning has. People are out there and don't have a system or a process for learning.** We got tossed into the information ... **The teacher took us there**. We have different stages of our country's development, of our human development. We had the industrial age. And now we're in the technology age. We were thrust into that. And what's amazing when you think about it is that the real personal computer that started creeping into people's homes was developed in 1985 or around 1985. There were computers around way back when but it was so far away from people's minds to actually have a computer that could access that kind of information and was something only smart people do. And most of them carry a library card. They were the people who could get access to this information. And I think cable television started a whole revolution. Because now there're more channels. Now we have more choices. And, by giving us more choices, it makes us want even more choices. That's why I think that whole Internet went crazy. At some point, the personal computer came into play and people started to feel more comfortable with it. And then, when they opened up the Internet, and you could access this information, we ran with it. Ran blind! And still are! **That's the key word. Blind. We ran *blind* with it.** And we still are. There've been a lot of attempts by search engines to try to organize that information the best way possible. A lot of portal sites popped up like WebMD, Goggle, Ask Jeeves, to try to organize that information. Even then, it isn't enough. Because, you can still overload on information. You can search on any subject like weight loss. There are three million websites to go find information. Do you think you'll ever read through all that stuff? So, what you're going to do is skip around. And then, you don't know if you're getting the best information or the right information or the information that's right for you. **And that doesn't ever lead you to the end or to another place?** Right. **Or, do you just get stuck in the circles.** And that's why you need someone to organize your thoughts before you even get in there and start doing the research for certain things. And that's why I think it's a big benefit when you can decide what you're going to do and how you're going to do it. And, then you have it detailed enough to look for information on very specific things you want to do in your plan. You're not just looking at everything in general. It's much quicker to get the information you need and get started on your plan and not get overwhelmed and give up because of information overload. And, I think especially for older adults it's real critical because it's way too much information for older adults. Older adults need a slower approach. And, by having a plan like that, they can follow at their own pace, get the information they need when they need it. There're not going to be like the younger folks, even younger than myself, who overload themselves. **And that's not a good thing to overload your self. It doesn't move you forward in the way of learning anything.** So, did I get way off the subject? **No, you didn't. We were talking about other types of learning.**

7. Were there any surprises or ah-ha experiences during or after the development? For me there was. I read that script. I read it 3, 4, 5, 6 times. Then we extracted what we thought would be good monologue for [the animated character] without really understanding the whole process and program. Without understanding the Susan Isenberg concept (little laugh). And, it clicked one day. And I remember, I was working on an idea for structure and tossing some things back and forth and I think I came to you, I called you and it just all started pouring out, how to plan this whole thing. And you said, "That's it, that's it"! You had nothing bad to say. Just all of the sudden everything clicked all at once. **It was so wonderful. Like Helen Keller finally saying "Water" (both laugh).** And that's how it felt to me. I get it. I think at that point, I became such a champion or co-champion of the project. It was like I get it, I could argue it. I could sit at the military meetings and argue this program and process and *effectively* because I understood it that well. **And suddenly, that allowed you to be able to make critical decisions even without me from that point on.** Right. **Once you really understood it, we would talk to one another, but you could really make decisions about the everyday work on this thing because of the fact that you really did understand the concept of it.** Yeah. That was the big ah-ha experience.

8. What one piece of the development was most important to get right?
I'm going to say flow. I'm going to say the whole flow of the thing. It was so important to get it right. I think if we had structured it any other way than it is right now, I don't think it would be as effective. I've had personal experience with it. I just think that was the most critical thing. That it flowed properly. That people felt what they were supposed to feel when we wanted them to feel that way. So people knew when they got past the science and theory, looking at their pasts and that they really did feel encouraged after they finished section four. They really do feel it. They feel even more confident after they get through [section] 5 and they get through 6. Because, they've answered a lot of questions and read through a lot of information but at that point they really do feel "I have a chance at this, I have a chance to change". And, I think they're looking forward to making a plan at this point. We succeeded there. I think if we had done it any other way, I don't know if it would have worked. **And I think even though it's been two years, today, I don't think I would go back and change it. I feel good about it. It's like a good book. Even though it was written in**

the 1800s, if it's a good book, it has application to the present. And I don't think that this is going to be anything that could be obsolete. I think if you strip out the content, the basic structure and flow is perfect. Now, I can see all kinds of improvements in content. I can see a ton of that. I can see more [animated character] or more information here, updates ... We reference Jerry Seinfeld and he hasn't been around in four years. There're things in there but that's content. I think if you strip all that away, you could fit the health coach on a single sheet of paper–its structure and flow. And that's what's so unique about it and nobody else is doing it. **Even two years later.** Yeah. It's still old thinking. Very old thinking. And, they're just missing it. I thought it was really funny when we went to the [St. Louis based consulting company] and you started talking about the whole virtual coach and he said, "Finally". Here was a forward thinker we were talking to and he's like, "That's what I've been waiting for all this time. I've wanted to do this entrepreneur school forever but I never knew where to start". He didn't know how he was going to make it work. And that was it. He was into the new thinking but he just didn't know how to get his information into a format with technology that would be specific to adult education. He didn't have a clue about how to get there. But I think that the basic structure and flow is the key and it's perfect as it is. I can't imagine it could be any other way. **Would you call what you were just talking about the climate of it? Have we set a climate for learning? When you get in there, does it feel different than any place you have been? Climate can be psychological and it can also be physical. Physical, you can walk into a room and the right colors can make you feel good. Psychological means it's respectful, inviting, you want to experiment. Those kinds of things. So, talk about the physical and psychological climate. This isn't on your list of questions! (little laugh).** I think it's a different climate than what everyone's used to. We certainly didn't create a traditional climate for learning. But, that wasn't our goal. **No, it wasn't.** The goal was to create a new climate for learning with some traditional aspects. We threw in things like graphics of clipboards, and chalkboards, and things that people are familiar with. **Almost a link to past experiences.** We created a virtual traditional classroom (laugh) if that makes any sense. And the reason is that we wanted them to realize that it is a learning climate. So, we had to flash things in front of them that they remember as part of the learning climate. That's what makes it a learning climate. It's those bits of history. Even the chalkboard we used was very old. I don't know if you noticed that. It wasn't a white board. It was the traditional chalkboard on wheels, which is even older so that it reaches a wider audience. So that people who are familiar with the old learning stuff ... So, I think that helped create that, establish that up front. Even when you first get in I think we titled the sections with a clipboard in the background to represent learning. You typically see people with a clipboard keeping track of things like a coach on the sideline with his game plan on it. That was kind of important to us. We would use some of those things like even on some of the images. What looks like a game plan for a football team, which actually you had come up with too, to try to create the climate of being on a team or working with a coach, working with someone other than yourself so you felt you aren't doing this by yourself. **But in reality, you really are. You're out there. It's all you. The coach is just to cheer you on, to motivate, build confidence, check in with you, show you the process, to show you the plan.** So, all those elements are there which create the right environment for learning on both physical, I guess in the individual sense and psychological because you're seeing these past school references and stuff flash in front of you.

9. Discuss the difference between the process and the content of VHC. I think we just talked about that. Because I think we already talked about the flow and structure is the process. And the content you can strip it all out or change it. But it can be consistent from one application to the next. The content can change completely but the structure and flow always remain the same. Because, if it changes in any way, I don't think it can work. It's so unique it wouldn't work. The whole concept wouldn't work. I don't know if that's the difference between ... **Yeah, I think that's what I was trying to get from you. You saw them as separate, you see them as separate, the content and the process.**

10. Discuss barriers to the project's progress and how you coped with them. Well, there were all kinds of barriers. First and foremost, there was time and money. **Those are tangibles.** Time, which were deadlines that seemed to be impossible because we didn't have the staff. We *had* the staff but then we *lost* the staff right when the project started. So, what would have been three people programming turned into one. What would have been two people doing Flash assembly, turned into one. But, what's impressive to me was that we built that entire project in the time allotted and met the deadlines. We were slightly off. **But, they were off, too.** To me, it was just amazing. But, I guess it was not amazing because we put a lot of hours into it. It was not done during normal working hours. It was done with a lot of 12-hour, 16-hour days including weekends. All the animation was done at midnight and on weekends for [graphic artist]. The animation process is slow. It's every little movement, every hand movement, everything had to be created as a graphic element and then they had to be assembled to match the voice. Of course, we recorded all the voice first, and then we went back and animated to it. And it's just a very, very slow tedious process. The fact that we managed to pull off probably about an hour's worth of animation in the short time that we did is pretty amazing. Considering that it takes Disney years to do a 2-hour feature film. Of course, there's a lot more animation involved … a lot more than what we did. We took about two months to do an hour's worth of animation. That's a lot of hours. **And we didn't even use it all.** A lot of it's on the shelf. We just need to put it back in. There's a lot that we didn't even do. There's audio recording that we never animated either. The biggest barrier was probably time and money. **Any emotional barriers? Not feeling that you had the right stuff to do this or fear of not accomplishing it.** No, there was never any fear that we couldn't do it. I knew we could pull it off. There was worry, anxiety about certain deadlines. But, I think we handled it correctly. We did a lot of shifting of deadlines and responsibility back to the military for items that bought us time on others. It was a juggling act to move things that way and really manage them [the military]. Unfortunately, we *had* to manage them more than they managed us. **And they didn't realize that.** No, they didn't. We had to do a lot more of that than we should have had to because that was even more responsibility than any of us really needed with trying to build this thing. But we did manage to juggle things and shift them around and deliver some things in advance just to get their reaction while we were busy working on some other stuff. **It took them awhile to disseminate it, get it out, and then wait for the people to get back to them. So, then it would be in *their* court, which bought us some time.** It was a very fun project. All three of us were enthusiastic all along the way. I don't think there was ever a time except at 2:00 a.m. on a Sunday night when you have to get up at 5:00 the next day and you're not where you want to be at that point. Those times would get really aggravating but we got past it. **I think one of the barriers was the military and their conservatism. We had to pull out some pieces that they didn't like. Remember the fluffy floaters?** Even using the original terminology. When you talked about the learning styles. They didn't want that at all. They had us dumb it down. I thought that what we had originally was right on. And the fact that we had the real term and we included a description. **That was a compromise. To keep those words in.** Right. That was because we insisted. That was something we stood up for because people need to know these. If they're taking this kind of a learning style assessment that's been around for several years and developed by a lot of other people who are involved in this. They may want to go back and read about it or may be exposed to it at a later time. **Well, it has to be the right information if it's going to have staying power.** And to be credible. I think if you dumb it down too much you start losing that. That's not where we want to go and I think we prevailed on that one. **And I think the military is smarter than they used to be, but on the whole they have a reputation of having smart leadership but they were talking about the enlisted people and that's why they were trying to dumb it down.**

11. If there had been no budget or time restrictions, what would you have done differently? More [name of animated character]. More animation. Other than that, I don't know. **We talked about him talking back, doing more of the talking himself but there was the question that the military raised their hand on about the capability of the users. And this is two years later now. So people have more of an ability to use this kind of a program. That's another reason why less animation was ok because it would have moved faster for them.** But there were still spots at the end, especially at the beginning and the end of each section. I think he's

Appendix D 237

required in certain areas but when you start getting into barriers, emotional and physical barriers, I don't know that he has to be there all the time. He should get you started in that section. Those [barriers] are long sections, they take probably the longest of the whole program. He should get you all pumped up and ready to go and set it out so you understand what you're going to do without having to read it. There's an introduction paragraph and they can read that but people don't like to read. **But, they'd be more entertained if they were talked to.** And at the end when they finally get through that they say, "Ok, now why did I do this?" We list everything out. Here are your past barriers, here's what you felt in the past and here's what you think you'll feel in the future. I think it's a great spot for [the animated character].

12. With the same budget and time restrictions, what would you have done differently? No regrets. I thought what we came up with was just amazing with the time and budget restraints we had to deal with. Having a room full of Ph.D.s involved with their ideas, I thought that what we came up with was just a great project. I don't think there's anything I would have done different. **I was presenting it at school all along the way, too, if you remember in the TLC [Technology Learning Center] with Ph.D.s. The professors were looking at this, as well.**

13. Describe your relationships with the other stakeholders and how they affected your work (author / researcher, Air Force lieutenant colonel, and pharmaceutical company regional account manager). You were crucial every step of the way from beginning to end. I think our relationship was a perfect open working relationship. I don't think there was ever … It was very open. You were open to ideas and I was open to trying to do things you wanted to do and I think it made it a very pleasant project. It wasn't so rigidly defined that we couldn't go outside the boundaries of it from time to time and do something. If you look at the beginning of the project, from the script or your whole concept to the script to our original scope, if we wrote a detailed scope of how to build this thing to where it is today, there's a lot of things in between that changed, a lot of back and forth, a lot of things we didn't do, a lot of things we added because of that close collaboration along the way. I don't know that this project could have ever been defined that perfectly up front. **No. Well, no. It was an idea.** And the fact that you were open to change and to "let's try this" and "here's something that someone else is doing" or somebody might suggest something, even the military. And you were open enough to do it. We made a lot of improvements to the original description of what we had both on our side and on your side. So, with the Air Force, I think that relationship was not critical to the project except for the financial situation. The Air Force and [pharmaceutical company] can be lumped together. Because [pharmaceutical company] was completely useless to the project except the finance. **They received no benefit from it. They didn't take any benefit from it. They could have but they didn't even pick up the CDs.** Yeah. They're still here. They never got involved at all. The only time they did is when it came down to … well, just to pay for it. **It became a line item for them on the budget. It looked good on paper.** Yeah, they were just not a factor in the project at all. **So you think the military was slightly positive, more positive than negative?** Oh yeah. They did nothing to hinder the project whatsoever. **Less than what I thought.** Yeah, me too. I was really surprised. I thought not only, just from the theory … Here are other doctors in whatever field they're in whether medicine, psychology and whatever, who were involved in this, and I thought we'd get a lot more input than what we wanted. Then, I thought on the technology side, the military likes to over-spec everything. So, I was sure we'd be hit with every spec in the book that we couldn't possibly meet. It just would not happen with the budget we had. That's why everything costs so much when the military buys it, because they over-spec it, way over-spec it. But, they didn't care. They weren't that involved. We made a very critical decision early on that probably saved that whole technology thing and it was that we made this thing totally, *totally* anonymous. When [lieutenant colonel] used it, he didn't ask for anything specific. I think that's what saved us. If we would have attempted to get their name and address, phone number and everything else *that* would have changed the whole scope of it. And we would have had to do some military encryption technology that nobody has access to. We, as a company [technology company] would have had to go through some kind of an approval process because we were getting access to military encryption.

There's so much responsibility when you start collecting personal data. I thought that was just a brilliant move on our part. Because I think that saved us on a lot of things. **We had to talk them into that. They were going down the health assessment track.** We basically, put it on them. That's why the final decision was, well, here's what you can do. You set up your website, let them log in and you can collect all that information and then you can provide a link to our program. But, we're not going to collect all that information. We're just not going to do that. That was a wise decision on our part. That saved us from a lot of that (hesitation) meddling (little laugh). **Yeah, that would have just gotten out of hand, so we put the stake in the ground right up front. That whole thing just helped us define ourselves and how we work together. I came to you because of [previous partner], because of his mother. I think that project really forced us to be collegial real quick. We had to do this and we had to do in a short amount of time and we were kind of forced to be a team. And I thought we got to that point really quick because a lot of people couldn't do that.** Right. Real quick. When we went to meet military, we always spoke with one voice. It was clear from their point of view that we were on the same page all the time. There was no ... **Even when you were thinking something else (big laugh), you were always ... (both laugh).** But I'd never admit it. **I was the Big Toe remember?** We were open enough that we knew ... **We would go *back* and chew on it.** Exactly. It was just handled the right way. It could have been horrible. It could have been you in the middle, military demanding things from you, you having to communicate with us, then we'd get back to you and you go back to the military. But it never happened that way. I think it's because of the way *you* approached it. It had nothing to do with us, or the military necessarily. It's the fact that you made it a partnership right from the beginning and you dragged us to the meetings ... not kicking and screaming but whenever there was a meeting or anything, no matter what it was, we were always present and part of it. Just by creating that climate up front (little laugh), we avoided a lot of that stuff. **You owned it all along the way. You were never just working for me. You owned this right from the beginning and were a part of everything and that's the only way you ... Taking ownership is the only way you were ever going to really support it.** I believe that wholeheartedly. I've seen that. I've seen it both ways. **Me too. Like, "this is mine, and this is hers, but we'll get it done".** So, we're going to do our part and throw it over the fence. And that never happened.

14. List 3–4 guidelines you could give to future technology companies partnering with an educator of adults to create an Internet-based learning program. It's a tough one. That's a real tough one. If I was going to tell another company like us, just have somebody like me there. I'm not bragging on myself but ... I've always had the ability to see other people's visions and be able to translate it into technology and design. I've always had that ability. I don't know if that's unique or just that ... There are a lot of people who can see the big picture and I think that if you had a lead programmer who wasn't a real big visionary, I don't know if that person could pull off a project like this. I think there's a lot more to it than that. **So, someone who was too concrete, less abstract thinking would have a much harder time. This whole thing was dreaming. That's all it was.** Which you discovered early on. From early on you actually showed us an example of a program sort of like this, which was very ... there was nothing unique or dynamic about it at all. It was pretty cut and dry. **I can't remember what it was.** It was as boring as it could be. You could tell that a technology person did it. I'm sure they were very proud of it and they should have been. But I think they lacked the creativity. I always see creativity, especially in programming, with how it functions but not how it looks and feels. And on the other side of the thing, if you have a graphic designer, or someone who is very creative, they don't understand the technology, therefore, they're going to do things that you really can't make work. You either have to have somebody like me that has a little of both or you have two people. You have a very creative person working side-by-side with a technology person, a programmer who understands it working side-by-side throughout the entire project. And they have to work as one building it. **And that would be very hard to do. If that situation ever happens, you're not working side-by-side. You have your company and the other person has their company. [Graphic artist] was the graphic artist and I was the academic and you were like half-and-half.** Right. **Truly, that's why I chose you because you did have that strong creative side and you**

had that technology side. **What I'm finding out is that the combination is unique. That's what makes you so good at what you do. You can put things together in your mind. You're not just one little detail after another.** Well, my approach is different, too. That would be one thing that I would put on the list of guidelines, is that the look and feel and flow is first and foremost and programming is secondary. And I think that 99.9% of programmers out there are more worried about the functions. And so they develop every piece of it and then they throw it together. And they assume that the common man is going to be able to use it. And they're very proud of what they've done, they wrote these very complex programs but there's no good flow. The look and feel is always secondary and it's so hard to go back. That's just from experience because I worked with somebody who was heavily a programmer and didn't have a creative bone in his body. I had to go back and try to make it look right and feel right and it was very difficult. Going in after the fact. You should always do it first. That's what we did. A different approach than this one. The way [previous partner] structured it originally was as a big giant database program, where you go in and create the questions, and it would display each question on each page. But it would be no unique experience. Everything's exactly the same. That was the opposite of what we needed to create here. We needed to create an experience and climate rather than a program to just gather information. **From the beginning to the end, whatever the end means.** But, did you experience anything along the way? No, except you got bored, terribly bored. So, that would be my number one ... My guidelines are that: You get the right people, build the look and feel and the flow first, and worry about all the functionality second. **What you just said is huge. It's huge. You could write a book about that.** Actually, somebody has. **Really?** Yeah. He used to work for Microsoft and he wrote a book about the right way to program and it's not the way everybody is doing it. But, nobody's doing it that way. They still are not doing it that way. You know, where they do the flow first and functionality second, except for like Corel. That corporation probably has the most user-friendly software. They do kind of follow that philosophy. **Two very, very different approaches. That makes me think of the difference between deductive and inductive reasoning. You start with the answer and you back up and try to** figure out what happened based on reality. The other is you collect information and you come to a conclusion after that.

15. Was there ever a time during your work on this project that you wanted to quit and walk away from it? If so, why? And, if so, how did you stop yourself from quitting? Every day (both laugh). No, not this project. There have been projects like that. Not this one. We knew we were doing something different, it was fun, it was a challenge, but it was a fun challenge along the way. And, I was always excited to work on it rather than not. I couldn't wait to do the next thing. **I never felt that at all. There was always so much energy. It was always fun to come over here in the middle of all your mess because you were churning ... Particularly when you had [voice actor] come in.** It was real exciting.

16. Compared to other projects you have been involved in, how would you rate the perceived value of this project on a scale of 1–10 with 1 representing least value and 10 most value. Explain your answer. Do you mean to myself personally? Financial value? **Ummmm ... let's say, professional value for you and your company.** I would give it a 10 for experience, for personal experience. We were able to do something unique, so its value was very high in that respect. Financial ... ummmm ... **Well, financially ... I'm going to jump in and say, this has been a rocky road for us as companies. I engaged your company when you were just a tenderfoot. And you experienced rough times along the way as you were building this thing. And you had sense and are really doing well now. And I have really been everywhere off track trying to make a living and trying to go to school. I sometimes think about what it would have been like if we had done this and you would have been a settled company and I would have been a settled company and ... Could we have jumped right into it? But, maybe the market wasn't ever ready for it! I don't know.** Well, chances are it's not quite ready. I think that it will be. These sorts of things happen at the right time, the right places at the right time. And this is the right time, I think. Who knows where we'd be if we had money to throw at it. If we had all the financing we needed. We certainly wouldn't have to do what we have to do now. Back then when we first did the project, we had financing to support doing nothing but *that* because we could live off the money. Now, we're trying to expand up to the next level and there's no money behind it except for our *own* time, money, and energy that supports it. Neither you nor I have it so we have to find it wherever we can. But, when you do that, it's like well, a very small amount of time and a very small amount of money. That means the overall end point ... **Low risk, so low return, actually. So, it's got to grow organically instead of getting a jump-start.** Right. But, there are a lot of things in place that could help finance it, so ... **It's given us time to do it right, I think. It kind of reminds me of how authors will write a book, and then they'll put it in a drawer unpublished for a couple of years and then go back and read it two years later and they gain some insights from that. I think that's what's happened with us, too, as time has past.** Well, every time we make a big jump, every time we get together and say, we're going to move this thing forward, we're going to do this and that and we start scrambling and getting stuff together and we're ready to roll something out. We kind of get our feet wet. Feel the waters and see how it is. **EAP, remember?** Yeah. And we say, gosh, that was bad. It didn't work. That was the wrong idea. We need to take a different approach. And, can you imagine if we had signed a deal with her? **I know.** Where would we be right now? Because it wouldn't be right. We had the wrong kind of structure. **Well, they don't have any money so ...** We rethought that ... We would have been ... It would have been a disaster for us. We would have been providing services for free. We would have been just losing money right and left. **We would have given it all away and would have had nothing to show for it.** So, I think that over time, there was another ah-ha moment. We've had quite a few of those along the way. When we thought about pricing. Well, the whole point of rolling it out to the public ... **That was a new thought as of six months ago.** That was sitting at the beauty shop getting a haircut and everybody is going, "Ok, how'd you lose weight?" Well, I'd tell them about it and everybody ... I could have sold 10 people that night on the health coach. And I guarantee every beauty shop in the country would all join the band wagon and so it was a big ah-ha moment that we really should ... when you think about the trillions of dollars spent every year on weight loss alone there could be a lot of potential for financing just from the general public. If we get it out there and get just enough people using it to really make this thing into something just tremendous ... But unfortunately, we have to get to that first level. So it makes it worth it for them to get involved. So they don't feel like they're *not* getting their money's worth. **Which requires more development.** And that's the hump we got to get over. Once we get past that, then the financing will come in just from the general public. We'll have all the financing we need to roll it out into corporate environments and everything else. **Add staff.** Yes, add staff, and content, develop new versions. Even along the way, we stopped and said, "Let's form a company called Virtual Coach". We were already forward thinking about other things we can do. **Because, I picture one of the options is a generic coach, just as we talked about where they can apply their own content to it. Just a guide for how to go to the Internet and learn something.** And, we're not that far away from the technology to do what my old partner was saying. And still maintain the unique experience. There's already text-to-speech technology and Microsoft has this little guy, this little helper that talks but the speech is generated from text. So, you could type something in and they just read the text. Right now, they have no emotion. The problem is that [animated character] has all kinds of emotion and these guys don't. Until they can learn how to do emotion, we can't quite build this generic thing. We can offer a basic plan, the basic structure and apply any content to it but it involves some human intervention and creative work. We'd have to be involved with it. I don't think it can be generic. **It would be like it is right now but we'd take the health component out of it. Making a change, just not around anything in particular. I think about that a lot. I just need to put pen to paper.**

17. Did this project ever seem to drift from a serious vein that should have been more prominent? In other words, were important aspects of this project ever at risk of being lost in the midst of the fun? I don't think so because I don't think any aspects were lost in it. It *was* fun. We always knew that there was something serious behind this. We were very conscious of it all along the way. That there was something important to this. That we had to reach these people. It had to help people. And that was an important goal even though we were having fun with it ... we got to hear [voice actor] and all his out-takes were just hilarious. I think that we always kept that in mind. I don't think we lost anything. I think if anything, we gained. Because, the fact that we were having fun built fun into it. If we hadn't built fun into it, then it would be very, very dry. **And that's the nature of creative people. You have to have fun, too.** If someone was being a taskmaster, it probably wouldn't have turned out like that. You would have gotten this built and we would have put it together but it wouldn't be like it is. **And we had the military pushing us. I think that's the part they played best. That was the reason why we had to keep moving, because they kept us going. We had deadlines. They gave us money. We had to give them that return on their investment. And, that's what's kind of happening now. There's nobody saying you have to get this done now because we're paying you money to do this so we find it easy to put off. We just push it back.** Oh yeah. We don't have a choice. That's the problem. **If someone had deposited a big pot of money here ...** Or, even if one of us did, if I didn't have to worry about paying bills ... **And the same with me.** Or losing my house, or losing my business because I wanted to focus on this for two months straight, then I would do it. I *want* to do this. And that's the thing ... this thing about walking away. Most of my days I want to walk away from here I get so aggravated. But that's a project that I want to continue and I just can't wait to be able to. I look forward to the day. It's trying to get to that point. It will be nice to say; well I don't have to worry about it. I can just focus on it and have fun and make it happen. I can't wait for that. I think it's closer but it just takes that money. It's going to be buying the time. **That's right. That's exactly right.** I mean, really buying the time. **If someone would pay me a salary to sit and do nothing but this, that would be heaven for me as well. I'd love to dive back into it.** And in my situation, without having [administrative assistant and project manager] here or ... my responsibilities are just overwhelming. So, back when I had someone dealing with customers, not me, I could step away because these two guys here can do good enough work to support all of us but the problem is that I always have to bring the work in, someone has to deal with the customers ... **Make sure the bills get paid.**

18. What other questions do I need to ask that you think would provide important information for this process? I can't think of anything else.

Lieutenant Colonel Interview

The interview questions are in bold.

Virtual Health Coach
Interview Questions for the Project
Stakeholders

1. Describe your initial interest in participating in the development of this program. My interest was born of a long-standing belief in the value of health risk appraisal and the provision of assistance for individuals interested in reducing their level of risk. Additionally, I was motivated by a desire to capitalize on available technology to provide health coaching to a large number of people without investing substantial human resources. Another motivating factor was a desire to demonstrate that quality, educationally and technologically sound products could be developed quickly and at a modest cost.

2. Discuss the return on your investment of time, money, or intellectual contribution. The return on investment (ROI) was, in my estimation, exceptional. Given the dollars, person hours and intellectual capital invested, the VHC product is of high technical and professional quality and fulfills the spirit and intent of the "virtual" coaching agenda. When compared to other products I have had experience with, the "bang for the buck" is substantial in terms of the quality of content, appearance, usability and comprehensiveness.

3. What were your plans and goals for using the product? Having retired from the military and accepted a position in academia, I am presently negotiating an arrangement for the use of the VHC to serve university faculty and staff through the office of human resources.

Appendix D 247

4. How did the program fill a void, add value, or accomplish a goal for you? First, and foremost, the VHC demonstrated the merits of close, collegial collaboration between the product's technical developers, the product's originator and intellectual property owner, the project funder, and the end user community representatives (MDPR). The shared responsibility and accountability that emerged was efficient, effective and rewarding to the team members. The goal of providing a product that Health and Wellness Center (HAWC) managers throughout the military health system could utilize to extend the reach of their staff was realized.

5. Discuss how the program integrates adult learning principles and Internet technology. It is obvious the VHC integrates adult learning principles. This is apparent if one considers the six characteristics of adult learners enumerated below and as outlined by Malcom Knowles, a pioneer in adult learning who popularized the term adragogy.

1. Adults are *autonomous* and *self-directed*.
2. Adults have accumulated a foundation of *life experiences* and *knowledge* that may include work-related activities, family responsibilities, and previous education.

In pedagogy, the concern is with transmitting the content, while in andragogy, the concern is with facilitating the acquisition of the content.

3. Adults are *goal-oriented*.
4. Adults are *relevancy-oriented*.
5. Adults are *practical*, focusing on the aspects of a lesson most useful to them in their work. They may not be interested in knowledge for its own sake. Instructors must tell participants explicitly how the lesson will be useful to them on the job.
6. As do all learners, adults need to be shown *respect*.

The VHC design accommodates these six characteristics very nicely, and does so within the context of an Internet-based delivery system. The Internet technology has been astutely leveraged to incorporate adult learning principles and the VHC goal of helping to "coach" individuals who are interested in changing their lifestyles and seeking assistance in doing so.

6. List and elaborate on other possible applications for this learning system other than making behavior changes to improve health. The basic premise behind the VHC was to provide a product that permitted individuals to assess their health status and address specific behavior change opportunities by developing a plan for doing so. The VHC model is applicable to most any arena wherein the objective is to "coach," to "plan" and to "act." A good example would be coaching individuals wishing to address their financial planning (or lack thereof). Another would be career planning, especially for adults seeking to make a career change. A third might be to facilitate various forms of mental health counseling to include depression counseling and marriage and family counseling. Yet another might be guidance counseling for high school students.

Personal Note: It was indeed a pleasure to collaborate on the development of the Virtual Health Coach with a team of professionals who brought to the table an exceptional collection of health education, marketing, management and computer technology skills and experience. The VHC represents more than the product people will see and use. It represents the outcome that can be achieved when people of intellect, experience and enthusiasm unselfishly join hands to accomplish a common goal.

Graphic Artist Interview

The interview questions and the interviewer comments are in bold.

1. How did the thinking and planning process for this project differ from other Internet-based learning projects you have created? I *did* work with a company that did this sort of thing briefly and I was pretty much just involved in the animation / illustration side of *that* project. And really didn't have much to do with the overall look, navigation or any of those things. So, this one I actually did get to think about laying this thing out. How people will navigate through it and how it will flow and how to make those links easy to find and kind of walk people through. Planning for the animation was a lot more in depth because we had far longer narratives that we had to animate than we had on the project I worked on before, which was just simple little movements. So, this one was a bit more involved from the get-go. And, it required me to think a lot more in terms of how the character would be, and how engaging it would be and then behind the character, how we would set the scene and where would the information go and how would this thing be basically laid out in an easy-to-navigate way. So, I would say that it was more involved, definitely. But, I admittedly only have a little bit of experience with this sort of thing. This was the first big one.

2. Describe in detail your tangible and intangible goals for this project. My goal for this was for it to be engaging (and I knew we could pull that off) and I would have preferred to do more in terms of animation but that wasn't really possible. But when I look back, it probably wasn't needed anyway. But, of course, I wanted to blow things out in a big way. My attainable, reachable goal was to get something that would appeal to a mass audience and that wouldn't alienate anyone and would get the point across and not overly entertain because you had to learn something, too. I didn't want it to get lost with the bells and whistles ... I didn't want the message to get lost in that. So, my main goal was to make that happen in a timely manner. We had time constraints and financial constraints. We had a very limited pool we could pull from in terms of talent and bringing people in to this to make it happen meaning voice-over and stuff like that. So my goal was really just to get something as animated as we could get and flowing as we could get with the software, the technology, the time, the money, and the talent pool to pull from. That was my main goal. I was just involved with the entertainment factor. [The programmer] was involved with the functionality. So, my goal was to have that happen with those restraints.

3. What did you do differently with this project than with previous projects? (laugh) I animated a whole lot, a whole lot more! **Is that not something you were doing on other projects?** I was doing a little bit of it but not to this level, which you know I always wanted to do anyway. I aspired in my youth to be a cartoonist when I was growing up so it's something I wanted to do anyway. But, I don't do a lot of that. It's only when we get projects like this that I really get the opportunity to use that. Anything I do on a daily basis, if there is animation involved, it's not to that level, it doesn't involve creating a character usually, it's more animating simple shapes and animating text and things like that. **Had you ever animated to match a voice?** No. No. That was the first time I ... I've known we could do it. And you know the theories involved and you know what it would take to do it but had there been a call to do it? No, so this gave me the opportunity to actually do it.

4. What new learning did you come away with from the experience? So, would you say *that* was one of the new learning you came away with from this experience? How to put animation to voice? I think, yeah. And there were other technical things involved, too, like we realized that this would have to be downloaded in some cases, people would be downloading this information through the Internet at some point so we knew we wanted to keep the size of this thing down. When you add audio, you're automatically making this a big, big file. There's no way around it. So, that meant that I couldn't go too crazy with the animation because then we would run the risk of making it too big to download or taking such a really long time that people wouldn't hang out. And granted, this was a few years ago when not as many people had high speed Internet. We either had to approach it using a lot of vector graphics, which are easier for a computer to process than bit maps, which are photographs. It processes them as individual pixels, it lines them all up as pixels where as vectors recognize shapes and not pixels. It doesn't rely on pixels. So, it's a lot easier to download and to process. So, I used as much of that as I could. And, I just had to do some tricks like that. I had to recycle a lot of elements of [the animated character]. I had basically four body shapes that I would rotate or kind of shift a little bit. But I always stuck with those four. That meant you only had to download those four body shapes. Then, once they're downloaded, I could just play with them a little bit. So, we kind of worked some tricks like that because of all the graphics involved.

5. What one problem was hardest to solve? Probably setting the stage. I look at it like we set up a scene on a theatre stage so to speak. And where we positioned everything because we knew that [the animated character] would be popping up occasionally and would be saying things. We didn't want him to just POOF, show up with a cloud of smoke or something and he's there. So we kind of had to make space for him but how do you make space for him and still not get in the way of the content. *That* I toyed around with a little bit trying to figure out how to see how to make that happen and how to make it look balanced and nice and not be cluttered and not get in the way. **I remember a time when he was covering something up. When he turned, he covered up text. And we didn't catch it immediately. We didn't see it until later. That whole concept of a stage was all yours. My first thought of the graphic was just non-gender eyes, an expression really versus a real character. So, that whole thing about being on a stage was your idea and I think it works very well.** I think it does. And it remains there throughout that first whole section while it's sort of stepping you into this and getting you prepared for it. And, I think it's good because you always know it's going to be there and it stays out of the way. And, I think it was just a good way to handle that problem. We could have approached it a lot of ways. **So, it was where to position the character.** Where to position everything. But, the character was a big one because that was probably the biggest obstacle. Where to put the navigation? How to step people through? The way we did it was the sections were almost like arrows, they all had a point at the end that kind of walks you through it, forces you through it, kind of like reading a sentence word by word. **So it moves you from left to right. That was part of what we wanted to communicate was left to right so they won't jump around.** There was only one way to do it and you had to go through these processes. Plus, it helps them to chart their progress. So they say, "I've done these and I have these steps left." I think that was good. Some of that was subliminal, though. Working on it, you get those happy accidents that you happen upon something and you go, "Just keep that. Don't lose it. Don't touch it!" **Isn't that serendipity?**

6. In your thinking, is this "system" for Internet-based learning more appropriate for a particular type of learning and why? Well, yeah, I think that there are some people ... I'll put it to you like this. When I was in college, I had a problem with math, if you can imagine that. Mathematics is not a strong point for me. I took college algebra in a classroom setting and, of course, I was young and I wasn't paying attention anyway so I didn't do very well. So, I thought I would take it ... they were offering it on the computer at that time. You basically went in and you were on your own. You had a scheduled class time but you really could work on it anytime you wanted to get in front of the computer to work. I did not do well with that because I wasn't disciplined enough at the time to do that. And so, for me, the computer wasn't a good way for me to go. Maybe now, I would stand a better chance. But at the time, I wasn't really interested in it at all on the computer. So, there are some people that for what ever their hang-ups were, whether they are impatient or whether they need to be instructed by a person, which some people do prefer that. I think there will be some people who it just won't appeal to them. And there are people who live on their computer who do everything on their computer. Now you can get your whole degree on the Internet if you want to and for those people I think it's very effective. And, I think those people are growing in numbers. The people who don't feel comfortable with a computer are shrinking. **But, what if the computer was your only option? Do you see that this system for learning is better for some curricula versus others? Are there some things that would be a better fit for this kind of learning on the Internet?** I don't think so. Is there another system that's more appropriate for this particular type of learning? That's what the question is. Is there a better way to do it? **No, I'm asking is this system better for a certain curriculum versus another?** If there's something that's hands-on, has to be ... If you had to learn bow hunting or something and you'd have to learn the feel. **Behavior change**

to improve your health ... Is there anything else that would really do well with this format? I think just about anything. If you could do it in this way ... If you're trying to teach someone with something, and you give them some knowledge, and give them whatever format, this way will work for just about any system that you don't really need physical props to learn to do it. If it's just learning something and all you need is your brain to learn it, then sitting in front of a computer to do it is a very good way to do it. **I think I was leading you on for that one.**

7. Were there any surprises or ah-ha experiences during or after the development? I think there were probably more for [the programmer] than for me because he really knew this new technology. The way that he did it. My end was just pretty tedious. I took a recorded wave file and brought it to Flash and just started basically lining up body movements and mouth movements with the audio, so it was very tedious in a way. And, there wasn't a lot of room for ah-has. It was pretty much going through the motion frame-by-frame working through it. Some of the surprises were those happy accidents like the buttons and the arrows. Some of them made me step back and say, "Oh, that works!" But, they're more design things, just little things like putting in the progress bar at the bottom in that open space, "That'd be great if we could throw that in there" ... and we did. So, there were maybe one or two but I'm sure [the programmer] had a lot more. Because he was making it up as he went. He was having one language write to another language and all programming stuff where he was kind of on the cutting edge of that. Now, the software, if we were to do this again, it would be incredibly easy for him but he was kind of making it up as he went. Because it wasn't as easy as it is now. It was a lot more complex when we did it. I think we got two new versions of Flash since we did this and they've worked in almost all of these features now with just simple button clicks that we could have done. It required him to be a lot more inventive. I think he probably had more of those ah-has.

8. What one piece of the development was most important to get right? In my mind? **Yes.** Overall, it would be the character. I think we could have really screwed that up. We might have been able to do a better job with it. And, like I said, if we were to do it again, and we had more money, I think we could have put it in front of the people. It was very important to get that character right. It will turn people on or turn people off. And so, you had to be more mindful ... you didn't want to alienate anybody. It had to be one size fits all so people could relate to it. So, for me, that was the most important part was getting that decided. **That speaks to the importance of the role that you played. If they went to that site, if they didn't like what they saw immediately, they wouldn't stick around to view the content or see if the functionality was good. You're the reason why they stay, or opt to stay. So, it was an extremely important role.** Like I said, it will either draw them in or it will push them away. **People today are information surfers and** ... Short attention spans! **If you don't catch them immediately, then they're gone and they don't come back.** Yes, you got to hit them up front. And they don't read. They make instant decisions on what they visually see right off the bat. **And they couldn't even tell you why sometimes.** Yes! Subliminal. They form an opinion. Yes, that was probably it for me. Getting that character right ... or as best as we could in the time and what constraints were ... *He* [the animated character] could have screwed up the whole thing. People might not have taken it seriously. It could have caused a lot of reaction. And we just wanted to get the best possible reaction. I don't think everyone is going to have a great reaction to it. That's just the nature of ... the statistics that some people will and some people won't. **I think color was involved as well.** Yes. **There are a lot of emotions with color.** Yes. **You picked primary versus pastels. Is there a reason for that?** I think simplicity. In this case, if you want to entertain somebody and just entertain them, well then, you can flash all kinds of pretty colors and all kinds of pretty images in front of them and it will spark something in their brain and it will get their brains going ... they're seeing pretty things, but will they retain anything from that? Probably not. I think with this, we were kind of walking a two edge sword and we wanted it to be ... we wanted them to learn something so we didn't want to clutter it up with too much craziness that would take away from the content. **That would distract ...** I think solid color ... that solid blue ... is calming. It kind of helps you. If it were warm colors, I think it would have been too much for the eye and it would have taken away. **Very interesting.** The colors that we used were simple. **And when you say the word simple, I now** have a granddaughter and she's six months old. And when you go to the store to buy a toy for a six month old, 3–6 months, they're always in primary colors. When you read the research, the first colors they are attracted to are the primary colors. So, it's yellow and red and bright green and blue and just all the colors of Virtual Health Coach that you see in infant toys. So, I wonder if there's something in that description you just gave about simple. Simple meaning back to basics. You don't have to figure that out. It comes in easy, and allows you to ...** Well, I think it frees your mind and lets you focus on what it is you really need to be focusing, which is the content. And, if we got too crazy and had some funky lines, and some curves and some weird angles and all sorts of hip artistic high dollar ad firm kind of stuff and we just went crazy, you would lose that attention to the content. So, I thought if we kept it real simple, that we'd get the point across and people would focus on what they really needed to focus on. **And, and I noticed that your screens were not cluttered either. The prop is there when needed and then it's gone. Immediately gone.** Right. **It's like a little short message and then gone.** Just pops in to take a point home or make an illustrated way of doing something. Just little things like that. Add a little something but not too much. I've seen a lot of people that ... In design, I see it all the time where people lose the message because they're ... Especially in these big ad firms. They just want to show how creative they are. Nine times out of ten, they miss the message by being really, really creative. And, I didn't want to do that. It wasn't meant to be a creative juggernaut piece. It was meant to instruct people and I figured the best way we could do that was to keep it simple and not cluttered up with all that stuff. **Because there were plenty of messages rather than the graphics that they had to figure out.** There's a lot of writing, there's a lot of lettering to read on that screen and you wanted to make that as easy as possible. Because with people's short attention span, if they're looking at all of that, they might just decide, "Aw, it's just too much and there's just too much going on for me to focus." So, Keep It Simple Stupid (KISS) was the theme there. **And you were successful in doing that.**

9. Discuss the difference between the process and the content of VHC. I don't think there really was. I mean, I think it's a complete package.

Your content is your process (little laugh). **Which one do YOU think is most important? If you had to rank them ...** So, this style of learning? Boy, I don't know. Because, I think that process is real important. So, I would kind of lean that way. But, you can have a process but if you don't have the right content ... But, for this, I think the process is what's really good about it. You set people up, you explain things to them, you entertain a little bit up front, you have the [animated character] kind of telling them some things, you know ... Then, you move on to the next section where you start to learn how people learn, make these changes ... So, I think that *that* step-by-step type of deal is good. You kind of feel like you've read a book or something or you've accomplished something at the end. You've gone through all these stages and then at the end, you get your reward, which is this plan to do all this. That process is probably the most important thing. **Well, that was the right answer! The whole drive of adult learning is to move from content to process.** Oh. **The process takes on a lot more importance than the content. It's all about trusting in the process.** Right. But, the content is real important to have. You can't just put anything out there. But, the process is what makes it successful. **But, if you take the process and lose the content, then, it's not near as effective.**

10. Discuss barriers to the project's progress and how you coped with them. We had some barriers. Money, time. It was a staffing thing, too. It was just [the programmer] and I that did this whole thing (laugh). [The programmer] admittedly did more than I did. **And the Air Force?** Yeah, there were barriers there. **"Take that out!" [they would say]** Yes. Well, there wasn't much we could do about the Air Force. I mean all we could really do was negotiate that. And, that's just ruled by committee. Anytime you have rule by committee, you have to pick your battles because you're going to win some and you're going to lose some. So, we just had to work around that with them. Barriers of time? We wanted to get this thing knocked out real quickly. So, what it meant for me was doing all the animation as quickly as I could, doing it on the weekends, I was knocking it out as fast as I could so [the programmer] could get moving on his part. So, it just required a lot of overtime to get that stuff done in a timely fashion. Money? Like I said, going back to the talent, I thought [the voice actor] was good for it.

But, we could have used other people if we had the money that those other people wanted. If you go through some of those agencies, they charge you an arm and a leg. We could have put it in front of focus groups. But we didn't have that ability. So, what we really did to overcome that was that we just kind of went somewhere in the middle. He had some extreme voices and some not extreme voices. We just kind of went somewhere in the middle and hoped for the best. And that's really all we could do with what we had and hoped for the best and hoped that it appealed to enough people and hoped enough people got it, hoped enough people were not offended or turned off by it. **I think we used our intuition. Intuition is what you use when you don't have all the facts. You go with what you know!** That's what we did, totally.

11. If there had been no budget or time restrictions, what would you have done differently? I think there are possibly some areas where we could animate it again. If we could have done more characters like we're talking about now to give people an option. That would have been interesting. If we could have put these characters in front of focus groups and got some feedback from people of all walks of life, all races, creeds, colors, ages, if we could have put it in front of a lot of people and just got their thoughts on it, it would have helped to form the final character and voice. We could have done a little more animation. If we had the money, that would have been interesting. If you didn't want one particular character, you could use another (laugh). **It would be like watching a movie then. It would address the people who are not attracted to the content that is in print. So, they could just listen and then answer a question.** People are more apt to do that. Thanks to computers and television, people are getting very lazy and very visually orientated. We go to that and we don't want to work real hard for anything, and that's even reading a paragraph. **We want to understand it just from an image.** Yes, I think if we had a bigger budget and no time constraints, we would have done those things. We would have taken more time working on the character and deciding on the voice and putting it in front of people, getting feedback from it. Just doing more upfront stuff to plan for this. Really, really plan for this. And get good numbers on what people like and what they don't like and adjust accordingly. We could have developed the character with more feedback, which would have been nice. We still don't really know if that was the best way to go. **Now that it's out there, we'll find out!** We WILL find out. And that *will* be interesting! I don't know how far off we were! We could be *way* off.

12. With the same budget and time restrictions, what would you have done differently? With what we had to work with, I think that it's really as good as it could be for what we had and where we were at the time. From the technology side where we were at, the money side, just all the way around, what we had to work with, I think it's the best we could have done. **Well, you went beyond what your resources allowed. You were working weekends. And so you were given x amount of money and you went beyond that. You pushed it yourself to the limit.** [The programmer] and I both did that. That's just because we really liked it. I was cursing it at the time (laugh) when I was going frame by frame and trying to line up the mouth to say "and" so it would look right. I was cursing at that point but overall, it turned out very good. So, I didn't mind doing that. And, I don't think there's anything I would have changed.

13. Describe your relationships with the other stakeholders and how they affected your work (author / researcher, Air Force lieutenant colonel, and pharmaceutical company regional account manager). I think my relationship and how you guys affected me was mainly in developing the character because that went in front of everyone. And everyone had to make a determination on that. Everyone determined the feel of the character, which determined how it was animated. If we had all agreed on a voice that was sort of dry and monotone, that would have affected the character and that would have affected how I potentially handled that character because … working with [the voice actor] his voice was animated enough that it was kind of easy too to make it entertaining because … and we were limited by "I have to download it so I can't make it too …". Because people have to download all those nutty things that I throw in there. And so I think the voice was real animated so it made it a little easier. But you guys had a say in it. We put a couple of characters in front of you and I think the Air Force

Appendix D

looked at them, too. Did they or did they not? **Yes.** So that totally affected my work. Because that determined what I was going to be working on. Am I going to be working on a [computer] monitor with feet and legs or was I going to be working on the whistle? I just didn't know how that was going to go. All in all, I think it was good and it was good to get the feedback. I liked having that feedback. I liked the fact that everyone was involved. I think it helped the project. It affected me in a good way. I think that it was good. If one person developed this whole thing without say from anybody, it would have just been that one person's ... **I think that ... The longer I think about it and write about it, the more I know that it was a real good example of teamwork. It truly was teamwork.**

14. List 3–4 guidelines you could give to future technology companies partnering with an educator of adults to create an Internet-based learning program. The guidelines that I think would be important to follow when doing something like this are the ones that we kind of just talked about. Keep it simple, don't clutter it up to take away from the message, make it entertaining but not too entertaining, and make sure that it actually functions the way that it needs to function. We were lucky because we had [the programmer] dealing with the functionality and setting this all up because if you had [the original co-owner], or those other guys do it, it would be a totally different project. I don't think it would have been near as effective. I think [the programmer] really understood what it had to do. That would be one of the biggest guidelines. Make sure you really know what this needs to do and what the user needs to walk away with once they've viewed this. I think they really need to have a big grasp of that. If they don't have it, you're going to get a useless program out of them. **In other words, take the time to understand it.** Really understand it from all sides and really take your time with that because if you don't, it doesn't matter how you animate it, how it looks, if the function's not right and it's not doing what it really needs to do, then it's useless. This could have potentially *been* useless. Luckily [the programmer] understood this. Better than a lot of us understood it. The process, you know. **He had to figure it out.** He got his head around it and made it happen in a way that I think is good. But, I think it could have been a disaster. If you really don't grasp it ... Because

I didn't fully grasp it until I saw it come together with what he had done. With tech firms, that is a danger because people think differently.

15. Was there ever a time during your work on this project that you wanted to quit and walk away from it? If so, why? And, if so, how did you stop yourself from quitting? Only when I was in the full-on animation ... When I had the headphones on going frame-by-frame trying to sync up vowel sounds with the right mouth on [the animated character]. That gets real tedious (laugh). It gets really agonizing after awhile. And I think at that point I was just Awwww ... Tired of even looking at it. I wouldn't have quit so that wasn't the question. But, that was one thing that got me ready to pull my hair out. **Is that why you had it cut so short?**

16. Compared to other projects you have been involved in, how would you rate your perceived value of this project on a scale of 1–10 with 1 representing least value and 10 most value. Explain your answer. Compared to other things I've done, I'd have to value this at a 10 because the only other thing I ever did that was even close to this was a project with [a Web-based learning company in Central Missouri]. I did some stuff with them before I moved back to St. Louis and when they found out ... I talked to [the Web-based learning company employee] on an email once and he had said that it was far above what he had seen in the industry. And he's in that industry. Web-based learning and stuff like that. He said it was very much beyond what he had seen before. And so that made me feel that this really is a step above. I think a lot of it is that the technology of companies like that is a little bit behind. **He's university-based. And they don't have money. Unless they get grants or something.** And this project would have been way more money had we taken it ... **But you just ran right past that barrier. Meaning, you gave it what it needed.** Because we wanted to see it work. So, I think it's a 10 because we really put everything into it that we could. And, I think we went above and beyond. It's informative, and it's easy to use and it's entertaining and it's all those things. Could it be better? Probably. Anything could be better if you really wanted to put the effort and the time into it. And to hear someone like [the Web-based learning company employee that graphic artist used to work with] say that ... And to have been in that environment and to have seen what they were doing, and then see this, it's way above that. I think it's definitely up there in terms of its value.

17. Did this project ever seem to drift from a serious vein that should have been more prominent? In other words, were important aspects of this project ever at risk of being lost in the midst of the fun? They were when we were recording it! There were a lot of things that didn't make the cut that were pretty entertaining. I think because you wrote it before we ever started planning ... This was already done before we did anything on our part, which was good in that we had a complete script to pull from. Your words are what we had this character say. So really, the only way we could have messed that up and pulled away was to get a little cartoony with it sometimes or a little cluttered up with props and goofy things like that. So, I think at times maybe it pulls away from the serious vein because of the make-up of the character ... being a whistle. I think anytime you do that, it's going to somewhat make it less serious. You don't watch Bugs Bunny and think of that very seriously. In a way, it's very good because people relax and it seems like more of a fun approach to things. The message is very serious and everything you wrote is very serious so the only way I could have screwed it up was to have the character, have [voice actor] read a voice that was like very Mickey Mouse that was not believable and not stern in any sense and totally way out there. We tried some of those and it didn't work. I think the only way we could have done that was to mess up the voice and have the voice too "out there" or to clutter it up with props that weren't really necessary. And we didn't do that. I don't think we had a lot of props that got in the way. I think what we have are more illustrative and not goofy. They're more to help the message than to make a goofy statement making it look more like a cartoon. I think they aided it. **So, your answer is that you don't think it *did* drift because the content was already done.** The content was there. It was your content and it was very serious. But your content wasn't too professional, medical, didn't cloud people's minds with meaningless stuff, talk over their head, kind of ... It was on a very good level. It was on a level where most people could understand it. It's not too complex and they're not going to lose interest in it. You weren't boring them with countless stuff they don't care about. I don't think we could have screwed it up. Only if we had done the character's voice differently I think we could have. And, I think if we had done it differently, we would have taken more time *on* that voice because I'm really close to this so it's tough for me to say but maybe it's not the best voice and maybe if we had the opportunity to put it in front of focus groups, try other voices, bring other talent in and get kind of a mix of voices and then put those in front of people, there would be a better voice out there that we don't know about. But that wasn't an option for us. We just went with what we got. I don't think it takes away from the serious vein. **As you said, it's entertaining. And that had to be a factor.** Definitely, or you're going to bore people.

18. Are there other questions I need to ask that you think would provide important information for this process? Not really. I don't think so.

Author / Researcher Interview

The interview questions are in bold.

1. How did the thinking and planning process for this project differ from other Internet-based learning projects you have created? I have never created a Web-based learning project. So this really doesn't apply.

2. Describe in detail your tangible and intangible goals for this project. My goal was to have a program that worked yet engaged people, kept them there long enough so that they went through the process and hopefully that they would then change behaviors, make behavior changes to improve their health. So, those are my tangible goals. The intangible goals were to make a success. I really wanted to create something that had impact to give me academic attention, would earn some money, would work based on what I've learned about adult learning and what I knew about behavior change modification in the area of health.

3. What did you do differently with this project than with previous projects? Well, I haven't done a Internet-based project and with this project there were so many players that needed to be listened to and satisfied.

The partnership with the Air Force required that I dance with the Air Force as well as the development company all at the same time. And, I was kind of the go-between. So, if I could just relate that experience to any other project I've done, on my own outside of work, it truly was a joint effort team process collaborative approach where one piece doesn't move ahead without the other without complete understanding and agreement. I had to learn patience and I had to learn to say it a different way, write it a different way, do it a different way when it wasn't satisfactory the first time. Because, my first time out of the chute was not always accepted by all.

4. What new learning did you come away with from the experience? I learned that they all [the other stakeholders] had value and a unique contribution to this thing that was different from mine and was going to be the reason for its success. And I think I learned that just because you have the process doesn't mean you have all the answers. Having the process and the content, I thought, well, I'm the Big Cheese, I don't need them in order to finish this but I truly needed them and could not have done it without them. I'm really happy that I was thrown into a situation where the work was forced due to the contract. We were forced to be on schedule and forced to do this together. It was a wonderful experience of give-and-take.

5. What one problem was hardest to solve? (hesitation) I think how much to put in and how much to ... It was so hard to not to put everything in that I had written. Therefore, it has a lot of words in it. But, when you're trying to get a certain affect, and you think you've created that affect through writing, to say you can't do it that way, you have to do it another way, that was the hardest problem. Once I'd made a decision about how it should sound, what it should say, and then to hear you have to do it another way, because it won't jive with this piece of it, that was very difficult. It was kind of like the author of a book when the editor says you have to rewrite the whole first chapter, or we're going to take chapter three out or we're going to change your title, or write out a character. "Wait a minute! This is my treasure, this is my creation, don't mess with it." But, it got messed with a lot.

6. In your thinking, is this system for Internet-based learning more appropriate for a particular type of learning and why? I *do* think that it's more appropriate for intentional learning, learning that happens not by chance but because you need to learn something now for some particular reason. That's why I think it would be particularly good for not only behavior changes to improve healthy lifestyle habits but also like preparing for a GED class, course, and test. Getting your financial affairs in order, something that you know you need to do but you just can't figure out how to do it. You need to learn a system for accomplishing it. I think that ... The answer is anything that is particularly difficult, has an emotional component, and you know you have to do it. You know you have to learn it.

7. Were there any surprises or ah-ha experiences during or after the development? Well, I think [the programmer] was my only surprise. It was a funny thing because it was as if overnight he figured it out. He read and read and read this program and tried to analyze the process to decide how best to create this program. And literally, overnight figured out what this was all about and the magic of it. And, once he got it, he's been the biggest supporter of it. So, he was able to problem solve in the creation of it and thereafter around how to sell it, how to add new features to the program, which is data collection and email function afterwards and creating a resource page that allows an organization to tailor a page based on the action plan or the behavior change plan so that individuals will only see those options, those resources that align with their plan. It would not have been possible had [the programmer] not really, thoroughly understood it. Because, if you don't, it's *real* obvious. But when somebody really understands how it works, then, it's also very obvious. He *did* have that ah-ha experience. And therefore, I had the ah-ha experience watching him have that ah-ha experience.

8. What one piece of the development was most important to get right? Umm. The others wouldn't agree with me but I don't think it was the character. I think that was a very important piece ... the character. The look and the feel, not necessarily just the character. But, the look and the feel of it. The flow of it, I think more than anything. How it could be navigated. But, I have to agree with [the graphic artist] though, that the initial character, if he turns you off, then you're not going to go back and you're not even going to look, wait around long enough to know what the process is all about, much less the content. So, truly, the look and the feel are most important to get right. I needed help with that. I had no idea what I was doing so I appreciated their help with that.

9. Discuss the difference between the process and the content of VHC. Well, the content can vary. The process will remain the same. That way, as I hope to describe in the paper, this is a process that can be applied to any curriculum or content that is a piece of intentional learning and the content changes according to the curriculum, what it is you want to learn, whether it's finishing your GED, whether it's how to build a house, learning to manage your stress or getting your finances in order. All that content changes but the process remains the same. What do you do first, what do you do second, what do you do third.

10. Discuss barriers to the project's progress and how you coped with them. Well, first of all, it was money. They didn't want to give us the money that it would take to build it. So, they scaled it down and we ended up building something less than what we originally planned to with less animation. And also, they built a more expensive program than what they were paid for. So, I had the buy-in of the creators who were willing, *more* than willing, to give *more* time and talent than what money was allowed them. They wanted to get this thing right because they felt ownership of it. So, that was a restriction. Time. I would get up very early and work on that before I'd work on anything else. I'd allow myself a little bit of time every morning to do the work and I'd set a goal for myself and made sure I accomplished that before time was up to get ready for this other work of mine. So, building in time everyday, getting up early to build it in. And, a lot of emailing back and forth, using my best communication skills in emails and with the Air Force. And making sure to respect everyone. I just bent over backwards to be kind and collaborative. Come their way, make it 50/50 to be sure that it was always a win-win situation. They would always feel like they were winning even when I was winning as well. And, that's the only way I figured out how to get around the lack of agreement on something was just to somehow turn it into a win-win situation. Like the name [the animated character]. [The lieutenant colonel] was not crazy about the character initially and all this time had been put into creating this character. So, I thought long and hard about that and I opted to give him the name [the animated character] because it was named after [the lieutenant colonel]. And once he knew the character was named after him, he loved him. That worked in my favor. You always catch more flies with honey than you do with vinegar. So, I was just the sweetest thing you could imagine. I really worked *hard* to communicate assertively and not aggressively.

11. If there had been no budget or time restrictions, what would you have done differently? Well, the issue is that if I had more time, I would have taken more time. And I don't know if it would have been any better. There's something about working under constraints that lights a fire under you. Like today. I have an interview with [the pharmaceutical regional manager] this afternoon and so I'm up at 3:00 a.m. getting my interview done before his interview because I have to do this before his. When I know I've got something to do, then I do it. Somehow, it's always been good for me to get where I'm at today. I don't think I would have done anything differently.

12. With the same budget and time restrictions, what would you have done differently? Nothing.

13. Describe your relationships with the other stakeholders and how they affected your work [author / researcher, Air Force lieutenant colonel, and the pharmaceutical company regional account manager]. They're all very unique characters. All with their special contributions and their special talents and different personalities. The relationship was very good with all of them. And, I learned from every single one of them. They affected my work with their involvement and all of their comments. And, don't ask unless you want an answer and you're ready to act on that answer. And, I learned that too. If you don't want to know, then don't ask! If you ask, then you best pay attention and move forward accordingly.

14. List 3–4 guidelines you could give to future technology companies partnering with an educator of adults to create an Internet-based learning program. The guidelines, and I'm talking from the educator of adults' point of view. I'll speak to that part. If you, as an adult educator, go to work with a technology company, it would be best to not try to run their show. You only have one show and that is the content and the process. The process more than anything. So stick to your guns about the process and let a few other things go because they know just as much as you do about what their business is. So, don't try to run the show. Don't try to tell them how to do their work because they know how to do their work. Give them latitude. Don't be close-minded. Be open-minded to possibilities or you won't let in all the good creativity and the possibilities that can come out of all that wonderful flow of creativity. So be sure and keep your mind open and not your ears closed to new ideas. You have to remember that they're busy people and they're not always on your time frame so be respectful of that. Let them do what they do best.

15. Was there ever a time during your work on this project that you wanted to quit and walk away from it? If so, why? And, if so, how did you stop yourself from quitting? No, there really wasn't a time. And I was the biggest stakeholder of all in this because this was my life and it wasn't just a contract to keep the pay coming in. This is my life's work so I had the biggest stake in it and I was never ... I was disappointed at times and I was tired, and I was kind of depressed about the progress and about stumbles along the way. I had a discussion with [the technology company] kind of chewing it over after the fact especially when it came to the Air Force issues, especially with [the programmer], I would get clarity and get new energy based on us processing each time something would happen—the good and the bad of it, what are the possibilities based on what we just heard. So, I would get energy from the group any time I would feel like I wanted to quit. I'd just *say* anything at all, they would just jump right in and we'd boost each other.

16. Compared to other projects you have been involved in, how would you rate your perceived value of this project on a scale of 1–10 with 1 representing least value and 10 most value. Explain your answer. Well, 10 obviously. It's my life work and it's going to be my doctoral dissertation. It's really how I live my life. It's what it's all about. And, I do live the lessons that I teach and I live the process of learning everyday in my own life with my children and how I coach them and with my communications with my husband and with my job at work. I'm a manager of an education department at a hospital. With my staff, I use all that I know every day and it never fails me! The process never fails me. So, it is absolutely a 10. Because it's kind of a fulfillment of everything I do and everything that I am.

17. Did this project ever seem to drift from a serious vein that should have been more prominent? In other words, were important aspects of this project ever at risk of being lost in the midst of the fun? No. Never. There's never too much fun ... at all. Especially with a project like this. It was like theatre. You know, if you can't have fun, then you lose the energy and the creativity and so we *absolutely* had fun in every possible term. Never, ever, ever ... never too much fun.

18. What other questions do I need to ask that you think would provide important information for this process? I don't think there's additional information other than the fact that it was about the most impactful thing I've ever done in my life, meaning it was all-consuming. It's become a part of who I am. To be able to tell the story of how that happened, how it came to be that I was working as a one-woman company, had a contract with the military to create a piece of software and by-God, I got to pick my own development company and I thought I was just the most fortunate person in the world. I got an education grant, $70,000, from the biggest pharmaceutical company around and I'm just blessed. And I think because I felt that way, I wanted to give it everything I had. I somehow understood, Susan, this is a once-in-a-lifetime opportunity. Don't blow it! I don't care if you're tired, I don't care if it doesn't make any sense right now, just keep working at it, keep talking, keep working, keep problem-solving, keep creating face-to-face meetings and it will happen. And, there's no option to fail. And that's how I looked at it. There was no option to fail. And, I think *that* was the driving force. And, I felt like the Big Toe, as [the lieutenant colonel] called me, he called me the Big Toe, everything had to run through me. And so, the Air Force didn't make a move without me. And [the technology company] didn't make a move without me. And [the pharmaceutical company] didn't make a move without me. It was kind of a grandiose feeling that I was the Big Toe. Never had I been treated so respectfully. That's one thing you can say about the military. And of course I was a client of [the technology company] so I was treated very well in this whole process in a very respectful manner. Perhaps there was once or twice that I felt a little disrespected but I assertively came back and came out feeling like it was a win-win. So, anyway, it was just the most impactful experience in my whole life ... to date! So, there you go.

REGIONAL ACCOUNT MANAGER INTERVIEW

The interview questions and the interviewer questions and comments are in bold.

After the interviewer's introduction on the audiotape but before the interview started, the regional account manager said: At the time, I was regional account manager but now I am the national account manager for [the same pharmaceutical company]. However, a key component of me *going* to a national account manager was Virtual Health Coach. **Really? You want to talk more about that?** Sure. When I was regional account manager, I was on a federal team. It was a new concept that had just been established. And about a year afterwards, when we had the merger with [an earlier pharmaceutical company], we became [the current pharmaceutical company]. And, at that time, I came up for national account manager and because of the types of programs I had been doing like Virtual Health Coach, which was a really new way of working in that federal field, that was really what positioned me and set me apart from the rest of the group in order to get the job as national account manager. That and there were several other projects I worked on that were similar. As a matter of fact, every time I see [the Air Force physician who worked on the Virtual Health Coach project under the lieutenant colonel], I pat him on the back and he pats me on the back because we were responsible for each other's promotions [both laugh] **That's good to know! Thank you for that detail. That's great!**

1. Describe your initial interest in participating in the development of this program. There were a number of things that came together all at the same time. [the Air Force physician] and I had just met. He had just taken his new position there at the MDPR at [the Air Force base]. I had just taken the new position as regional account manager for the federal group and they had just met you at the same time. In our discussions, we were trying to find some common ground where we could really work together to benefit patients in a new way that they had not been used to working with pharmaceutical companies before. And so, when I presented them with a test or the challenge to present to me a number of needs that they felt [pharmaceutical company] could have an interest in and that would be a benefit to the Air Force and a benefit to patients most of all. I gave them that challenge and one of their first responses was the Virtual Health Coach and that was the one that they really seemed most interested in. So, that was how I got interested in it. And, at that time, I didn't have a belief in the world that we'd ever be able to get that through because I had been told by the company to go forth and really work with the customers to try to develop these new relationships but it had really never been tested in the company. Would they really back up something like this that was not product related, had no type of advertising in it but would benefit the three [Air Force, patient, and pharmaceutical company]? **So, have there been other things since then that have been similar initiatives that were unrelated to a product but would be a way to talk with physicians?** Yes. As a matter of fact, because of my success with this one, I got bolder and was able to do a couple of other ones that had major national consequences for, in that case, the VA [Veteran's Administration]. So, I've been able to work the system well. **Good!**

2. Discuss the return on your investment of time, money, or intellectual contribution. It's kind of a challenge with this one because traditionally, people expect a return on investment and a lot of times it's measured in dollars or some type of value. In this particular instance, it was being set up in a way that return on investment could really not be measured with any dollars or potential for a contract or things like that but really the value that I was attaching to it was it was allowing me to build a new environment to create in the minds of the customer a different level of interaction with the pharmaceutical industry, something they had not been accustomed to before. And doing it in such a way that it was going to have a benefit to the customer as well as to the patient. My belief at that time was that we didn't have to have anything attached to a contract or any type of product or anything like that because I really felt that by using this type of system, introducing more people to like the Virtual Health Coach in terms of recognizing that they perhaps had a problem that just by default we would start to see some benefit without any direct intervention. And, I think it's held true. **So, that was the return on investment that you anticipated? What was your return? Did you actually ... If I recall, the packets didn't actually get out like you expected them to get out. What was the end result of all of that? Did it actually happen the way you thought it would?** Not quite the way I thought it would. I was hoping that it would be embraced a little bit more. No fault of the program, but with [the pharmaceutical company]. Right at the end when we were trying to do that is when the merger took place and so the resources that we would have had to introduce it were really not there. The merger of [one pharmaceutical company] with [the other pharmaceutical company, thus forming the new bigger company where the regional account manager then worked and now works]. At that time, there really were no regional account managers, enough of them to go forth and do that. However, we still were very successful with it in terms of being able to have account managers that we *did* have use it and for me personally to introduce it to a number of places. People who we were trying to introduce it to were maybe people you were not thinking about when you were designing it because I know the MDPR [Medical Defense Partnership for Reinvention] was a physician or clinical-based operation and the other arena that was important for this was the pharmaceutical clinics. Most of the major pharmacies *do* some clinics. Like they'll have weight reduction clinics, diabetes clinics, heart failure clinics ... So, we were using it to introduce that as a new tool. **So, is anyone still using it?** As far as I know, they are. **Like who?** I do know that if you check on some of the websites of the major military bases they have a link to Virtual Health Coach on their Internet. I know that in that TriCare region of the Southwest United States, they have asked for us to come in and demo it for them to roll out. **So, you've been involved in that piece of it?** Yeah, I've continued. **Okay, because, I've been getting contacts from people kind of all over asking, What is it? We'd like to have it. How do we get it? I've been referring them to [the programmer] because he's the one who can tell them how

to access it and then we had to work with [a preventionist on the Air Force base] but then he left. They closed that down so we lost our contact person. They sent me on to the Air Force Surgeon General's Office and they didn't know much about it. They just knew they had this thing. So, when I finish the dissertation, which is soon, I'll have a little more energy and time to actually try to jump back in to the military thing. That's what one of my advantages will be that some of my customers *are* the Surgeon Generals. **Ah, then, maybe *you're* the one I should continue talking to. We have new features that allow the tracking of the data, collecting and tracking of the data, and reporting features now. So, in other words, for the person who is responsible for it, who is the sponsor, whether it's the VA [Veteran's Administration] Hospital or whatever, who is putting this out for users will be able to collect data and be able to create reports on-the-fly. You can slice and dice it any way you want. And always know on any date at any time how many users you have, what they have signed up to work on, and what their anticipated barriers are whether it's time, whether it's money or whether it's stress and it will also tell you what their preferred learning style is and how to create the curriculum with the best methodology to deliver the services and it will also help you know what they are planning to do. You can also ... then customize their resource page. And, the resource page will match their action plan. So, they create a behavior change plan that says I'm going to attend a class for quitting smoking and then they hit the next button and the resource page will come up and show them all the available classes. So, the sponsoring facility can feed people into their own programs because not only will they have people who have created a plan, now they'll also be able to get immediately in front of them with the resources that match their plan.**
I think that particularly the Surgeon Generals and consultants to the Surgeon General probably are going to be very interested. I know there are a lot of features of the Virtual Health Coach that lean toward mental health—depression, substance abuse ... I know that now with the war going on, things going on all over the world ... There was an article just the other day about the number of soldiers that kill themselves in Iraq and it's a major issue. They *do* address that at a very high level. And, so a number

of people I get to talk to ... those are issues. So, since we already really did the big work ... **It's already created, you've already invested the money, let's issue the new features.** Right, because we also have the resources. I spent a lot of my time the first year of my new job to build the case to get the resources to increase the federal team. So, we *have* done that. So, we've now got 10 new regional account managers who have all been armed and trained on the Virtual Health Coach. And I've really been on them to get in front of people with this tool. You really don't have to sell anything. Just make them aware ... **It has to be the Internet version to use all these wonderful new features because it will allow us to collect the data. It also has an email function now and they're pre-programmed. [The animated character] will come in, if they opt for it. If someone has created an exercise plan, a plan about their stress or their alcohol, or whatever, and then if they opt for an e-coach, then [the animated character], at whatever time they want, for example at 6 weeks, they'll automatically get an email. [The animated character] will know what they said they will do, how they're going to do it. He'll know what their barriers were and he'll give them a tailored message. So, it's still confidential, they've not reached out to any person but the program knows and will automatically give them a reminder.** Cool. What I'd like to do is continue to remind and maybe help introduce those new features or introduce *you* to introduce those new features to people because the program is just as important now as it was initially. It's even *more* important now because of all the things going on in the world. **It could be tweaked for your needs if you could identify things that you really want in there, we can tweak it for your purposes.** And, maybe I'll be in a position to facilitate. Probably, it'd be more difficult this day and age to take over the funding issues as much as we did at first. Changes in client laws and things like that. When I travel, I now travel with three lawyers. It really makes it difficult. But still, people I have a chance to relate to now, these are all huge issues and any time I've mentioned it to them, it tweaks their interest. We just haven't had the manpower to push it through. So, maybe we can work together to find some ways to push that. **Well, initially, the ROI [return on investment] on this was that you hopefully get people to make behavior changes to improve their health and that's** very hard to measure. Even if someone quits smoking, how do you know they're healthier six months later? But, the additional piece now is that we have ... we can sell people data. In other words, you're getting all this data to help you use your resource dollars very wisely. Instead of the shotgun approach, you'll have the rifle approach. In fact, if no one is planning to exercise and they're working on something else, then don't build a fitness center. Put your money into classes if that's what they say they want, for example. Especially when wellness dollars are at a premium and you don't have a whole lot ... how do you spend them wisely? You don't just throw something out there just because it sounds like a good thing to do. The other key point to be brought up, too, is the data. The most important part to these people is showing outcomes. Not just doing something, but being able to show the value of doing that. And by having the data ... it's always been the missing link. That will be a big help. **And knowing their perceived barriers ... the tangible and the intangible. Emotional barriers, the fear of failure ... is it not being successful in the past, or is it money or time, or lack of opportunity.** One thing that will make it easier this go 'round is ... There used to be seven TriCare regions. And, TriCare regions were really responsible for these types of programs. That's now been narrowed to three TriCare regions. And, there's also a company that won the contract for medical education and training, and patient education and training for TriCare. So, it may be a tool that they can now embrace and use, as well, in a very controlled fashion. And they got the bucks! **Even better!**

3. What are your plans and goals for using the product? For me, more than just being able to talk to physicians, it was one way to find out a little more about the customer, find out what their needs were. So that when we were *in* a position to talk to physicians, we would have a better message that was more in sync with what their needs actually were. That's kind of what we were looking like there. That and being a new team, not knowing a lot a people within the federal sector, it was also a way to introduce ourselves in a non-traditional way. **Not as selling something but giving something.** Right. Not just being there to say, I'll give you this and you can give me some sales. But, it was truly a unique way to create an interest on the part of the pharmacy staff or the medical staff we were working with to show that we're doing things just a little bit different. And it did pay off very well. Excellent. Extremely high profile contacts (little laugh). And again, not tied to anything in specific but just that we were able to demonstrate that we were looking for different ways to do things. It always had to come back to the patient being the main person to benefit from it. Now, even by law, we have to have some type of interest with it, and we do. Because any of the disease states associated with Virtual Health Coach, we have products in. For example, we were talking about smoking cessation. We have a couple of products for smoking cessation. Not everyone has to use ours but if you identify more people, chances are that ... **Your product sales will go up. Throughout the program, one of the options is always, talk to your doctor. Ask your health care specialist. Constantly we are referring people into the health care system.** It turned out to *be* the biggest benefit. It was not the tool itself. For me, it was the process. It was the process of working so close with [the lieutenant colonel], [the Air Force physician] and some of the other support staff. Matter of fact, it's been four years since I first called on [the Air Force base]. I came into the airport about a month ago and someone was screaming across the baggage and it was somebody from [the Air Force base] from that team! That makes me feel good. **It was an impactful time.** Right! I met my objective about learning more about what some of their needs were because working on the project introduced me to ... they actually brought me into another team there, where once a month, they would bring in the whole primary care team to discuss issues and ways to work with [the Air Force physician]. I'm probably the only one in the industry that was able to sit in on ... just to learn. **The happenchance learning was probably great.** Right. **You didn't anticipate ...** Because that way I could go to the meetings I was attending back internally at [the pharmaceutical company] and I could build or present a case on behalf of the customer. So, when I was talking with Product Management, I could get them to think about things they needed to do perhaps different. Enlighten all the way around. It was the process. **That's very interesting. In adult learning, the process becomes more important than the content. Truly. So, you just said that in another way. So, it's interesting.**

4. How does the program fill a void, add value, or accomplish a goal for you? Did it fill a void for you? It did. There was a very vague concept being presented by our department at that time, our Managed Markets division. Very vague in terms of account management style, where you were able to meet with the customer to really present [the pharmaceutical company] as a solutions-oriented company so that you're not just pharmaceuticals but you had more than the drug. You've got the education materials. So we were trying to develop that as a solutions orientation. Really good when your standing in a meeting in Philadelphia and people start talking about that, but had never seen anything concrete that was really like that. **So, ... How do you translate that into what I do everyday?** So, Virtual Health Coach *was* the first out of the box. And, I remember when I presented it for the first time. I had a new pretty impressive boss. Here, I'm asking for a significant chunk of change to get this thing going. I was surprised. At first, there was no rolling of the eyes but just some frustration because there wasn't enough detail. So we went back and got some additional detail. And, another good learning experience was, put 30 pounds of paper on your boss' desk about a week before Christmas ... **I remember that (both laugh). Timing is everything.** Timing is everything. So, another critical lesson learned. And, by doing that, we were able to really demonstrate what the value of the program would be in very general terms and you can get the charitable grant to do that. **Charitable grant?** It's a charitable grant and that's why I have to go through great lengths to make sure that when I'm talking to any of my customers about it, they know they own it, not me. I just help facilitate and when I also introduce this through my regional account managers, to make sure *they* understand it. This isn't tied into anything. This is *theirs*. But it's a good way for you to show that there are other ways for us to work together. And, that's what we've been doing. **And so, that truly is the value, too. It's another way to work with [the pharmaceutical company].**

5. Does the program integrate adult learning principles and computer technology? Absolutely! **So how did we do?** Oh, excellent! You couldn't ask for a better group to work with because the Department of Defense and the VA [Veteran's Administration] are probably the most technical groups you'll find out there in the health care system. As a matter of fact, we used to always kid them when I went over to [the Air Force base] and some of the other bases. I was always envious because they have the biggest computers out there. They're really into it! So, it was the right group. But also where I see, (maybe I'm getting ahead of myself), it really lends itself well to the military because of the deployments. Because, this is now something that's on the Internet. In a forward position, they may not have access to it but certainly when in Kuwait and some of the other places like that where they *do* have Internet access … So, as a tool, it's useful … **And so, it could be used by someone in the desert. And they do get to it. My daughter happens to be involved with a fighter pilot, a friend of my son's who went and was in the first wave over there. And that's one thing that she could count on. He'd get back to do email. He lived in a trailer and had a bath once a week when he was there but he did get to email.** I was just approached by someone. We have another program at [the pharmaceutical company] called [name of program] and it's for all federal pharmacies. It's another one of these types of programs that is basically a charitable grant that's for high-level Surgeon Generals. And we just had the meeting in San Antonio to present the awards. It's the people in the military and the VA across the world who have an opportunity to submit things that they have done. Programs that they have put on that have benefited patients. And, it may have been for medical readiness. There's a variety of criteria. So, we had that presentation. Dr. Bob Arnot from NBC, the physician who was imbedded with the troops. He's a physician and he's a reporter. He was the keynote speaker for this event. We had the 100 top military pharmacists, physicians … There were one or two of the Surgeon Generals in the room and there was very high brass walking around. Because that's the value *they* place on doing these types of things. And so, we were in there and somebody approached me who had just recently come back from the Middle East and caught smoking cessation [in the presentation] and how key it was for smoking cessation, drug abuse and things like that. So I said, have you heard about Virtual Health Coach? **You said that?** I said that with this meeting because, we've got this tool there that's not lending itself to the troops just now but I gave him the information. Because when I had my discussion with some of these higher ups, you know, if you've got this problem and you already have this tool, it could be tweaked to put it in the hands of the people. This guy was really pleading that it was such a significant problem that these people are getting deployed for long periods of time. **What did he say to that?** Forward lines don't have the Internet. But, when they pull back, perhaps ... **Well, they wouldn't have time to do anything like quit smoking when they're on the forward line. They just have to survive.** But what they consider forward line, it's like the pharmacy. It's well away from the actual fighting. So, there are opportunities. **I think they'd be very interested in hearing about the Web-based program ...** There may be an opportunity for us to ... Maybe I could help identify some people to facilitate that happening. **That would be great. I'd just love to do a presentation on what we have now because that's going to be open to the public. But, they aren't going to collect any data. See, but then there's the corporate membership and that's who gets to collect the data and understand the information about the population they're giving it to. That's very different from the individual who gets their printed report and they get their resource page and email.** So, there are opportunities there. I probably took you way off ... **No. This part of me is in school and this part of me is in the business. Because I'm still trying to grow this business and to do something with this ...** I'm enthusiastic about the program and also I'm now responsible for all of the Department of Defense so it's neat for me to be able to know that ... **There's a second version [beyond the CD version], which is so much more because it's Web-based and it collects data and it gives you reports. So you do think it integrates adult learning principles and Internet technology?** Oh absolutely.

6. Are there other appropriate applications for this learning system? If so, what are they? It didn't take me very long to come up with a couple totally unrelated to pharmaceuticals. The one I have a very high level of interest in is preparing for retirement. I actually could use ... I'm seeing a need out there for developing a plan for change for retirement. And, I can even see the tools in my head that you could put together to do that. **So, what are you going to do to retire? How are you going to do that?** Probably like right now! I have an immediate need ... **I think**

Appendix D 279

we're about the same age. So, for me now, I work so hard and put so much into my job and career, I haven't given a whole lot of thought to what I would do when I retire. I was presented with an opportunity for early retirement [little laugh] six months ago and so it started me thinking. I really need to spend some time thinking about what I want to do and I can think of using a tool that would help me do a review of where I've been and what are my strengths, what do I really care about and do an analysis there and start to develop opportunities from that. Right now, we're doing it by the seat of our pants because my wife and I are moving to a retirement community, an active adult community. And that's why it's on the top of my head because I see people are moving into this ... Actually it's a new place down there ... They're going to have 6,000 homes. More and more of the people I met ... Some know they want to play golf all the time and some don't. **Another?** Return to the work force. Right now, my daughter would need to use it, for example. Right now she's bringing up the kids. At some point, she may want to return to the work force. You see this all the time. **Or a spouse suddenly loses his or her job.** Absolutely. Or you want to return to the workforce. And unless you spend some time knowing where your strengths and weaknesses are, you could use a tool like this to help that ... to really analyze where your strengths lie. **And create a plan. What do you do first? And how do you get around those barriers that you expect to get in the way. Very good. Anything else?** One more! Career development. Career or personal development. Not medical development. I'm talking more along the lines of ... You know, I've been in enough management positions now that I know there're people who just don't have a clue how to relate to other people. They may be top-notch scientists but they just *do* not have a clue. It's not to say that can't be changed. It's a whole concept of first identifying steps necessary to do it. And, I spend a lot of time on the Internet and I've never seen anything again like Virtual Health Coach, that type of concept. **I haven't either. And I've spent a lot of time looking. Very good ideas!** So, I came up with that one because I'm going down to Texas and I want to collaborate with you and do that. **I have a friend who has a business consulting company and he is a consultant for small businesses and he and I have been talking a long time about**

an entrepreneurial coach so, if you're going to be an entrepreneur, what do you need to know to do that? Intentional learning. Because a lot of people go about it willy-nilly and don't do the things you need to and you make mistakes and there's a lot you need to know. And, he's got it all figured out. He's got it done. It's just that the content needs to be put in the process. I also thought of a GED coach. What steps do you need to take to accomplish that? Financial, also. A financial coach. There are a lot of people in debt who don't even know where to start to get out of it. The military was very interested in that ... the financial coach. Because they have a lot of young people who've gone way over board. The military owns their people so if you have a person in the military who has a lot of debt, it becomes a liability for the military. The process is done. The reason why I used health coaching as the content was because that's what I knew a lot about. But, it's very easy to take a different curriculum and apply it to that process. The concept is there ... the Internet is there. **Actually, we've done seven in one here. So, to just do financial or just do career, personal development, retirement ... I love that. With the baby boomers. My husband and I are faced with the same thing and we're trying to figure it out all by ourselves. Every time you meet with a financial planner, they try to sell you a product. This is not a product.** No, this is a process. And more and more what you see is more and more people not ready to retire. **And that goes back to Prochaska [stages of change]. Readiness to change. Learn about** *that* **first of all and then you understand that, well, then, if I'm not ready to do** *that***, what am I ready to do? What am I willing to work on that will lead me down that track so that I** *will* **be ready.**

Is there anything else you'd like to say that I haven't asked a question around? I just want to congratulate you because the program *does* have tremendous value. And, I think that we've only just scratched the surface, even with the DoD [Department of Defense]. Even with version one ... But they're constantly undergoing change and then you throw in a few terrorist attacks and a war and it makes it harder but I wouldn't let that be a deterrent because those very events make the program even more important. Depression is much more a major player right now and when I'm talking about the military, I'm not talking about just GI Joe, I'm talking about the entire family. It's huge. In fact, I've had some documentation, some of the major military bases look at the communities surrounding them ... the incidence of depression has increased. And, being in the military, having depression, they sometimes don't want to go to a base physician. And everything else that goes along with the depression. Like smoking. **Well, sure. They do have to pay for all of that. The effects of all that.** It's very, very important. **Well, they [the Department of Defense] already own it, they already own version one. It's just knowing how to use it. Again, it would be just an upgrade. We wouldn't give it to them but it certainly wouldn't be like a brand new ...** Well, I'll put that on my to-do list, to see who we can interact with. There are some significant meetings coming up. **And, I would be happy to talk with them about any customization that we could do to really zero in on what they're finding to be of concern.** I would like to see it taken to the level of Washington. Someone with more clout that we can give it to. Be rolled out and stick. The avenue to look at is the VA. A lot of times, we don't think of the VA as being Internet savvy but times are changing. **Everyday things are changing and you can't hardly do anything anymore without the computer.** The face of the VA system is not that much different from the Department of Defense. The World War Two-ers have pretty much died off and now we're talking about the younger folks about my age that are from Vietnam that are really populating the ... So, if there was ever ... **And the best part is that it's going to give them solutions. Help them through that process of deciding to do something, and then making a plan for how to do it, and then resources. So, all in one fowl swoop. It will lead people directly to resources.** The VA has major needs and they're increasing. There's a greater population going into the VA with all the wars going on, again, that's likely to increase. They need expensive treatments including pharmacy and all other things are exceedingly high. And, they have a fixed budget. So, they have to find ways to spend money wisely and they have to do a good job of motivating the patients that go there. And, to a good extent, I think they understand that. **And, it *does* reach**

those hard-to-reach people. Those who would not come out otherwise to attend a program or see a doctor. They can do it at 2:00 in the morning in the privacy of their own home. Low risk. I've had some discussions with the top mental health people at the VA on the concept. I don't have any money to do it but there is interest at the VA for this type of thing. **So, we'll stay in touch about that.**

APPENDIX E

Author / Researcher's Virtual Health Coach Implementation Kit Letter

August 19, 2001

To all those in receipt of the Virtual Health Coach[SM] implementation kits, As you plan for the implementation of the Virtual Health Coach[SM], a product of For A Change, LLC, let it be known that the military services (Air Force, Army, Coast Guard, Marines, and Navy) have unlimited reproduction, distribution, and use rights to the Virtual Health Coach[SM] (both CD and Web versions) and the same rights to the accompanying Virtual Health Coach[SM] promotional materials (brochures, letters, posters, CD cover, etc.) within the military health care system without paying licensing and royalty fees.

Let it also be known that the above military services have no rights to reproduce, distribute, or use the Virtual Health Coach[SM] or its accompanying promotional materials outside the military health care system without paying licensing and royalty fees.

Respectfully,
Susan Isenberg
President
For A Change, LLC
P.O. Box 372009
St. Louis, Missouri 63137
Phone
Fax (314) 972-7914
s_isenberg@forachange.com

APPENDIX F

MILITARY SURVEYS ON ANIMATION AND VOICE OF VIRTUAL HEALTH COACH CHARACTER

Virtual Health Coach Focus Group

Please rate (circle a number 1-7) and comment on the following from an "audience" (i.e., person being "coached") perspective, NOT from a technical perspective.

Animation:

1　2　3　4　5　6　(7)
Poor　　　Average　　　Excellent

Comments: Entertaining, Clean, Clear

Voice:

1　2　3　4　5　6　(7)
Poor　　　Average　　　Excellent

Comments: Clear, Clean

Combined animation and voice:

1　2　3　4　5　6　(7)
Poor　　　Average　　　Excellent

Comments: Entertaining

Overall impression of the "virtual" coach (i.e., the talking whistle):

1　2　3　4　5　6　(7)
Poor　　　Average　　　Excellent

Comments: Very talented people created this.

Appendix F

Virtual Health Coach Focus Group

Please rate (circle a number 1-7) and comment on the following from an "audience" (i.e., person being "coached") perspective, NOT from a technical perspective.

Animation:

1　2　3　4　5　(6)　7
Poor　　　Average　　　Excellent

Comments: Well coordinated & appropriate for the voice text.

Voice:

1　(2)　3　4　5　6　7
Poor　　　Average　　　Excellent

Comments: Don't like the Brooklyn accent.

Combined animation and voice:

1　2　3　4　(5)　6　7
Poor　　　Average　　　Excellent

Comments: Somewhat distracting with all the hand movements

Overall impression of the "virtual" coach (i.e., the talking whistle):

1　2　(3)　4　5　6　7
Poor　　　Average　　　Excellent

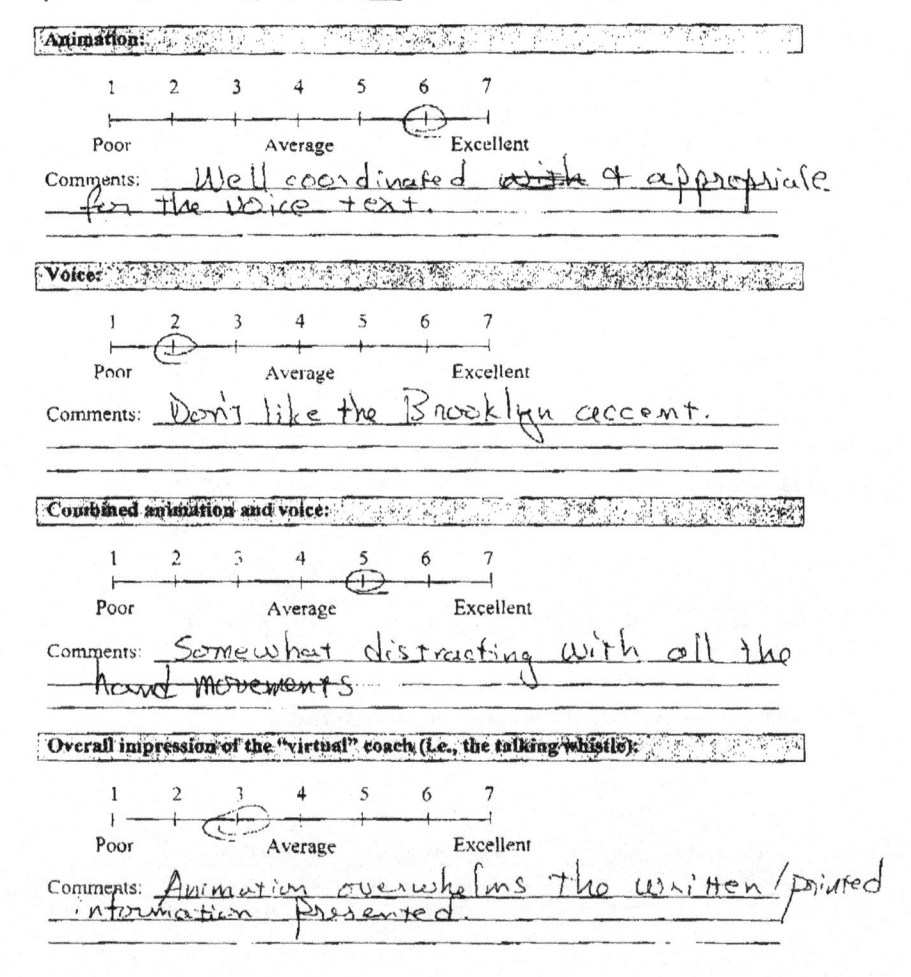

Comments: Animation overwhelms the written/printed information presented.

Virtual Health Coach Focus Group

Please rate (circle a number 1-7) and comment on the following from an "audience" (i.e., person being "coached") perspective, NOT from a technical perspective.

Animation:

1 2 3 4 5 ⑥ 7
Poor   Average   Excellent

Comments: Overall - Quite well done

Voice:

1 ② 3 4 5 6 7
Poor   Average   Excellent

Comments: Do they have a "midwest" or accent-neutral version?

Combined animation and voice:

1 2 ③ 4 5 6 7
Poor   Average   Excellent

Comments: That "Snotty New Yorker" voice is distracting

Overall impression of the "virtual" coach (i.e., the talking whistle):

1 2 ③ 4 5 6 7
Poor   Average   Excellent

Comments: Good Idea & approach! Execution is too cutesy.

Virtual Health Coach Focus Group

Please rate (circle a number 1-7) and comment on the following from an "audience" (i.e., person being "coached") perspective, NOT from a technical perspective.

Animation:

1 (2) 3 4 5 6 7
Poor   Average   Excellent

Comments: _Animation is distracting_

Voice:

1 (2) 3 4 5 6 7
Poor   Average   Excellent

Comments: _Voice is too regional_

Combined animation and voice:

1 (2) 3 4 5 6 7
Poor   Average   Excellent

Comments: _____

Overall impression of the "virtual" coach (i.e., the talking whistle):

1 (2) 3 4 5 6 7
Poor   Average   Excellent

Comments: _I don't like the and the forth_

Virtual Health Coach Focus Group

Please rate (circle a number 1-7) and comment on the following from an "audience" (i.e., person being "coached") perspective, NOT from a technical perspective.

Animation:

1   2   3   4   5   (6)   7
Poor   Average   Excellent

Comments: No problem with animation. Vivid, vivacious, entertaining.

Voice:

1   2   3   (4)   5   6   7
Poor   Average   Excellent

Comments: Extremely cheery. Does not perhaps convey empathy with how hard the changes can be. Quit smoking and having a constantly cheery thing like that would have made me want to put a brick through my computer.

Combined animation and voice:

1   2   3   4   (5)   6   7
Poor   Average   Excellent

Comments: It works technically, but is somewhat insincere.

Overall impression of the "virtual" coach (i.e., the talking whistle):

1   2   3   (4)   5   6   7
Poor   Average   Excellent

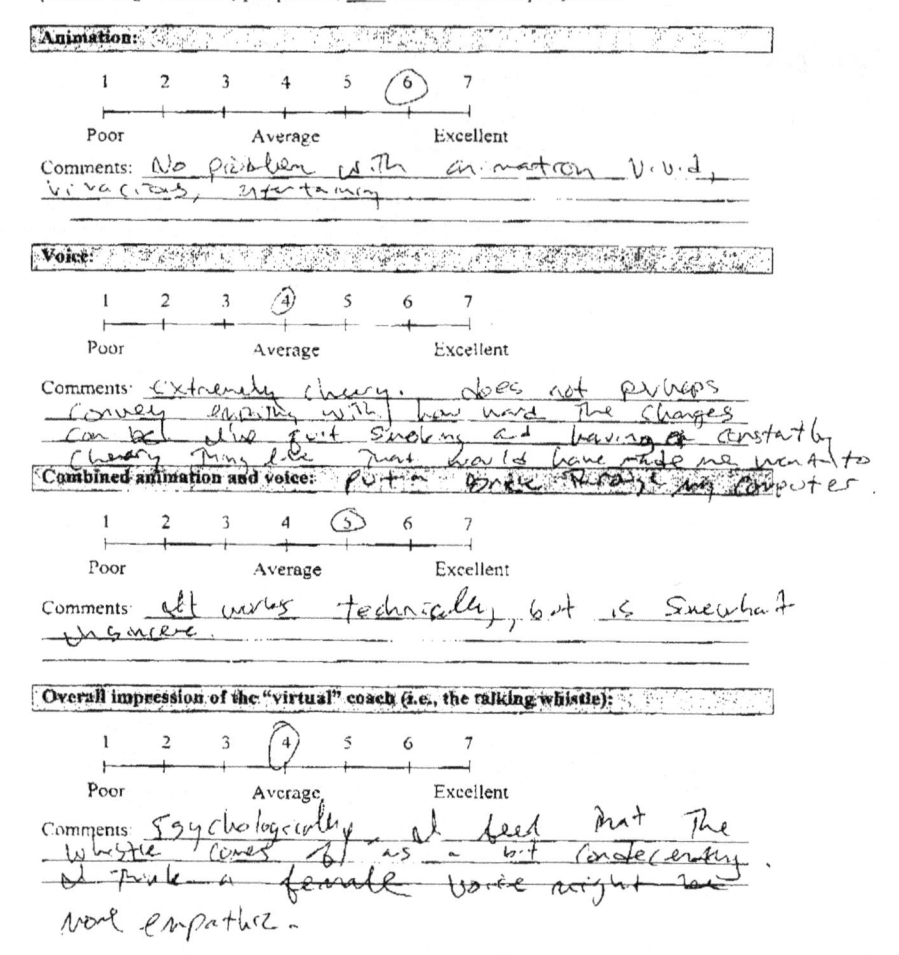

Comments: Psychologically, I feel that the whistle comes off as a bit condescending. I think a female voice might be more empathic.

Virtual Health Coach Focus Group

Please rate (circle a number 1-7) and comment on the following from an "audience" (i.e., person being "coached") perspective, NOT from a technical perspective.

Animation:

1   2   ③   4   5   6   7
Poor   Average   Excellent

Comments: What is the little guy supposed to be? Doesn't look like a whistle

Voice:

1   2   ③   4   5   6   7
Poor   Average   Excellent

Comments: He's from Jersey — which is annoying."

Combined animation and voice:

1   ②   3   4   5   6   7
Poor   Average   Excellent

Comments: Good idea, don't care for the presentation

Overall impression of the "virtual" coach (i.e., the talking whistle):

1   ②   3   4   5   6   7
Poor   Average   Excellent

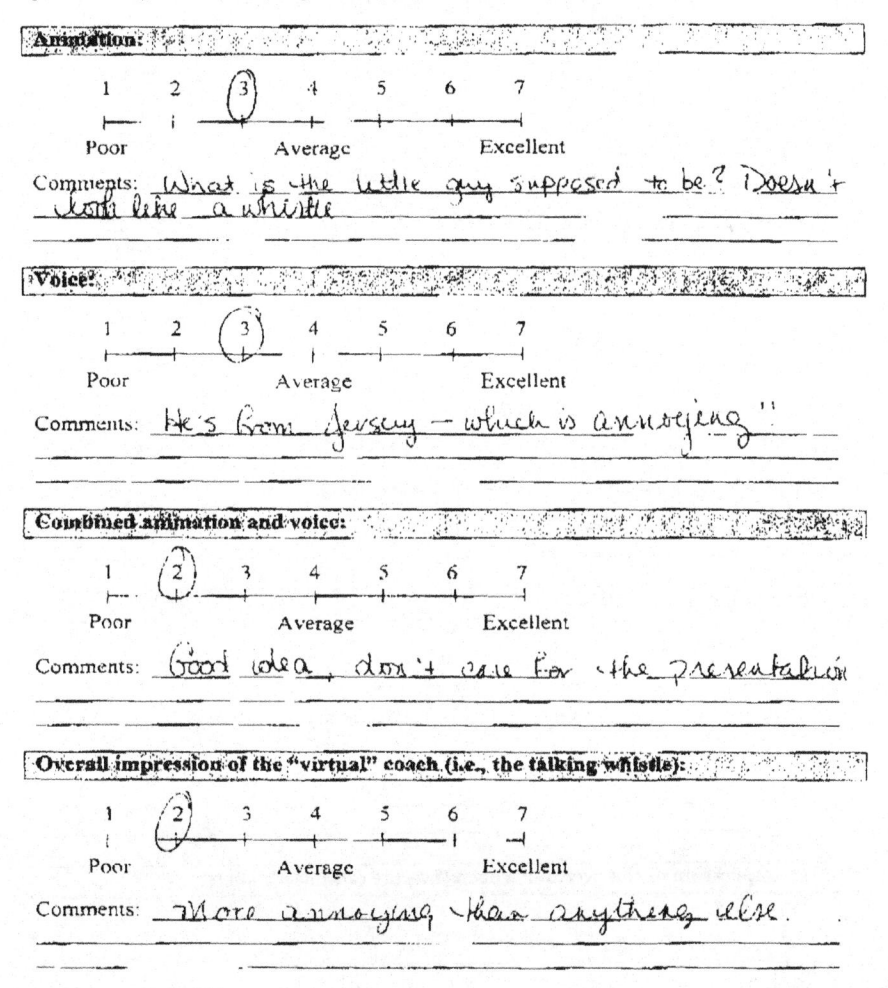

Comments: More annoying than anything else.

Virtual Health Coach Focus Group

Please rate (circle a number 1-7) and comment on the following from an "audience" (i.e., person being "coached") perspective, NOT from a technical perspective.

Animation:

1   2   3   4   ⑤   6   7
Poor   Average   Excellent

Comments: _cute --- why a whistle? looks like a Vaudeville character in "blackface" with a Bronx accent_

Voice:

1   2   3   4   ⑤   6   7
Poor   Average   Excellent

Comments: _enthusiastic --- why the Bronx accent?_

Combined animation and voice:

1   2   3   ④   5   6   7
Poor   Average   Excellent

Comments: _____

Overall impression of the "virtual" coach (i.e., the talking whistle):

1   2   3   ④   5   6   7
Poor   Average   Excellent

Comments: _not sure the animation adds to the presentation aside from being "cute"_

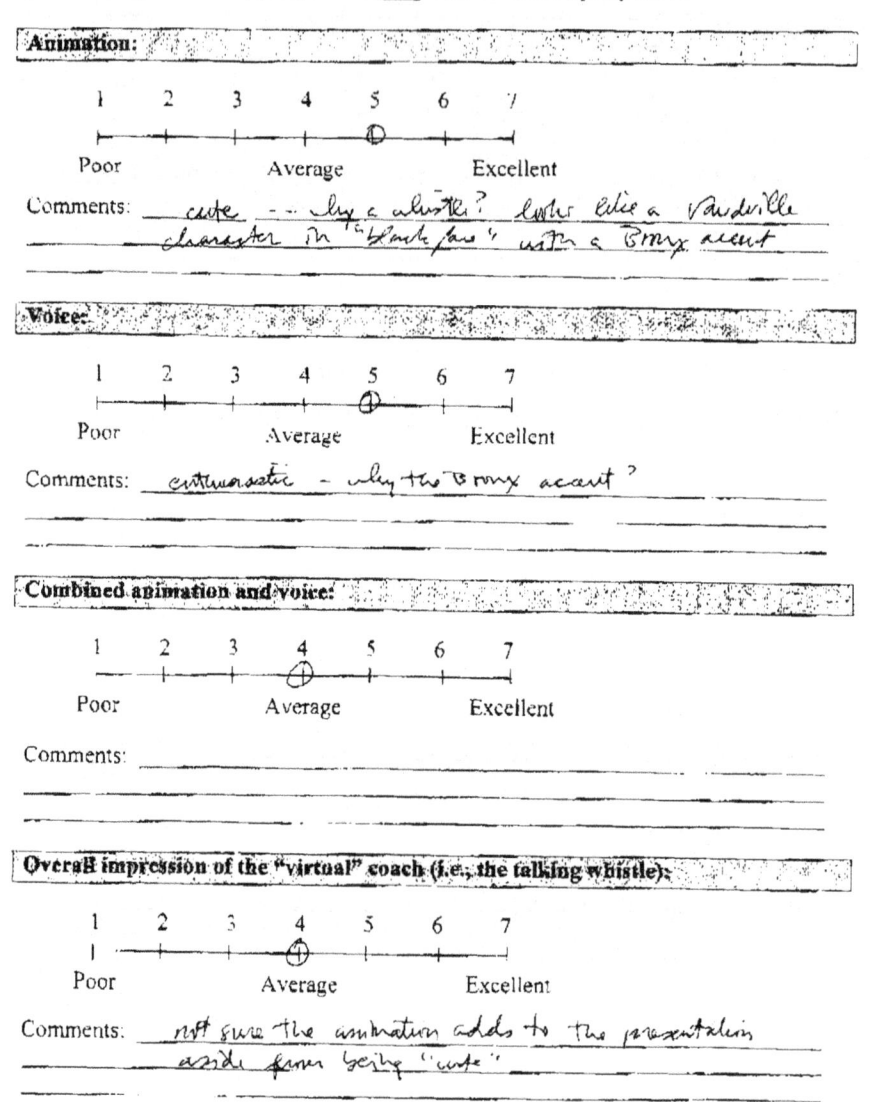

Appendix F

Virtual Health Coach Focus Group

Please rate (circle a number 1-7) and comment on the following from an "audience" (i.e., person being "coached") perspective, NOT from a technical perspective.

Animation:

```
1    2    3    4    5    6    7
|----|----|----Ⓐ----|----|----|
Poor      Average        Excellent
```

Comments: _The "floating hands" were distracting to me — they didn't always seem in sequence_

Voice:

```
1    2    3    4    5    6    7
|----|----|----|----|----|----|
Poor      Average        Excellent
```

Comments: _Sounds like a gay guy from the East Coast — I think to appeal to a wide population — No accent + a definite male or female voice would be better. I couldn't listen to this long_

Combined animation and voice:

```
1    2    3    4    5    6    7
|----|----|----Ⓐ----|----|----|
Poor      Average        Excellent
```

Comments: _____

Overall impression of the "virtual" coach (i.e., the talking whistle):

```
1    2    3    4    5    6    7
|----|----|----|-✓--|----|----|
Poor      Average        Excellent
```

Comments: _It's ok but the voice is so irritating to me — I lost my attention sometimes._

Appendix F

Virtual Health Coach Focus Group

Please rate (circle a number 1-7) and comment on the following from an "audience" (i.e., person being "coached") perspective, NOT from a technical perspective.

Animation:

1   2   3   4   5   (6)   7

Poor   Average   Excellent

Comments: I think it is a cute animation. I think that it is a whistle and appears friendly and excited. I do not find it annoying @ all

Voice:

1   2   3   4   (5)   6   7

Poor   Average   Excellent

Comments: The voice is very understandable, but it does have a strong "New York" accent. Some others might find it difficult to understand

Combined animation and voice:

1   2   3   4   5   (6)   7

Poor   Average   Excellent

Comments: The whistle talks when the voice does. ☺

Overall impression of the "virtual" coach (i.e., the talking whistle):

1   2   3   4   5   (6)   7

Poor   Average   Excellent

Comments: I like it and find it interesting and exciting

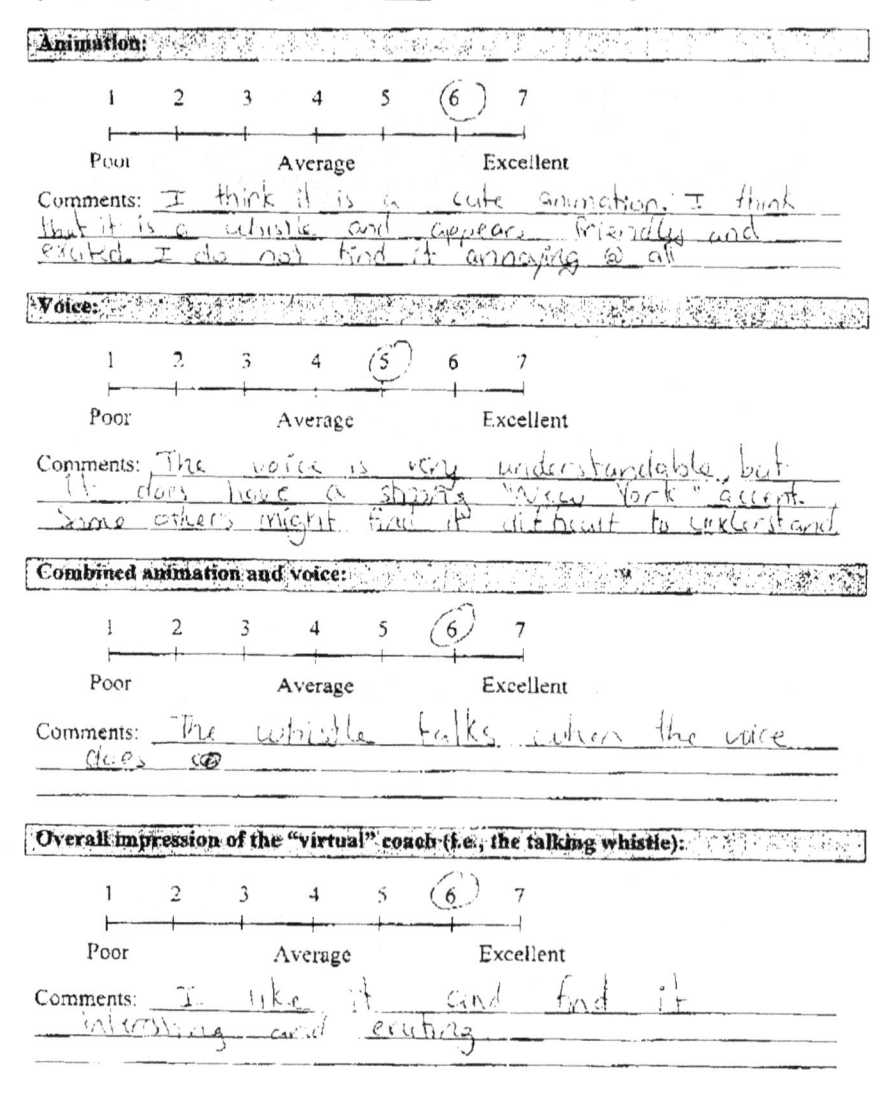

Appendix F 293

Virtual Health Coach Focus Group

Please rate (circle a number 1-7) and comment on the following from an "audience" (i.e., person being "coached") perspective, NOT from a technical perspective.

Animation:

1   2   3   4   ⑤   6   7

Poor   Average   Excellent

Comments: animation character does not well with voice

Voice:

1   2   3   4   ⑤   6   7

Poor   Average   Excellent

Comments: _____

Combined animation and voice:

1   2   3   4   5   ⑥   7

Poor   Average   Excellent

Comments: Good combination implementation

Overall impression of the "virtual" coach (i.e., the talking whistle):

1   2   3   4   ⑤   6   7

Poor   Average   Excellent

Comments: _____

APPENDIX G

Example Provider and Patient Letters in Virtual Health Coach Implementation Kits

Virtual Health Coach

Example Provider Letter

Note: The letter below may be used with your modifications. The idea is for the medical facility leadership or a wellness professional to send the letter to providers along with a copy of the virtual health coach (1) or guidance on how to use the web version if available. The purpose is to enlist their support in using the Virtual Heath Coach with their patients with health risks.

November 15, 2001

Dear Doctor,

Please take a moment to consider how much patients' lifestyle influences their general health. There is little your patients can do about environmental and hereditary health risks. There is, however, much they can do about lifestyle induced health risks. Excellent intervention programs are readily available at health and wellness centers and in the community. Helping your patient to work through barriers that might keep them from entering or completing an intervention program and developing a plan of action many times requires more time than you have available. This "health coaching" step has been found to significantly influence the outcome of intervention.

Appendix G 295

The large number of your patients with modifiable health risks makes it unlikely that you or health and wellness staff can provide traditional health coaching to each individual, preparing them for an intervention program. While maintaining other key health promotion programs, even though individual health coaching could significantly lower health risks and annual health care dollars.

To help you in managing your patient's health risks, the Medical Defense Partnership for Reinvention, a DoD Health Affairs unit, in partnership with Susan Isenberg, MEd. RN. has developed a computer multimedia interactive "virtual" health coach program available on a compact disk. This program leads your patients through a series of steps, based on adult education concepts, resulting in a plan of action. The cost of finished CDs and CD jackets (less than $1.00 each when purchased in quantities of 5,000 or more) is affordable for clinic health care delivery team members and base wellness programs to give each beneficiary with identified multiple health risks their own CD, which could include a customized package insert listing locally available intervention programs along with pertinent contact information.

You are being provided a master copy of the finished CD and an Internet web version for unlimited, no licensing fee reproduction and distribution. DoD has unlimited rights to the program for military healthcare beneficiaries and owns the program computer code. As a result, additional copies of the CD can be purchased directly by your organization from Expressive Tek. www.expressivetek.com or any company of your choosing. A separate CD in the virtual health coach kit contains a printable format for the patient brochure and a patient letter that can be modified as you choose as well as the installation information for the Internet web version.

We hope this new prevention tool will be of use to you in continuing to deliver the high quality health care we know military medicine provides.

Yours truly,

REFERENCES

Ardell, D. (2003). The other end of nutrition: Why high fiber diets are so important. *Seek Wellness*. Retrieved October 29, 2006 from http://www.seekwellness/reports/2003-05-14.html

Agarwal, R., & Day, E. (1998, Spring). The impact of the Internet on economic education. *Journal of Economic Education, 29*(2), 99–109.

Arlin, P. K. (1975). Cognitive development in adulthood: A fifth stage? *Development Psychology, 5*, 602–606.

Ausubel, D. (1967). A cognitive structure theory of school learning. In L. Siegel (Ed.), *Instruction: Some contemporary viewpoints*. San Francisco: Chandler.

———. (1968). *Educational psychology: A cognitive view*. New York: Holt, Rinehart & Winston.

Baumgartner, L. M. (2001, Spring). An update on transformational learning. In S. B. Merrium (Ed.), *New directions for adult and continuing education: The new update on adult learning theory* (No. 89, pp. 15–24). San Francisco: Jossey-Bass.

Bear, J. H. (2004). *Desktop publishing—Color meanings: Color meanings and colors that go together*. Retrieved October 7, 2004, from http://desktoppub.about.com/cs/color/a/symbolism_2.html

Beck, H. (2006, February). The role of ontologies in e-learning. *Educational Technology, 46*(1), 32–38.

Becker, S. P. (1977, December). Competency analysis: Looking at attitudes and interests as well as technical job skills. *Training HRD*, 21–22.

Beckhard, R. (1997). *Agent of change: My life, my practice*. San Francisco: Jossey-Bass.

Bier, M., Gallo, M., Nucklos, S., Sherblom, S., & Pennick, M. (2001). *Personal empowerment in the study of home Internet use by low-income families*. Retrieved March 20, 2001, from http://www2.educ.ksu.edu/Projects/JRCE/v28-5/Bier/article/textonly.html

Billington, D. (2000). *The adult learner in higher education and the workplace: Seven characteristics of highly effective adult learning programs*. Retrieved June 20, 2000, from http://www.umsl.edu/~henschke/henschke/seven_characteristics_of_highly_effective_adult_learning_programs.pdf

Bogdan, R. C., & Biklen, S. K. (1998). *Qualitative research for education: An introduction to theory and methods* (3rd ed.). London: Ally and Bacon.

Brookfield, S. (1984, Summer). The contribution of Eduard Lindeman to the development of theory and philosophy in adult education. *Adult Education Quarterly, 34*(4), 185–196.

———. (1986). *Understanding and facilitating adult learning: A comprehensive analysis of principles and effective practices.* San Francisco: Jossey-Bass.

Bruner, J. (1990). *Acts of meaning.* Cambridge, MA: Harvard University Press.

Bullen, M. (n.d.). *Andragogy and university distance education.* Retrieved January 18, 2003, from http://www2.cstudies.ubc.ca/~bullen/bullen1.html

Carlson, R. (1999, Spring). *Malcolm Knowles: Apostle of andragogy. Vitae Scholasticae,* 8:1.

Carr-Chellman, A. (Ed.). (2005). *Global perspectives on e-learning: Rhetoric and reality.* Thousand Oaks, CA: Sage, 194.

Casella, R. (1997). *Popular education and pedagogy in everyday life: The nature of educational travel in the Americas.* Unpublished doctoral dissertation, Syracuse University.

Casper, K. (1996). *Thoughts on life, liberty, and the pursuit of happiness.* Retrieved January 28, 2003, from http://www.freelaunch.com/essays/libery.html

Cavalier, J., & Klein, J. (1998). Effects of cooperative versus individual learning and orienting activities during computer-based instruction. *Educational Technology Research & Training, 46*(1), 5–17.

Chapnick, S., & Meloy, J. (2005). *Renaissance e-learning: Creating dramatic and unconventional learning experiences.* San Francisco: Pfeiffer.

Chelimsky, E. (1987). The politics of program evaluation. *Society, 25*(1), 24–32.

Claywell, L. G. (2003). *The lived experience of licensed practical nurse (LPN) to registered nurse (RN) transition.* Unpublished doctoral dissertation, University of Missouri, St Louis, MO.

Columbia Electronic Encyclopedia. (2000). Columbia University Press. *Comenius, John Amos.* Retrieved April 27, 2003, from http://www.infoplease.com/ce6/people/A0813016.html

Cooper, M., & Henschke, J. (2003, February 27–March 2). Andragogy: The international foundation for its research, theory and practice linkage and HRD. In S. A. Lynham & T. M. Egan (Eds.), *Academy of Human Resource Development AHRD: Vol. 1. 2003 Conference Proceedings* (pp. 427–434). Bowling Green, OH: Bowling Green State University.

Cooper, M., Henschke, J., & Isaac, P. (2003, March 13). Conversations in teaching and technology. Andragogy: In teaching adults and non-traditional students. *The art and science of helping adults learn.* St Louis, MO: University of Missouri.

Coruthers, J. M. (2005). American Lung Association Launches Freedom From Smoking Online. *The New York Times*. Retrieved May 5, 2005, from www.nytimes.com/ads/marketing/smoking/pg12.html

Creswell, J. W. (1998). *Qualitative inquiry and research design: Choosing among five traditions*. Thousand Oaks, CA: Sage.

Csikszentmihalyi, M. (1996). *Creativity: Flow and the psychology of discovery and invention*. New York: Harper Collins.

Cuban, L. (1993, Winter). Computers meet classroom: Classroom wins. *Teachers College Record*, 95(2), 185–210.

Delors, J., & The International Commission on Education for the Twenty-first Century. (1998). *Learning: The treasure within* (2nd ed.). Paris: UNESCO.

Denzin, N. K., & Lincoln, Y. S. (1994). *Handbook of qualitative research* (2nd ed.). Thousand Oaks, CA: Sage.

Deshler, D., & Hagan, N. (1989). New educational technologies for the future. In S. B. Merriam & Pm M. Cunningham (Eds.), *Handbook of adult and continuing education* (pp. 147–167). San Francisco: Jossey-Bass.

Elias, J., & Merriam, S. (1980). *Philosophical foundations of adult education*. Malabar, FL: Krieger.

English, F. W. (2000, October). A critical appraisal of Sara Lawrence—Lightfoot's Portraiture as a method of educational research. *ER Online*, 29(7). Retrieved March 16, 2004, from http://www.aera.net/pubs/er/arts/29-07/englis07.html

Ermath, M. (1978). *Wilhelm Dilthey: The critique of historical reason*. Chicago: University of Chicago Press.

Ethnographic Research, Inc. (2002). *Ethnography: What's going on?* Retrieved September 22, 2002, from http://www.ethnographic-research.com/research.html

Evers, K. E. (2006, March/April). Practical information to make programs more effective. *The Art of Health Promotion in the American Journal of HealthPromotion*, 20(4), 1–7.

Field, J. (1997). The adult learner as listener, viewer and cybersurfer. *Electronic pathways: Adult learning and the new communication technologies* (Report No. ISBN-1-86201-008-0). Leicester, England: National Institute of Adult Continuing Education (ERIC Document Reproduction Service No. ED423439).

Fox, S. (2005a, October 5). *Digital divisions*. Washington, DC. Pew Internet and American Life Project. Retrieved June 25, 2006, from http://www.pewinternet.org/pdfs/PIP_Digital_Divisions_Oct_5_2005.pdf

Fox, S. (2005b, May 17). *Health information online.* Washington, DC. Pew Internet and American Life Project. Retrieved June 25, 2006, from http://www.pewinternet.org/pdfs/PIP_Healthtopics_May05.pdf

Fraley, G. (2003). *David C. Morrison: Creativity and innovation.* Retrieved June 20, 2003, from http://www.greggfraley.com/David%20C.%20Morrison.html

Freire, P. (1973). *Education for critical consciousness* (English language edition). New York: The Seabury Press.

Galbraith, M. (Ed.). (1991). *Facilitating adult learning: a transactional process.* Malabar, FL: Krieger.

Gay, L. R. (1996). *Education research: Competencies for analysis and application* (5th ed.). Upper Saddle River, NJ: Prentice Hall.

Glaser, B. G., & Strauss, A. L. (1967). *The discovery of grounded theory: Strategies for qualitative research.* Chicago: Aldine.

Henschke, J. A. (1987). Preparing non-experienced teachers of adults: Research issues. In J. Levine (Ed.), *Proceedings of the 6th Annual Midwest Research-to-Practice Conference in Adult, Community and Continuing Education, 64–68.* East Lansing, MI: Michigan State University.

——— (1998, Spring). Modeling the preparation of adult educators. *Adult Learning,* 11–13.

Henschke, J. A., & Cooper, M. K. (2003, November). *An update on andragogy: The international foundation for its research, theory and practice linkage in adult education and human resource development.* Paper presented at the Commission of Professors of Adult Education International Conference, Detroit, MI.

HIPAA Compliance Regulation Training. (2002). *HIPAA compliance regulation training.* Retrieved July 14, 2004, from http://www.hipaacomplianceregulationtraining.com/hipaa-info.html

Hornbeck, D. (1991). Technology and students at risk of school failure. In A. Sheekey (Ed.), *Education Policy and Telecommunications Technologies.* Washington, DC: U.S. Department of Educational Research and Improvement, 1–2.

Hultgren, F. H. (1989). Introduction to interpretive inquiry. In F. Hultgren & D. L. Coomer (Eds.), *Alternative modes of inquiry in home economics research.* Peoria, IL: Glencoe.

Isenberg, S., & Titus, T. (1999, September 22–24). The impact of the Internet on research-to-practice in adult, continuing, extension, and community education. *Proceedings of the 18th Annual Midwest Research-to-Practice Conference, St Louis, Missouri,* CD Rom.

James, W. B., & Galbraith, M. W. (1985, January). Perceptual learning styles: Implications and techniques for the practitioner. *Lifelong Learning, 8*(4), 20–23.

Jia Qi, J. (2005). The gap between e-learning availability and e-learning industry development in Taiwan. In A. Carr-Chellman (Ed.), *Global perspectives on e-learning: Rhetoric and reality* (pp. 89–100). Thousand Oaks, CA: Sage.

Kidd, R. (1982). In Introduction to A. Tough. *Intentional changes.* Chicago: Follett.

Knowles, M. S. (1973). *The adult learner: A neglected species.* Houston, TX: Gulf.

———. (1975). *Self-directed learning: for learners and teachers.* Chicago: Follett Publishing Company.

———. (1980). *The modern practice of adult education.* Englewood Cliffs, NJ: Cambridge.

———. (1995, November). Designs for adult learning: Practical resources, exercises, and course outlines from the father of adult learning. *American Society for Training & Development Handbook.* New York: McGraw-Hill.

———. (1996). Adult learning. In Craig, R. L. (Ed.). *ASTD training & development handbook: A guide to Human Resource Development, Fourth Edition.* (pp. 253–265). New York: McGraw-Hill.

Knowles, M. S., & Associates. (1984). *Andragogy in action: Applying modern principles of adult education.* San Francisco: Jossey-Bass.

Knowles, M. S., Holton, E. F., & Swanson, R. A. (1998). *The adult learner* (5th ed.). Houston, TX: Gulf.

Kouzes, J. M., & Posner, B. Z. (1993). *Credibility: How leaders gain and lose it, why people demand it.* San Francisco: Jossey-Bass.

Kraut, R., Patterson, M., Lundmark, V., Kiesler, T., Mukopadhyay, & Scherlis, W. (1998, September). Internet paradox: A social technology that reduces social involvement and psychological well-being? *American Psychologist, 53*(9), 1017–1031.

Latchem, C. (2005). Towards borderless virtual learning in higher education. In A. Carr-Chellman (Ed.), *Global perspectives on e-learning: Rhetoric and reality* (pp. 179–197). Thousand Oaks, CA: Sage.

LeDoux, J. (2002). *Synaptic self: How our brains become who we are.* New York: Penguin.

Lewin, K. (1948). *Resolving social conflicts: Selected theoretical papers.* In D. Cartwright (Ed.), New York: Harper & Row.

———. (1951). *Field theory in social science*: Selected theoretical papers. In D. Cartwright (Ed.), New York: Harper & Row.

Lindeman, E. C. (1961). *The meaning of adult education.* Montreal: Harvest House (originally published in 1926).

Long, H. (1983). *Adult learning: Research and practice.* New York: Cambridge.

LoveToKnow Corp. (2002a). The method and doctrine of Socrates. *Socrates—The life of Socrates.* Retrieved August 1, 2003, from http://www.2020site.org/socrates/method.html

———. (2002b). The socratics (after Socrates). *Socrates—The life of Socrates.* Retrieved August 1, 2003, from http://www.2020site.org/socrates/method.html

MacKeracher, D. (1996). *Making sense of adult learning.* Toronto: Culture Concept Books.

Marotta, P. (1999, April). Power the quest. *Women of wisdom: Strategic planning for women to maximize success.* Retrieved October 8, 2004, from http://www.womenofwisdom.com/thequest.html

Mayo, N., Kajs, L., & Tanguma, J. (2005, September). Longitudinal study of technology training to prepare future teachers. *Educational Research Quarterly, 29*(1), 3–14.

McBride, J. (2003). U. Va. Career office changes name. *Inside UVA Online.* University of Virginia. Retrieved February 8, 2003, from http://www.virginia.edu/insideuva/2000/03/career.html

McLagan, P. (1978). *Helping others learn.* Reading, MA: Addison-Wesley.

Merrill, H. S. (2006). Best practices for online facilitation. *Adult Learning, 14*(2), 13–16.

Merrium, S. B., & Caffarella, R. S. (1999). *Learning in adulthood: A comprehensive guide.* San Francisco: Jossey-Bass.

Mezirow, J. (1978). *Education for perspective transformation: Women's re-entry programs in community college.* New York: Center for Adult Education, Teachers College, Columbia University.

———. (1981, Fall). A critical theory of adult learning. *Adult Education, 32*(1), 3–24.

———. (1991). *Transformative dimensions of adult learning.* San Francisco: Jossey-Bass.

———. (2000). Learning to think like an adult: Transformation theory: Core concepts. In J. Mezirow & Associates (Eds.), *Learning as transformation: Critical perspectives on a theory in progress.* San Francisco: Jossey-Bass.

Miles, M. B., & Huberman, A. M. (1994). *Qualitative data analysis: An expanded source book* (2nd ed.). Thousand Oaks, CA: Sage.

Mills, C. W. (1959). *The sociological imagination.* New York: Oxford University Press.

Muirhead, B. (2004, March). Research insights into interactivity. *International Journal of Instructional Technology and Distance Learning*. Retrieved June 28, 2006, from http://www.otheredge.com.au/klogs/toolkit/archives/002405.html

National Center for Education Statistics. (2003). *Institutions offering distance learning courses*. National Center for Education Statistics. Retrieved June 28, 2006, from http://nces.ed.gov/surveys/peqis/publications/2003017/

NTIA and the Economics and Statistics Administration. (2002). *A nation online: How Americans are expanding their use of the Internet*. Retrieved February 10, 2004, from http://www.ntia.doc.gov/ntiahome/dn/

Ormrod, J. E. (1999). *Human Learning* (3rd ed.). Upper Saddle River, NJ: Prentice Hall.

Ozmon, H., & Craver, S. (1995). *Philosophical foundations of education* (5th ed.). Englewood Cliffs, NJ: Prentice Hall.

Papert, S. (1993). *Mindstorms: children, computers, and powerful ideas* (2nd ed.). New York: Basic Books.

Parkes, C. M. (1971). Psycho-social transition: A field for study. *Social Science and Medicine, 5*, 101–115.

Pike, B. N. (1992). *An ethnographic action research study: Undergraduate, adult learners' perspective on the learning process*. Unpublished doctoral dissertation, University of Missouri, St Louis, MO.

Polkinghorne, D. E. (1989). Phenomenological research methods. In R. S. Valle & S. Halling (Eds.), *Existential-phenomenological perspectives in psychology*. New York: Plenum.

Prochaska, J. O., Norcross, J. C., & Diclemente, C. C. (1995). *Changing for good: A revolutionary six-stage program for overcoming bad habits and moving your life positively forward*. New York: Avon Books.

Radhakrishnan, S., & Bailey, J. (2000). *Web-based educational media: Issues and empirical test of learning* (ERIC Document No. ED4295420). WebNet 97 World Conference of the WWW, Internet & Intranet Proceedings, 2nd Toronto, November 1–5, 1997.

RAND. (1999). *Documented briefing: Predicting military innovation*. Retrieved December 2, 2003, from http://www.rand.org/publications/DB/DB242/

Ratinoff, L. (1995). Global insecurity and education: The culture of globalization. *Prospects, 25*(2), 147–174.

Riegel, K. F. (1973). Dialectic operations: The final period of cognitive development. *Human Development, 16*, 346–370.

Ross, B. E. (n.d.). Integrating andragogy with current research on teaching effectiveness. *Proceeding from conference on andragogy at University of Maryland (as recalled by author)*. B. E. Ross is Professor Emeritus in the Education Department at the University of Delaware.

Rossi, P. H., Freeman H. E., & Lipsey, M. W. (1999). *Evaluation: A systematic approach* (6th ed.). London: Sage. Retrieved December 15, 2003, from http://www.edu.uvic.ca/faculty/mroth/580/InterpretiveInquiry.html

Roth, M. (2001, January). *Interpretive inquiry*. Canada: University of Victoria. Retrieved December 10, 2003, from http://www.edu.uvic.ca/faculty/mroth/580/InterpretiveInquiry.html

Ryan, A. (1997, Fall). Exaggerated hopes and baseless fears. *Social Research, 64*(3), 1167–1190.

Savićević, D. (1991, October). Modern conceptions of andragogy: A European framework. *Studies in the Education of Adults, 23*(2), 179–201.

———. (1999). Adult education: From practice to theory building (Introduction, Forward, and Table of Contents only). In F. Poggeler (Ed.), *Studies in pedagogy, andragogy, and gerontagogy* (Vol. 27). Frankfurt am Main, Germany: Peter Lang.

Schwandt, T. A. (1997). *Qualitative inquiry: A dictionary of terms*. London: Sage.

Shön, S. A. (1983). *The reflective practitioner: How professionals think in action*. New York: Basic Books.

Simonson, M., Smaldino, S., Albright, M., & Zvacek, S. (2003). *Teaching and learning at a distance: Foundations of distance education* (2nd ed.). Columbus, OH: Merrill Prentice Hall.

Simpson, O. (2005). E-learning, democracy, and social exclusion: Issues of access and retention in the United Kingdom. In A. Carr-Chellman (Ed.), *Global perspectives on e-learning: Rhetoric and reality* (pp. 89–100). Thousand Oaks, CA: Sage.

Sims, R. R., & Sims S. J. (Eds.). (1995). *Learning styles: understanding the implications for learning, course design, and education*. Westport, CT: Greenwood Press.

Smith, R. M. (1982). *Learning how to learn: Applied theory for adults*. Chicago: Follett.

Solberg, C. (1999, September). Partners profit in parallel. *Healthcare Informatics*. Retrieved December 6, 2003, from http://www.healthcare-informatics.com/issues/1999/09_99/hits.html

Stites, R., Hopey, C. E., & Ginsburg, L. (1998). *Assessing lifelong learning technology— ALLTECH*. Practice Guide No. PG98-01. Philadelphia: National Center on Adult Literacy, University of Pennsylvania.

Taylor, M. (1986). Learning for self-direction in the classroom: The pattern of a transition process. *Studies in Higher Learning, 11*(1), 55–72.

Tennant, M., & Pogson, P. (1995). *Learning and change in the adult years: A development perspective*. San Francisco: Jossey-Bass.

ThinkExist. (2004). Albert Einstein famous quotes. Retrieved February 10, 2004, from http://www.thinkexist.com/English/Author/x/Author_1082_1.html

Tough, A. (1971). *The adult's learning projects: A fresh approach to theory and practice in adult learning*. Toronto: Ontario Institute for Studies in Education.

———. (1979). *The adult's learning projects: A fresh approach to theory and practice in adult learning* (2nd ed.). Toronto: The Ontario Institute for Studies in Education.

———. (1981). *Learning without a teacher: A study of tasks and assistance during adult self-teaching projects*. Toronto: The Ontario Institute of Studies in Education.

———. (1982). *Intentional changes*. Chicago: Follett.

Trends Report 2001. (2001). *Building the net*. Retrieved July, 9, 2003, from http://www.trendsreport.net/participate.html

Van Doren, C. (1991). *Benjamin Franklin*. New York: Penguin.

Van Manen, M. (1990). *Researching lived experience: Human science for an action sensitive pedagogy*. Albany: State University of New York Press.

Verner, C. (1962). *Adult education theory and method: A conceptual scheme for the identification and classification of processes*. Washington, DC: Adult Education Association of the USA.

Virtual Learning Space. (2006). Retrieved June 28, 2006, from http://www.itlearning-space-scot.ac.uk/campus/home/content.cfm

Yin, R. K. (2003). Case study research: Design and methods (3rd ed.). Thousand Oaks, CA: Sage Publications.

NAME INDEX

Agarwal, R., 43, 297
Albright, M., xxv, 304
Ardell, D., 132, 138, 297
Arlin, P. K., 31, 159, 297
Ausubel, D., 21, 45, 175, 297

Bailey, J., 42, 303
Baumgartner, L. M., 33, 297
Bear, J. H., 22, 186, 297
Beck, H., xxxiii, 297
Becker, S. P., 1, 297
Beckhard, R., 9, 297
Bier, M., 42, 297
Biklen, S. K., 60, 61, 297
Billington, D., 25, 155, 174, 189, 297
Bogdan, R. C., 60, 61, 297
Brookfield, S., xxii, xxiv, 4, 16, 19, 179, 189, 298
Bruner, J., 45, 55, 60, 63, 187, 298
Bullen, M., xviii, xxiv, 26, 27, 192, 298

Caffarella, R. S., 2, 4, 45, 302
Carlson, R., 4, 298
Carr-Chellman, A., xxviii–xxx, 298, 301, 304
Casella, R., 58, 298
Casper, K., 2, 298
Cavalier, J., 43, 298
Chapnick, S., xxxiii, xxxiv, 298
Chelimsky, E., 61, 298
Claywell, L. G., 58, 298
Columbia Electronic Encyclopedia, 15, 298
Cooper, M. K., 20, 26, 177, 184–186, 192, 298, 300
Coruthers, J. M., 210, 299

Craver, S., 35, 55, 169, 303
Creswell, J. W., 51, 52, 54, 299
Csikszentmihalyi, M., 37–39, 179, 180, 183, 189, 191, 299
Cuban, L., 43, 299

Day, E., 43, 297
Delors, J., 1, 2, 34–37, 167–173, 179, 181, 182, 188, 299
Denzin, N. K., 57, 299
Deshler, D., 6, 53, 299
Diclemente, C. C., 24, 175, 303

Elias, J., 21, 23, 24, 175, 299
English, F. W., 299
Ermath, M., 51, 299
Ethnographic Research, Inc., 55, 299
Evers, K. E., xxviii, xxxi, 299

Field, J., 42, 189, 299
Fox, S., xxviii, xxxi, 299, 300
Fraley, G., 38, 300
Freeman, H. E., 54, 304
Freire, P., 17, 176, 177, 300

Galbraith, M. W., 23, 132, 181, 184, 190, 300, 301
Gallo, M., 42, 297
Gay, L. R., 50, 51, 190, 300
Ginsburg, L., 44, 177, 180, 189, 304
Glaser, B. G., 52, 300

Hagan, N., 6, 53, 299
Henschke, J. A., 6, 21, 26, 28, 60, 157, 158, 176, 177, 182, 184–186, 192, 298, 300

HIPAA Compliance Regulation Training, 106, 300
Holton, E. F., 17, 175, 185, 301
Hopey, C. E., 44, 177, 180, 189, 304
Hornbeck, D., 43, 44, 180, 300
Huberman, A. M., 62, 302
Hultgren, F. H., 51, 54, 300

Isaac, P., 21, 184–186, 192, 298
Isenberg, S., xxii, xxiv, 4–6, 31, 36, 41, 64, 83, 153, 187, 218, 232, 295, 300

James, W. B., 132, 301
Jia Qi, J., xxiv, 301

Kajs, L., xxvii, 302
Kidd, R., 29, 301
Kiesler, T., 301
Klein, J., 43, 298
Knowles, M. S., xvi, xvii, xxi, xxii, xxv, 2, 4, 8, 9, 10, 17, 19–24, 26–28, 80, 154–157, 162, 175–177, 180, 182–186, 189, 190, 192, 193, 247, 298, 301
Kouzes, J. M., 28, 155, 156, 158, 176, 181, 183, 185, 188, 192, 193, 301
Kraut, R., 42, 301

Latchem, C., xxx, 301
LeDoux, J., 4, 25, 32, 36, 37, 41, 44, 155, 163, 164, 166, 168, 184, 301
Lewin, K., 7, 28, 53, 159, 181, 301
Lincoln, Y. S., 57, 299
Lindeman, E. C., xvi, xxv, 15, 16, 32, 38, 155, 164, 179, 184, 298, 302
Lipsey, M. W., 54, 304
Long, H., 31, 159, 302
LoveToKnow Corp., 14, 302
Lundmark, V., 301

MacKeracher, D., 4, 302
Marotta, P., 26, 192, 302

Mayo, N., xxvii, xxviii, 302
McBride, J., 3, 302
McLagan, P., 27, 154–158, 302
Meloy, J., xxxiii, xxxiv, 298
Merriam, S., 2, 4, 21, 23, 24, 33, 45, 175, 299
Merrill, H. S., xxxii, xxxiv, 302
Merrium, S. B., 302
Mezirow, J., xvii, xxv, 20, 23, 33, 37, 41, 166, 179, 180, 184, 185, 190, 302,
Miles, M. B., 62, 302
Mills, C. W., 58, 302
Muirhead, B., xxxi, 303
Mukopadhyay, 301

National Center for Education Statistics, xxix, 303
Norcross, J. C., 24, 175, 303
NTIA and the Economics and Statistics Administration, 3, 303
Nucklos, S., 42, 297

Ormrod, J. E., 31, 32, 36, 46, 159, 160, 161, 164, 165, 167, 168, 171, 175, 178, 180, 182, 303
Ozmon, H., 35, 55, 303

Papert, S., 24, 31, 41, 45, 160, 187, 303
Parkes, C. M., 24, 303
Patterson, M., 301
Pennick, M., 42, 297
Pike, B. N., 58, 303
Pogson, P., 33, 163, 164, 305
Polkinghorne, D. E., 51, 303
Posner, B. Z., 28, 155, 156, 158, 176, 181, 183, 185, 188, 192, 193, 301
Prochaska, J. O., 24, 175, 280, 303

Radhakrishnan, S., 42, 303
RAND, 56, 303

Name Index

Ratinoff, L., 4, 7, 303
Riegel, K. F., 31, 159, 303
Ross, B. E., 3, 192, 304
Rossi, P. H., 54, 57, 61, 304
Roth, M., 57, 304
Ryan, A., 3, 304
Savićević, D., 15, 28, 154,
Scherlis, W., 301
Schwandt, T. A., 52, 54, 59, 61, 304
Sherblom, S., 42, 297
Shön, S. A., 304
Simonson, M., xxi, xxii, xxv, 26, 304
Simpson, O., xxix, 304
Sims, R. R., 27, 157, 158, 176, 304
Sims, S. J., 27, 157, 158, 176, 304
Smaldino, S., xxv, 304
Smith, R. M., 2, 9, 10, 15, 19, 24, 27, 30, 42, 157, 159, 161, 162, 175, 180, 181, 183, 189, 194, 304
Solberg, C., 57, 304
Stites, R., 44, 45, 177, 180, 189, 304
Strauss, A. L., 52, 300
Swanson, R. A., 17, 175, 185, 301

Tanguma, J., xxvii, 302
Taylor, M., 14, 24, 25, 32, 41, 44, 155, 163, 174, 177, 184, 187, 304
Tennant, M., 33, 163, 164, 305
The International Commission on Education for the Twenty-first Century, 1, 8, 49
ThinkExist, 38, 305
Titus, T., 4–6, 31, 36, 41, 64, 153, 187, 300
Tough, A., 9, 10, 19, 29, 30, 41, 159–163, 178, 181, 182, 184, 187, 188, 193, 305
Trends Report 2001, 40, 305

Van Doren, C., 305
Van Manen, M., 59, 60, 62, 63, 305
Verner, C., 16, 17, 21, 23, 24, 175, 184, 187, 305
Virtual Learning Space, xxxiii, 305

Yin, R. K., 52, 54, 305

Zvacek, S., xxv, 304

SUBJECT INDEX

Advance organizer, 21, 45, 46, 175, 197
Ah-ha experiences, 66, 83, 164, 213, 231, 253, 264
Andragogy as learner centered, process model, xvi, 9, 13, 17, 19, 185
Asynchronous learning, xvi, xxxii, xxxiii, 40

Change readiness, 24
Climate setting, xxxiv, 4, 15, 19, 186
Cognition, motivation, and emotion in learning, 4, 8, 32, 47, 49, 163, 166, 197, 205, 208
Creativity, 13, 37–39, 46, 47, 71, 73, 74, 84, 91, 92, 113, 114, 117, 123, 124, 131–134, 138, 169, 170, 172, 173, 179, 180, 181, 184, 188, 189, 240, 267, 268
Critical consciousness, 17, 300
Critical reflection, 4, 23, 61, 190

Distance education, xvii, xxix–xxxii, xxxiv
Distance learning, xvii, xix, xx, xxx–xxxii, xxxiv, xxxv, 26, 27, 81, 163, 177, 192
Do what you say you will do, 28, 199, 205

Flow, 85

General dissemination of knowledge, 16, 17, 175, 194, 201
Gestalt theory, 21, 160, 161

Habermas' three domains of learning, 33
Happy accidents, 84, 124, 183, 252, 253
Heutagogy, xxxiii

Humanness, 22, 30, 127, 182, 184, 185, 197, 205

Interactivity, xxvii, xxxii–xxxv
Intersubjectivity, 60

Learner uniqueness, 13, 25, 94, 196, 203
Learning contract, 10, 21–23, 47, 180, 190, 195, 196, 202, 203, 208
Learning process, xvii, xx, xxi, xxiii, 4, 7, 15, 17, 25, 29, 31, 33, 37, 41, 43, 47, 50, 64, 65, 84, 121, 150, 155, 158, 161–164, 182, 185, 187, 194, 199, 200, 206, 230
Learning projects, 10, 29, 66, 75, 159, 162, 163, 196, 204, 213, 221, 249, 262
Lifelong learning, xxiii, 2, 55, 194
Lived experience, 47, 51, 54, 62, 63, 101, 155, 177, 194, 198, 200, 201, 202, 204, 206, 298, 305

Memory, 32, 35–37, 47, 55, 58, 61, 101, 106, 108, 114, 126, 133, 159, 168, 169, 189
Modeling, 28, 29, 182, 300
Mutual planning, 4, 17, 18, 19, 22, 82, 156, 175, 195, 201, 202, 207

Nonhuman planners, 30, 41, 47
Normal natural process for learning, 19, 20, 195, 202

Ontologies, xxxiii, xxxiv
Orchestration of emotional states, 32, 163, 184

Pedagogy as teacher centered, content model, 17, 19, 185
Philosophy of education, 23
Physical climate conducive to learning, 17, 21, 22, 23, 47, 184, 186, 195, 201, 202
Power-over, 26, 192
Power-with, 26, 192,
Preferred learning style, 15, 19, 27, 30, 132, 134, 157, 196, 198, 203, 272
Psychological climate conducive to learning, 21, 22, 47, 184, 195, 202

Self-directed learning, xxxiii, xxxiv, 24, 29, 31, 160, 196, 204
Self-paced learning, 28
Self-planned learning, 29
Self-teaching, 29, 30
Socratic method, 14
Speaking with one voice, 181, 192

Stages of change, 24, 134, 135, 138, 189, 190, 224, 230, 280
Synchronous learning, xxxii, 40
Systematic diffusion of knowledge, 16, 17, 21, 175, 187, 194, 195, 201, 202

Teaching tasks, 29, 162, 200
Theory and practice connection, 28
Theory of cognitive development, 31
Transactional learning, 9, 23
Transformational learning, 33
Triangulation, 61

Value-free / bias-free designs and researchers, 50

Whole-mind experience, 34, 197, 201, 208
Whole-Part-Whole Learning Model, 21

6.24.18

Page 16 Brookfield about Lindeman
+ contemporary relevance
+ intellectual elegance
+ inspirational vision

10.27.18

Page 16 Brookfield about Lindeman
+ contemporary relevance
+ intellectual also a dynamic
+ inspirational vision

ontologies = concept maps
―――――――――――――――――
heutagogy = ontology-guided
(Dr. Hase; Australia, w/ Self-directed
professor. Kenn.?)